the girl scout

promise

On my honor, I will try:
To do my duty to God and my country,
To help other people at all times,
To obey the Girl Scout Laws.

SENIOR

CADETTE

JUNIOR

BROWNIE

the *girl scout* laws

1. A Girl Scout's honor is to be trusted.
2. A Girl Scout is loyal.
3. A Girl Scout's duty is to be useful and to help others.
4. A Girl Scout is a friend to all and a sister to every other Girl Scout.
5. A Girl Scout is courteous.
6. A Girl Scout is a friend to animals.
7. A Girl Scout obeys orders.
8. A Girl Scout is cheerful.
9. A Girl Scout is thrifty.
10. A Girl Scout is clean in thought, word, and deed.

Girl Scouts of the United States of America
830 Third Avenue, New York 22, New York

Catalog No. 20-103 $1.00

cadette
Girl Scout Handbook

contents

Cadette *s*

couting

Welcome to the Cadette Girl Scouts! Here is a new world of Scouting for you, different from any you may have known before. Scouting has grown up...and you are ready for it.

Cadette Scouting is a way of living up to the best of your abilities. It is a way of learning about yourself and about others. It is a way of making the most of you, as you are now and as the person you would like to be.

Here are new ideas for your mind, new projects for your hands, new adventures for your soul. Here are the joys of working and playing, thinking and doing.

Here is Cadette Girl Scouting....

A Challenge to Cadettes

Cadette Girl Scouting is different because you are different. As a Brownie or a Junior Scout, you did a great many things under the guidance of your leaders. Now you are older and ready to do more, much more, on your own.

Cadette Scouting is different because it brings you the Challenge course for deeper understanding of yourself, development of your special abilities...and more fun than ever.

The dictionary defines a challenge as an invitation to a game or contest. There are four Challenges, each of which is an invitation to you and the other members of your troop to test your performance in a real-life situation. The Challenge of Social Dependability, for example, is to plan and carry out a social event to give pleasure to others.

Before you are ready to accept a Challenge, there are certain things for you to learn and practice in preparation. Some of these things you will already have learned as a Brownie or Junior. If you are a new Girl Scout you'll be able to catch up quickly. Many of these things will be learned as you earn badges.

The choice of advanced proficiency badges in Cadette Scouting is wide. If you already have a special interest, choose a badge that will help you develop it further. If you want to do something new, choose one you know nothing about. As you earn each badge, you will be using what you learn, either by giving service directly or by teaching or sharing it with others.

Each of the four Challenges is the framework of an idea, waiting to be translated into action by you, your patrol, and your troop.

The Challenge of Social Dependability develops you as a person in relation to others—old and young, friends and family, newcomers in your life. You gain poise and social graces that will help you be a successful hostess and a welcome guest. You bring helpfulness and cheer into a social setting by using the things you've learned and practiced as a Girl Scout.

The Challenge of Emergency Preparedness gives you a chance to learn and practice the skills of safe and comfortable living both indoors and out-of-doors. The mystery and suspense of the unexpected will test how well you have learned the lesson of self-reliance in a crisis.

The Challenge of Active Citizenship calls on you to show your understanding of democracy and your part in it. The democracy may be your troop, your community, your country. Your role as a citizen may have to do with neighbors across oceans or those at the other end of town. Here's a Challenge that evokes a true spirit of service to others.

The Challenge of the Girl Scout Promise helps you to understand how your Promise relates to your everyday life, by emphasizing the spiritual values that are basic to all Scouting, and by helping you to reaffirm and strengthen your own standards of everyday conduct.

Each Challenge has a special insigne which is presented at a Court of Awards to each girl who has met the Challenge.

First Class is the highest award in Cadette Girl Scouting.

The requirements for First Class are:

1. Earn a minimum of six Cadette Scout badges which show you have grown in your understanding, knowledge, and skill in each of these areas: arts, citizenship, health and safety, home, international friendship, and out-of-doors.
2. Meet all four Challenges.

It may be possible for you to achieve First Class in less than three years. In that case, in your last few months as a Cadette Scout, you will have extra privileges and responsibilities. First Class Scouts may attend Senior Conferences as special guests, plan Cadette Scout events involving a number of troops, or share their program skills with younger girls in troops or camps.

Begin now to map your course to fun and adventure. You will find the detailed framework for each Challenge in Chapter 16. The requirements for the badges begin on page 280.

Let's get started!

The Challenge Course

What will be your pattern as you progress through the Challenge course of Cadette Scouting? No two girls will travel in the exact same way. The course has:

SIX ATMOSPHERES TO EXPLORE

Arts, home, out-of-doors, international friendship, citizenship, health and safety.

Proof of Exploration—Earn a badge from each atmosphere

FOUR CHALLENGES TO PURSUE

Challenge of the Girl Scout Promise
Challenge of Active Citizenship
Challenge of Social Dependability
Challenge of Emergency Preparedness

Proof of Attainment—Earn insigne for each Challenge

There are opportunities to learn to manage troop affairs and to serve others along the entire course. As you pursue each of the Challenges you will cross in and out of the six atmospheres. Most of the time you will work with other girls in the troop, perhaps with your own patrol.

From the time you start, you will have many opportunities to take part in intertroop, councilwide, and intercouncil events and activities. Remember your most important navigational instruments are the Girl Scout Promise and Laws.

TARGET

First Class. And then? Take off for Senior Scouting.

The World Association of Girl Guides and Girl Scouts owns and operates three world centers. Although each is different from the other in appearance, each attracts Guides and Girl Scouts from many lands who always find the true spirit of international friendship there.

Our Chalet, *Notre Chalet*, or *Unser Chalet*, according to your language, is high on a mountainside near Adelboden, Switzerland. Skiing in winter or mountain climbing in summer are among the many activities offered to visitors.

Our Cabaña is near Cuernavaca, Mexico. Girls who go there may swim in the pool, learn crafts or traditional handwork, or explore the historical legends of the countryside.

Our Ark is a residential center in the city of London, England. Equipped by Guides all over the world, it serves as a temporary home for traveling members of the movement.

A Proud Heritage

Most Girl Scouts know the story of how, in 1908, Sir Robert Baden-Powell founded the Boy Scouts in England. They know, too, how a charming American woman named Juliette Gordon Low brought the idea from England to the United States in 1912, the idea that grew into the Girl Scouts of the U.S.A.

Since that time millions of girls from seven through seventeen years of age have enjoyed what Baden-Powell called "the game of Scouting." Your troop is part of a movement in the United States that has over three million members—girls and adults. In troops and camps, they too are exploring new ideas, learning new skills, having fun, and giving service to others. Together, you are making Girl Scout history.

Just as the idea of Scouting was welcomed here and grew, so also in countries throughout the world. Whether the girls are called *Bandeirantes* as in Brazil, *Padvindsters* as in the Netherlands, or Guides as in England, they share a common heritage with you. All enjoy the privilege of exchanging the sign and the handshake. Each association has an official pin such as the Girl Scout trefoil pin; each has an identifying uniform.

On Boy Scouting's 21st birthday, its Founder was made Lord Baden-Powell by the king of England. Scouts remember him as "B-P, Chief Scout of the World." His wife, Lady Baden-Powell, is our World Chief Guide.

The Girl Scout sign is a form of greeting exchanged when Girl Scouts and Guides meet or even pass each other on the street. Notice that only three fingers are extended; this is to symbolize the three parts of the worldwide Promise.

The Girl Scout handshake is a more formal greeting, used by Scouts and Guides when they are introduced. It combines the sign and a left handshake.

You and all the Girl Scouts in our country are united with these sister Scouts and Guides through the World Association of Girl Guides and Girl Scouts. Your national organization, Girl Scouts of the U.S.A., is a member, as are the associations in over fifty other countries. Juliette Low believed deeply in the power of Scouting and Guiding for international understanding and played an important part in the beginnings of the World Association. One of its aims is to encourage friendship among girls of all nations.

All over the world, Girl Scouts and Guides celebrate Thinking Day, February 22. To honor the birthday of both Lord and Lady Baden-Powell, girls of member countries symbolically join hands with each other in recognition of the spirit of Scouting that unites them in international friendship.

All over the world, the slogan is the same. *Do a good turn daily.* This reminds you that you can help, comfort, and gladden other people every day of your life. It doesn't matter if the kindness is only a small one, such as making a new girl feel at home in your troop. What does matter is your spirit of giving freely for the sake of it, neither wanting nor expecting a return. Of course, you needn't limit yourself to doing only one good turn

Here are the Guide pins worn by girls in the Philippines, Korea, and Greece. They all in some way symbolize the three parts of the Promise.

World Association pin, which may also be worn when not in uniform, identifies you to sister Scouts when traveling in other countries and at home.

Uniforms are adapted to climate and customs of the country. These are from Great Britain, Sudan and Pakistan.

a day. The more, the happier; the quieter, the more admirable!

All over the world, the motto is the same: *Be prepared.* Be ready to help, to do the right things when you are needed. "Ready" means willing but it also means able. You must have the know-how, as well as the will to help. For you can't save a drowning swimmer or bind a cut unless you know how. Knowing how to do things is the most important part of being prepared. Learning how to do them is part of the fun of Cadette Scouting.

All Girl Scout troops and Girl Guide companies may use the World Association flag; all Girl Scouts and Girl Guides may wear the World Association pin. They are the symbols of the worldwide bond of Scouting and Guiding. The gold trefoil on the bright blue background signifies the golden sun shining in a blue sky over all Girl Scouts and Guides. The wavy base of the stem stands for the Flame of the Love of Mankind, burning brightly in the hearts of all. The tiny center vein is a compass needle, always pointing the right way. The two stars stand for the Promise and Laws, cherished and honored by all.

The Promise

"Whene'er you make a promise, consider well its importance: and when made, engrave it upon your heart." The Girl Scout Promise has only four short lines. The words are simple and easy to memorize, but the meaning is profound:

> *On my honor, I will try:*
> *To do my duty to God and my country,*
> *To help other people at all times,*
> *To obey the Girl Scout Laws.*

Though the Promise is given in many lands and languages, the feeling behind it is always a heartfelt vow to live up to its meaning.

What is this meaning? It is your promise to do the best that is in you to honor God and rejoice in life. And as you worship God in your own

The Girl Scout Trefoil. The three broad leaves stand for the three parts of the Promise; the "GS" stands for Girl Scouts. The American eagle and shield, parts of the Great Seal of the United States of America, symbolize readiness to serve country.

and the Laws

way, you respect the beliefs of those who differ from you.

It is your promise to be loyal to the United States of America, to be part of it, to learn all you can about your country and to do all you can for it. What can you do now to show you are a good citizen? You might work on a troop project for the day nursery in your home town or give service to a national endeavor, such as the Red Cross. Take an interest in the government of your town, your state, and your nation. Begin to think of the government as "we," rather than "they."

It is your promise to offer your help and services to others, to give your skills and friendship, the understanding of a sympathetic word, a warm smile. These are very good

ways to become an important person to others and to yourself.

It is your promise to obey, as well as you know how, the Girl Scout Laws, keys to happy Scouting and living. You've already learned a great deal of this in your home, in your church or synagogue. As you accept and absorb the Laws, you become more the person you want to be. As you say the words, think about them.

1. A Girl Scout's honor is to be trusted.

As you grow into young womanhood, you understand this better than when you were a Brownie's age. Your honor is your word, the pledge of your character. When you say something is true, it is true. When you make a promise, you keep it. You are a person who can always be trusted.

2. A Girl Scout is loyal.

What is loyalty? It is being true to something, believing in it, protecting or defending it if you have to. You are true to your family and your friends, your religion and your country. If you have doubts or criticisms, you have the courage to try to find out what is wrong and correct it. You are not afraid to uphold your beliefs, even among those who disagree. You are not a gossip or tale-bearer and are careful never to say anything that might hurt another person or group. Friends know they may rely on your loyalty to them, even when they are not present.

3. A Girl Scout's duty is to be useful and to help others.

You offer your help freely, lending your hand, heart, and mind wherever they are needed. Wanting to help is not enough. Your help is real because it is practical. By living up to the motto, "Be prepared," you know what to do and how to do it properly. By doing a little more than is expected of you, you learn more and more every single day. By giving to others, you become a bigger person.

4. A Girl Scout is a friend to all and a sister to every other Girl Scout.

You care about other people's needs and feelings. Your kindness is sincere. It is not reserved for those near to you, but given to everyone, just as the sun shines on all. You are interested in people different from you in appearance, beliefs, and customs, for you value all human beings, strangers as well as friends.

5. A Girl Scout is courteous.

You are judged by your manners. The outward graces of gentle behavior, a pleasant voice, expressions of thoughtfulness reveal the kind of person you are. For true courtesy is genuine and comes from the heart. Your manners are a real part of you, equally good at home and away from home.

6. *A Girl Scout is a friend to animals.*

All animals, tame and wild, need your help and protection. They cannot speak for themselves. And so, you learn all you can of their ways and needs. You do all you can to spare them pain, cruelty, or neglect. Animals depend on you for love and care. And they may, for you are ready to help.

7. *A Girl Scout obeys orders.*

You are sensible about orders from your parents, your troop leader, and other people who are responsible for you. They are helping you develop self-discipline—one key to true happiness. Of course, you understand the need to obey without question such things as traffic laws, health and safety regulations.

8. A Girl Scout is cheerful.

Cheerfulness is an attitude you can develop. It means substituting a smile for a frown, optimism for a downhearted outlook, courage for retreat when things go wrong. Happiness is not a matter of clothes or money, but a way of looking at things, bringing a laugh to a situation even when the laugh is on you. Joy is catching. Your smiles and laughter will invite friends and fun into your life.

9. A Girl Scout is thrifty.

Whatever you have, use it wisely, not wastefully. This means your time and energy, as well as your money. You invest your time in working and playing at things that are meaningful to you. You invest money the same way.

You make the most of what you have. You are careful not to throw away anything useful, so that you have it when you need it. You give your body the rest, food, and exercise it needs. You care for your possessions, replacing buttons, mending rips. There is beauty in thrift, for it shows respect for the gifts of life.

10. A Girl Scout is clean in thought, word, and deed.

Certain things must be put into feelings, rather than words. Cleanness of mind and spirit is one of these. Of course, you scrub your body clean with soap, water, and brush. But *inside* cleanness is a way of viewing yourself and life. Baden-Powell believed every Girl Scout should train herself "to look for what is beautiful in everything, so that she may become strong enough in her mind to avoid listening to or taking part in anything that is ugly and unclean." Let these words find an echo in your heart.

These are the Girl Scout Promise and Laws. Let them become part of your daily life. Believe in them. Be guided by them.

Your Uniform

What does a Cadette Girl Scout wear?

Your smart uniform has been styled by a leading fashion designer who considered suggestions from girls all over the country. It is worn with pride, is always crisp, fresh, and spotless, with the hem at a becoming length for you. No jewelry, other than a ring, watch, or religious medal, should be worn with it. The picture on page 10 shows your uniform and the following pages show where to place your insignia.

Wearing a uniform is a privilege you share with all members of the Girl Scout organization—from the newest Brownie to the National President.

You should be aware of what your uniform represents to everyone who sees you in it. It is not merely a way of dress, but a statement that you are part of the Girl Scouts—a worldwide movement with high standards. With your uniform you wear the tradition of all Girl Scouts everywhere.

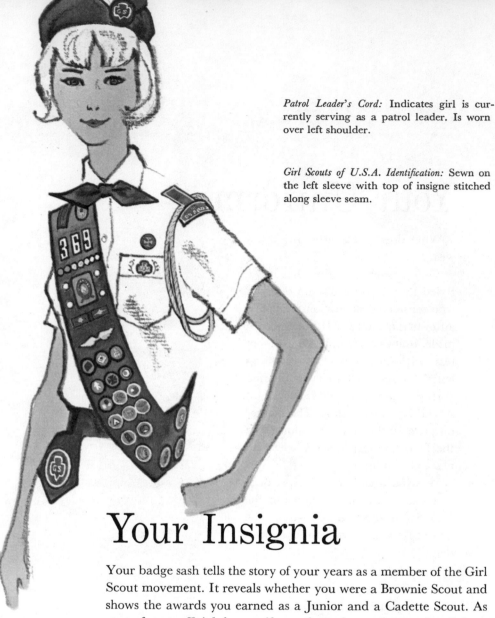

Patrol Leader's Cord: Indicates girl is currently serving as a patrol leader. Is worn over left shoulder.

Girl Scouts of U.S.A. Identification: Sewn on the left sleeve with top of insigne stitched along sleeve seam.

Your Insignia

Your badge sash tells the story of your years as a member of the Girl Scout movement. It reveals whether you were a Brownie Scout and shows the awards you earned as a Junior and a Cadette Scout. As part of your official dress uniform, the sash may be purchased from your local equipment agency. You will need your membership card or a note from your leader in order to buy the uniform, the council identification emblem, the Girl Scouts of the U.S.A. identification strip, and troop numerals. All other insignia must be purchased by your leader.

World Association of Girl Guides and Girl Scouts Pin: Centered over pocket of shirt. See picture on page 9.

Girl Scout Pin: Indicates membership in the Girl Scout movement. Pinned over embroidered emblem on the shirt pocket.

Identification Emblem: Curved strip embroidered with name of council or lone troop community. Worn by all members of the troop.

Troop Crest: May be selected from available stock, or troop's own design embroidered on blank oval. Design should be approved by leader and council. Worn by all members of the troop.

Troop Numerals: Indicates number of troop in community. Centered below identification emblem. Worn by all troop members.

Membership Stars. Each green star represents one year's membership as a Brownie; yellow, as a Junior Scout; white, as a Cadette Scout.

Challenge Pins: Indicates completion of each Challenge. The first earned insigne is pinned at top right of space for First Class patch; second, at top left; third, at bottom right; fourth, at bottom left.

First Class Patch: Indicates completion of the four Challenges and six badges required for First Class, the highest award in Cadette Scouting.

Sign of the Arrow: Indicates completion of Junior Scout requirements for the Arrow.

Sign of the Star: Indicates completion of Junior Scout requirements for the Star.

Brownie Wings: Signifies previous registration in a Brownie troop.

Proficiency Badges: Sewn in rows of three in order earned. Green borders indicate badges earned as a Junior; yellow borders, those earned as a Cadette Scout.

Ceremony by
Candlelight

header on right margin

Membership Requirements

To be a Cadette Girl Scout you must:
- Be 12, 13, or 14 years of age and/or be in the seventh, eighth, or ninth grade.
- Attend four meetings of a Cadette Scout troop.
- Pay the one dollar annual membership dues to Girl Scouts of the U.S.A.
- Make the Girl Scout Promise and subscribe to the Girl Scout Laws.

The day you formally become a Cadette Girl Scout is a great occasion in your life. For this reason, it is marked in a special way with a ceremony of welcome.

If you were a Junior Scout and are moving up into a Cadette Scout troop, your ceremony is one of rededication. This means that you reaffirm your acceptance of the principles of Girl Scouting as expressed in the Promise and Laws.

If you have never been a Girl Scout before, your ceremony of welcome is called an investiture. This means you have met the membership requirements and are ready to become a full-fledged member of the Girl Scout movement in the U.S.A. The Girl Scout pin you receive symbolizes this membership.

Not all ceremonies are the same. In every troop, the girls themselves plan the event and work out the details with their leaders, so that ceremonies differ from troop to troop.

It is quite likely, however, that yours will be a ceremony by candlelight, an impressive and moving performance in which the entire troop takes part. To the lighting of candles, you indicate your belief in and intent to live up to the Girl Scout Promise by saying it aloud. By the gleam of candlelight, you become a Cadette Girl Scout.

Often, a flag ceremony is included, and later, group singing by the troop, new members and old, joining voices as they have just joined forces.

Many troops invite families and close friends of new members to the ceremonies of rededication and investiture, so that they may share this stirring experience with you. Like you, they will long remember the dignity and beauty of your welcome to the Cadette Girl Scouts.

your troop

What is a Girl Scout troop?

It might be defined as a club made up of girls and their leader. But a Girl Scout troop is quite different from most clubs in its ideals and in the way it functions.

For one thing a Girl Scout troop is a democracy. Every girl in it is an important member. You are important. You make the troop work.

For another thing, girls from every variety of background, all girls, are welcome. Everyone has the freedom to express her ideas. Troop members respect each other and listen thoughtfully, even when opinions differ.

You and the other girls, with the help of the troop leader, make troop plans and see them through. Just as every citizen of the United States has the privilege of voting in the government, every girl in the

troop has a vote. As in every democracy, the majority wins, but the minority is always heard and always included in troop activities.

Most troops have from twenty-four to thirty-two members. In the country or a small town, a troop may have as few as eight girls. But large or small, each troop belongs to the girls in it. Learn how to take part in the planning and join in the fun.

The Patrol System

Your troop operates on the patrol system.

This is the representative form of government used by Scouts and Guides, boys and girls alike, in their troops in town and in camps all over the world. It consists of two parts: patrols and Court of Honor.

Patrols

The troop is divided into small groups, each consisting of six, seven, or eight girls. Each group is called a patrol. Patrols have interesting names chosen by their members. Some names are based on the patrol's special interests, the part of the country where they live, or the like; others may not mean anything but just sound appealing. A patrol interested in nature lore might be named "Treetops." A patrol on the coast of New England might be called "Clamdiggers." Patrols at Our Chalet are named for nearby mountains— *Wildstrubel, Lonner,* and *Engstligenalp.*

Patrols often invent an identifying emblem which they use on a patrol flag or on their patrol equipment.

THE PATROL LEADER

Each patrol has a patrol leader, elected by the girls in her patrol to serve for one year usually. You vote for her, just as any responsible citizen votes for a candidate for government office.

Before voting, read over the duties of the patrol leader, then ask yourself, "Will she do a good job? Is she the kind of girl who is fair and friendly to everyone? Will she let us, the patrol members, have our say, or will she be bossy? Will she speak for everyone in our patrol at the Court of Honor? Does she have ideas that are fun and exciting?"

These are important questions, for the patrol leader is in charge of seeing that things go well and smoothly. Here are the patrol leader's duties:

o Conducts regular patrol meetings (weekly in town, daily in camp) using agenda made at the Court of Honor with the troop leader and other patrol leaders.

o Learns what her patrol wants to do by leading discussions and offering suggestions.

o Represents her patrol at regular Court of Honor meetings by reporting on patrol progress and activities, getting needed assistance, and sharing ideas with other patrol leaders.

o Works with her assistant patrol leader and shares some of the leadership of the patrol with her.

o Helps herself and others in her patrol to learn or practice Scouting skills.

o Takes charge of any special assignment given her patrol.

o Assigns duties to patrol members and sees that they are carried out.

o Helps her patrol organize to get jobs done.

o Consults with troop leader for special help on plans or problems, and keeps her up to date on patrol activities.

You may say to yourself, "What a lot for one girl to do!" Remember, though, that the patrol leader should have the cooperation of all the girls in her patrol. She can always call on the adult leader for advice, too. So she has help whenever she needs or wants it.

THE ASSISTANT PATROL LEADER

Another girl elected by the patrol members is the assistant patrol leader. She serves for the same term as the patrol leader and her job is to help the patrol leader in every way she can. Here are some of the things she does:

o Takes over the job of the patrol leader in her absence.

o Carries out leadership responsibilities delegated by the patrol leader —such as making a kaper chart or organizing a flag ceremony.

o Serves as hostess when the patrol has a guest or consultant.

Every patrol needs a patrol leader and assistant patrol leader. But a patrol that really gets things done sees that every member has a definite, permanent job. This allows it to whirl into action—not confusion, to get the necessary things done quickly and save time for the real heart of a troop or patrol activity, to turn a spur-of-the-moment idea into a fun-packed afternoon.

Here is one plan for dividing the work of the patrol.

FINANCE MANAGER—in charge of patrol financial matters.

o Collects troop dues from patrol members.

o Handles all money.

o Keeps financial records of patrol income and expenses.

RECORDER—in charge of patrol records.

o Attends to patrol correspondence (invitation, thank-you notes).

o Keeps a log of patrol program.

o Fills in necessary information on permission slips.

o Keeps written record of each girl's progress toward First Class.

DANCES
FEB.
14-15
auditorium

TRANSPORTATION MANAGER—in charge of patrol transportation.

o Arranges transportation for patrol activities and troop events.

o Makes sure drivers receive thank-you notes from recorder.

o Works with health and safety manager to make sure patrol members understand health and safety precautions needed for traveling by car, bicycle, on foot, canoe, etc.

o Finds out about interesting places the patrol can visit, how to get there, and how much it will cost.

COMMISSARY MANAGER—in charge of patrol food.

o Arranges for refreshments for special occasions.

o Serves as shopper for the food.

o Sees that food is properly packed and stored.

o Makes sure food is attractively served, works out plan for cleanup.

EQUIPMENT MANAGER—in charge of patrol equipment.

o Makes up list of personal equipment if needed for program and gives a copy to each girl.

o Makes out list of patrol equipment needed.

o Secures, distributes, packs, and stores patrol equipment.

o Makes sure equipment is kept in good condition.

o Initiates making of patrol equipment (tin-can stove, cook kits, etc.)

o Returns borrowed equipment.

HEALTH AND SAFETY MANAGER—in charge of patrol health and safety.

o Makes and equips first aid kit, being sure it remains with patrol at all times.

o Alerts patrol to good health and safety practices.

o Makes sure patrol members know what to do in case of fire, storms, accident, lost persons, etc.

o Knows how to reach the nearest doctor and hospital.

o Gives first aid if qualified and keeps record of treatment.

o Sets up an emergency call system for patrol.

Whether you use this division or make your own plan, you should be able to answer "yes" to the following questions.

1. Does every girl in the patrol have a specific job?

2. Does she have a thumbnail description of what she is to do?

3. Will she really have an opportunity to do her job because it is based on actual plans of the troop and the patrol?

4. Are copies of each description with the name of the girl who has the job kept in one place so anyone can see who is responsible for what?
5. Is there a plan to evaluate the division after two or three months? Check to see if jobs need to be rearranged; if each girl has the job best suited to her talent; if it is working for both troop and patrol activities.

The Court of Honor

The Court of Honor is a vital part of the patrol system. Its members include all the patrol leaders in the troop, the scribe, the treasurer, and the troop leader. Each patrol leader represents her patrol faithfully at the Court of Honor. This means that, since all the patrol leaders attend Court of Honor meetings, every troop member is represented. This is what the Court does:

o Plans interesting troop programs, based on ideas submitted by patrols.
o Makes up ideas for activities and submits them to patrols through the patrol leaders.
o Hears reports on patrols given by patrol leaders (and from committee chairmen, when needed).
o Makes arrangements for patrol leaders to learn new things to teach their patrol members.
o Sometimes arranges for girls from different patrols to work together on special interests.

The Court of Honor meets before or after every regular troop meeting. These short—ten minutes to a half hour—weekly meetings are for quick reports of patrol reactions, reminders of responsibilities for next week, or adjustment of plans.

At special monthly meetings, the Court of Honor fills in the details of plans for the month ahead and considers ideas and suggestions from patrols brought to the meeting by patrol leaders. "The Revelers would like the troop to give a dance." "The Clamdiggers think we should have a project working with animals."

The Court of Honor thinks over the various ideas. Are they good? Will they work? How can we make them work? This is the way ideas are turned into action for the troop. Even the best idea needs planning and work to make it come true. The Court of Honor starts the planning so that "Let's give a party!" can become a reality.

The Court of Honor also holds long meetings at the beginning and end of the troop year. The first meeting is to get things going by deciding how many big events can be fitted into the year's calendar. (The big events might include: overnights, Court of Awards, council events, parties, trips, community service projects.) The last meeting is to see how the troop has fared.

Now and then, an "Open Court of Honor" meeting is held so that everyone will understand how the system works. All troop members attend as "silent watchers."

THE SCRIBE

"Scribe" comes from a Latin word meaning a person who writes. That is the job of the troop scribe, a girl who is elected by the entire troop. For one year, she is the official correspondent and secretary of the troop. Here are her duties:

o Takes minutes and notes at Court of Honor and business meetings.
o Answers mail.
o Writes invitations and thank-you notes for gifts and services to troop.
o Writes troop history, such as an account of a camping trip.

If she were kept very busy, the scribe would probably have an assistant to help her. Patrol recorders also help her compile troop history. All scribes should have neat, clear handwritings, so that their notes are easy for others to read.

THE TREASURER

The troop treasurer is also elected by the entire troop for one year. She has these duties:

o Keeps an account book, entering all the money that is collected by the troop and all that is spent.
o Receives dues from the patrol finance managers, records their payment in the account book and deposits them in the troop's bank

or gives them to the troop leader for deposit.

o Provides facts and figures to Court of Honor when the troop's yearly budget is made and to any group spending troop money (food buyers for camping trip, decorations committee for troop party).

o Makes financial report to the troop once a month.

o Is prepared to make a report of troop finances at any time when asked.

Just as your experiences as a Girl Scout are different when you are a Brownie, a Junior, a Cadette, a Senior, or an adult, so too do you play different roles in your troop government at various times and places. Whether you are in town or in camp, alone with your own troop or in the company of many troops, the patrol system is the successful system. In fact, it works so well that skill in the use of the patrol system is one of the requirements that qualifies you for all sorts of exciting national and international events.

Judge for yourself how well the patrol system is working in your troop right now. Is it just starting, or is it well on the way? Look at the chart and see. Check again every three months or so.

Each patrol has elected a patrol leader and assistant patrol leader. Members are proud of their patrol name and emblem. Some choices are made in patrol meetings, but troop program is mainly thought up by the troop leader.

Things are really beginning to happen in patrol meetings. The patrol leader has learned she's the representative, *not* the boss! Patrol leaders and troop officers meet regularly with the troop leaders in Court of Honor. Information gets from patrols to Court of Honor and back. The troop leader gives less direction.

Patrol leaders and their assistants share parts of the leadership job. Each patrol member has a specific permanent job in her patrol. Patrol leaders regularly teach skills or activities and all members share and practice skills with newcomers or younger members.

Patrols carry on some activities on their own, at a time and place apart from the regular troop meeting. During patrol meetings and Court of Honor, girls know how to pick up ideas, develop them into exciting program plans, and organize themselves so that plans become a reality.

Patrols are really self-propelled, and girls are able to evaluate their activities. Patrol and troop spirit is high. Girls take the initiative in planning troop program and are responsible for carrying it out.

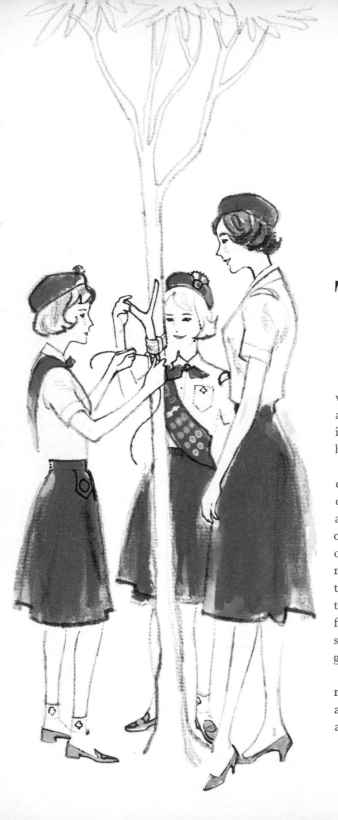

The Troop Leader

Every troop has an adult leader, who enjoys working with girls your age. Specially trained for her job, she is a volunteer, giving her time and help freely to you and your community.

The most important thing she does is to help you discover and develop the best that is in you. She works along with you to bring out your capabilities and talents, to draw you out, both as an individual and as a member of the troop. She also teaches the girls new and interesting things to do, or she finds experts in various fields to teach them. And, of course, she is always available for advice and guidance when the girls wish.

In some large troops, the leader may have the help of one or more adult assistants to share the work and fun.

Other Adults
in Girl Scouting

Although you, the members, run your troop, there are times when you need advice and help from grownups. At these times, you will always find two groups ready to help you.

The troop committee is one. This is made up of mothers and fathers of troop members and other adults who are interested in you and will lend a hand when needed. On a troop trip, for example, you might need several automobiles for transportation and several adults as chaperons. You could ask members of the troop committee for this kind of help. Sometimes members of the troop committee help a group of girls who are working on a particular badge. A father might help with the Handywoman badge, or someone who works in an office might help with the Clerk badge.

The Girl Scout council is the other. This is an organization of volunteers—men and women—who are responsible for Girl Scouting in your town. Although the council does not work directly with your troop, it does a great many things to organize, direct, and encourage Scouting. For example, the council starts new troops and finds meeting places for them. It trains leaders, runs camps, and helps to raise money for the Girl Scouts. Your troop leader will tell you more about your council and its work.

countdown for troop program

To launch a rocket takes careful planning; to launch an action-packed troop program also takes careful planning.

Planning is a way to think about the future, a way to get things done. People aren't born good planners, any more than they are born knowing how to read. But everyone can learn.

As a Cadette Scout on your way to First Class, you will be planning your Challenge course. Your troop will be planning its year's calendar of activities. Start with short, simple plans. After a while, with more knowledge and practice both you and the troop can make more detailed, elaborate plans. What's more, this planning experience will work for you not only in Scouting but all the time.

Follow the

On these two pages you will see an example of good planning by a Cadette Scout troop. The girls are meeting to make a decision about a troop trip. Although this is an example, the planning method they

PLANNING STEPS	EXAMPLE

1. STATE THE QUESTION OR PROBLEM.

Every girl should understand clearly just what it is you are trying to decide. State the question as simply as possible; it will help to keep the discussion to one idea.

"Which weekend in February will we take our troop trip?"

To make sure everyone sticks to the point, write the question where all can see it. A blackboard or large cardboard will do nicely.

2. COLLECT THE FACTS.

With the question firmly in your minds (and before your eyes), first consider the facts that limit your choice. In this case, rule out the dates you cannot go.

"We can't go on the first weekend of the month because two patrols will be away camping. Can't go on the last weekend either because we're going to see some films."

The choice is now narrowed down to real possibilities.

Next, state the facts that will be to your advantage.

"Washington's Birthday falls on Monday. If we pick that weekend, we'll have an extra day."

Be sure your information is correct.

"I'm sure we don't have school on Washington's Birthday because I checked it in the school calendar."

Don't let other subjects, no matter how tempting, get you off the discussion track. If you are bursting to tell about the attractive boy you met at Nancy's, don't. It is interesting but it won't help plan your troop trip.

Planning Steps

use has been carefully worked out, and it may be applied to almost any situation calling for a wise decision. Refer to this chart often as you plan activities.

PLANNING STEPS	EXAMPLE
3. CONSIDER ALL POSSIBLE SOLUTIONS. Once you have all the facts, think of all the ways you can use them.	"We could go the second weekend if we leave after school Friday." "If we go on Washington's Birthday weekend, we will have more time to do things."
4. MAKE A DECISION. After everyone has had a chance to be heard and all viewpoints are considered, it is time to decide. The girls have the facts and the choices before them.	Most of the girls vote for the Washington Birthday weekend.
5. MAKE A PLAN. Once the decision is made, start planning for it. List all the things that must be done to turn the decision into action.	From school closing on Friday Feb. 19 through Feb. 22 are marked on the troop calendar. The leader informs the troop committee; clears with council if necessary. The girls take home permission slips for parents to sign.
6. CARRY OUT THE PLAN.	The troop goes on the trip on the dates selected.
7. EVALUATE THE PLAN. This means to judge the way it went. Did it work out well? Could it have been better? How? What would you do differently next time? Record the answers to these questions to use for planning the next time.	After the trip all the girls give their opinions at patrol meetings. Patrol leaders report to Court of Honor. Scribe records the reports which will be used when troop plans next trip.

I especially liked	I liked least	Bright ideas for next time
IIII Music festival II Our quick and easy menus, so we had plenty of time for sightseeing.	III Sitting in the same seat in the bus all the way.	II Let's stay longer.

OUR TRIP

THIS WORKED WELL	CHANGE THIS NEXT TIME	FUTURE PLANS

Visit to:
    Historic block house
    Music Festival
    Canning Co. testing kitchen
Sufficient time for sightseeing
	Seating arrangements in the bus	1. Plan a chart to rotate the seating arrangements
		2. Again allow girls to choose what they wish to see and visit in advance planning of trip

Plans
Big
and
Little

At the beginning of the troop year, the Court of Honor makes the troop's "long-term plan" for the months to come. This is how the plan is worked out.

Each patrol leader gets ideas and suggestions from her patrol members. The troop leader finds out the dates for any councilwide events. Special occasions, such as troop birthday, Juliette Low's birthday, Thinking Day, and Girl Scout Week, are all noted. Of course cookouts, overnights, and holiday parties are included. When *not* to plan special activities should be considered, too—such as exam week.

The Court of Honor makes a Time and Events Planning Chart (next page, please) which is presented to the whole troop for its approval. Each patrol makes a copy of the final plan, so it can check before selecting dates for patrol activities.

The Time and Events Planning Chart is used by the Court of Honor throughout the year. It reminds them when it is time to start short-term plans. These are the detailed plans which make sure food is bought for the cookout, invitations for the party are sent, toys are made for children at Christmas, or whatever else the event in the long-term plan calls for.

Time and Events Planning Chart

MEETING DATES	SUGGESTIONS AND REMINDERS
SEPTEMBER Three meetings	20 School opens Troop meets twice before school opens, then skips a meeting during the first week of school. Discuss and decide upon Challenge grouping procedures.
OCTOBER Four meetings	24 U.N. Day Meet outdoors if weather is nice. Cookout with boys. Troop money-earning event.
NOVEMBER Four meetings	22 Thanksgiving Review badge choices with troop leaders. Good time for a party.
DECEMBER Three meetings	19-31 Vacation Special troop service project. Start planning for trip. Review Challenge progress.
JANUARY Four meetings	16-20 Exam Week Council Cookie Sale (review selling and accounting procedures). Final check on trip plans.
FEBRUARY Four meetings	22 Thinking Day Review progress on Challenge Preps. Troop trip weekend of February 22. Be sure to pick up camp folders.
MARCH Five meetings	11-17 Girl Scout Week Invite a Senior troop to send representatives to describe Senior troop program.
APRIL Four meetings	14-21 Vacation Invite 11-year-old Junior Scouts to a troop event. Brush up camping skills for Cadette Little Roundup.
MAY Five meetings	27 Little Roundup Plan troop Court of Awards and send invitations to parents.
JUNE Three meetings	14 Flag Day Make detailed plans for first two meetings before school starts next September. Troop Court of Awards. 14's attend Senior Capping Ceremony.

DURING JULY AND AUGUST—plans depend upon camp and family vacation plans.

As you progress toward First Class by earning badges and meeting Challenges, there will be many times when the success of your project depends upon your ability to turn an idea into a working plan.

Read the statements below to see how well you and your troop are coming along in the skills of planning. There's quite a difference, isn't there, between the first statement and the last? You can see how the planning depends less on the leader and more on the girls. Which one applies to your troop at the moment?

o The leader does the planning for the troop.
o The leader suggests several ideas and the patrols make a choice.
o The patrols begin to add their own ideas to the leader's suggestions.
o Patrols develop their own ideas, with help from the leader, choose among them, and plan some of the details to turn ideas into reality.
o The patrols do most of the planning, suggesting ideas and carrying them out. They plan well in advance. They know how to gather facts, make interesting plans, and sensible decisions. They judge the results of their own plans and consider ways to do better next time.
o The leaders and girls are in partnership.

The Kaper Chart

One of your handiest working tools in planning is the kaper chart. "Kaper," as you know, is the Girl Scout word for a temporary job or responsibility like chopping wood for a fire, conducting the flag ceremony at a meeting, serving refreshments at a party.

Kaper charts tell you who does what in any given project, so that each girl knows just what her job is. They also provide for rotation of jobs, so that everyone gets a chance to do many things, even the unpleasant ones.

Since kaper charts are so often used in Scouting, you will find it useful to know how to make one.

A SURPRISE!

BEAVER

LARK

CHIPMUNK

AN OPENING CEREMONY

A CLOSING CEREMONY

COOKS

	FRI. SUPPER SAT. BREAKFAST	SAT. LUNCH TO SUPPER	SUN. BREAKFAST AND LUNCH
COOKS HOSTESSES			
WOOD WATER FIRE			
DISHWASHERS CLEAN-UP			
FLAG AND CLOSING CEREMONY			

To Make a Kaper Chart

1. Write down the jobs to be done, listing just what each consists of. For example, do cooks or dishwashers clean the pots?
2. Count how many times each job needs to be done. For one meal or several; for one day or more.
3. Plan how to divide the work. Individuals? Buddies? Patrols?
4. Combine some jobs if necessary, keeping an equal amount of work in each if possible.
5. Make a chart which shows which group or individual does what and when. Rotate the jobs if they must be done more than once.

Let's Talk It Over!

Knowing how to take part in a discussion is important when you make plans with others. This is how ideas are communicated, problems thrashed out, and decisions made. How good a talker and listener are you? These questions will help you find out:

o Do you have ideas and opinions of your own?
o Do you listen respectfully to others, even when you disagree?
o Do you try to understand why another girl may feel or think differently from you?

If your answer is "yes" to these questions, you're doing well. If not, perhaps an example may help you.

Suppose your patrol is meeting to plan a campfire stunt. Do you make suggestions? By offering your ideas, you are taking an active part in the discussion. If you don't, is it possible you're leaving the planning to others? One way to overcome this is to give thought to the meeting beforehand and come prepared with suggestions.

Now, suppose you say, "Let's do a skit showing what we learned in first aid." Another girl may say, "I don't think that's a good idea." Don't be cross because she disagrees with you. Find out her reasons for objecting. See what suggestions she makes. There may be something to what she says.

Good discussion is give and take. You want the others to hear you out patiently and thoughtfully. Be prepared to return this courtesy.

Why Have Discussions?

Discussions may serve different purposes, so it is wise to be clear in your mind as to *why* you're talking about something. That way, you can get a great deal from the talk.

Your patrol is discussing next week's hike. The question is "Where shall we go?" One girl suggests the state park, another says the bird sanctuary, and a third says the beach. And there you are, plunged into a lively discussion with one purpose: to make a decision.

Or you might be talking about the movie you all saw last week. This discussion has a different purpose; to exchange ideas, to share your thoughts and impressions with others.

Some discussions are for the purpose of learning new things or learning more about a subject. Troop members might compare notes on different kinds of camping, so that a girl who has never been to day camp, for instance, can get an idea of what it's like. Or your patrol might stop, after packing a box to be sent abroad, to talk about the meaning of international friendship.

Whatever its purpose, a good discussion is a satisfying experience. Whether you've come to a decision, exchanged thoughts with others, or learned something new, you've accomplished something worthwhile.

The Discussion Leader

A good discussion leader is like an orchestra conductor. Using special knowledge and skill, she can direct an assortment of different girls with different ideas, opinions, and tastes into a unified discussion. She doesn't dash about, trying to play all the instruments herself. But, like a talented conductor, she does know how to get the most music from each player.

How does she get the talk going? How does she keep it going, bright, lively, and to the point? To begin, a discussion leader should herself be informed about the topic the group is going to talk about. If she doesn't have the facts in her mind, she should have them available for handy reference.

For example, if you're going to decide on a goal for a hike, she might provide a list of interesting sights to see and a map showing the distances to each. She might also inquire if any of the girls have been to these places before. If they have, they will be able to describe them to the girls who haven't. Other sources of helpful information are books, the Court of Honor, the troop leader, and other patrol leaders.

When it is your turn to be a discussion leader, you will want to know the best way to go about it. On the next two pages are some suggestions to help you lead a group in an interesting, rewarding talk.

Make everyone comfortable. Seat the girls in such a way that no one feels left out.

Start the ball rolling by stating, as simply and clearly as you can, the purpose of the discussion.

At first . . . listen! Let the others talk, so you can see if they know the purpose of the discussion, and if they have ideas to suggest.

Try to keep the atmosphere friendly and good-humored. "Here's a riddle. What's the difference between a discussion and an argument?"

Learn a few tactful phrases to soothe ruffled feelings, to soften your disagreement. "That's a lovely idea, but don't you think . . .?" "You're quite right, but on the other hand . . ."

Keep the discussion to the point. "Yes, a dance would be fun, but right now, we're talking about . . ."

Make sure every speaker gets respectful attention. Encourage shy girls to talk.
"Let's hear what Sheila thinks of this."

If things get noisy and confused, give the quiet signal. It works like a charm.

Be prepared with correct information when it is needed.
"It's eight miles to the bird sanctuary, not six."

Summarize the discussion. Repeat the main points that have been made pro and con.

If the purpose of the discussion is to make a decision, see that it's made. Sometimes, it's unanimous. Sometimes, the vote is divided.
"All in favor of going to the bird sanctuary . . ."

Be prepared to report the discussion accurately to the Court of Honor. Be sure to include . . .

1 The Vote
2 The General Feeling of the Girls
3 Minority Opinion.

A really good discussion leader has a special sense. She can hear more than is actually said. Does this seem mysterious? In a way, it is. For she has a way of sensing what the girls may be thinking, even though some of them may not be able to put their thoughts into words. This special sense might be called a sensitivity to others.

If, for example, she notices that Sheila is unusually silent, she may conclude that something is troubling her, perhaps something personal. Tactfully, she waits for Sheila to join in the talk when she feels up to it.

As you learn to be a good discussion leader, you are learning much more at the same time. You are learning to be a good companion, conversationalist, and hostess. That's why the art of discussion is more than a part of good planning.

It's part of good living.

A Matter of Money

Money, getting and spending it, is a necessary part of planning. Undoubtedly, your troop will need money for all sorts of things; special equipment and supplies, games, trips, cookouts. Where will this money come from? And who will decide how to spend it?

Usually, it will come from two sources. First, there are weekly dues paid by all troop members. These are not the same as the dollar membership dues, which are paid to the National Organization once a year by every member—girl or adult, but a smaller sum paid each week and kept by the troop. The amount you pay is decided on by the troop and is based on your plans and how much the girls can afford.

The second source of income is money earned by the troop in a special money-earning project (see Chapter 14).

All this money, dues and earned income, goes into the troop treasury. By the same token, it is spent by the troop to make your plans come true. This is where budgeting enters your plans.

A Budget Is a Plan

Many, many years ago, the meaning of the word "budget" was different from the way we use it today. It was a sack, pouch, or wallet. No doubt, a lady of long ago reached into her budget, jingling with coins, to pay for her purchases.

Today, a budget has come to mean a plan of estimating future expenses and working out ways to get enough money to pay for them.

How can your troop foresee expenses? In very much the same way your family might plan this winter for a vacation next summer. Remember the troop's long-term plans? Consult the Time and Events Planning Chart and you will get a clear picture of projects to come.

If you're having a cookout next month, you will see it on the chart. What will you need for the cookout? Will you have to buy food, cooking utensils, pot-holders? What supplies does the troop already own? This is how you gain an idea of what is available and what you will have to buy.

The same applies to any troop project. Are you planning to build up a library? What books and magazines do you own? What will you want to buy?

To start your troop budget, list the events to come and, taking them one by one, estimate how much money you will need for each project. Your troop leader will help you here. Will the regular weekly dues be enough? If not, what to do?

A yearly budget for a Cadette Scout troop of 32 girls might look like this:

PROPOSED OUTGO		ANTICIPATED INCOME	
Basic Expenses		*From Dues*	
National Annual Membership Dues..........	$32.00	Plan A 50c per month, 10 months..	160.00
Troop Meeting Equipment... (first aid kit, bulletin board)	5.00	Plan B 25c every 2 weeks, 40 weeks	160.00
Troop Library (books, records)	10.00	Plan C 15c per week, 40 weeks....	192.00
Ongoing Program.......... (long-term plans, service projects, cookouts)	60.00	Plan D 10c per week, 40 weeks....	128.00
Flexible Program........... (spur of the moment ideas)	20.00		
Basic Total Expenses........	127.00	*From Money-Earning Project*	
Highlights		To balance our budget we would need in addition to:	
Troop Trip...............	45.00	Plan A....................	57.00
Troop Camping........... (equipment, site fees)	45.00	Plan B....................	57.00
		Plan C....................	25.00
Highlight Total Expenses....	90.00	Plan D....................	89.00
Total Proposed Outgo.......	$217.00	Total Anticipated Income....	$217.00

You might consider increasing the dues to cover the cost. That would be one way of getting more money. But suppose the girls are against that idea. You still have two good choices to make.

You might decide on a special money-earning project to enrich the treasury. Or you could simplify your original plan, so it doesn't cost as much as you first reckoned.

How do you simplify a plan? Consider the troop library project. Perhaps your list of books is too ambitious. You might get the library started by borrowing books from the public library or another troop. This would be temporary, until you've saved money to buy your own.

By working these things out, you can manage to match your troop's income to its expenses and arrange to pay for projects you've set your hearts on.

The Beauty of Budgeting

Some girls are disappointed when a plan must be simplified. They feel some of the glory is going out of it. Actually, it's more fun, more of a challenge, to see how clever you can be, how well you can do with less, rather than more. More than half the joy of planning is making it work. There is great satisfaction in getting the most out of what you have. There's wisdom in knowing which things are important and which are not really so necessary, after all.

There is also great personal pride in handling your own financial affairs. It's an accomplishment to make a plan, work out the details, foresee the costs and the difficulties…and then do what you've set out to do. This is wonderful preparation for the time when you will be earning your own living, managing a household, or combining a job and a family.

Money Quiz

How well does your troop manage its money? Check the description that applies to your troop. Then turn the page upside-down for your rating.

1. There's no money-planning in the troop at all. The girls do not discuss or plan costs and expenditures.
2. The troop decides how much the weekly dues shall be.
3. The troop considers the cost of purchases, but makes no budget to balance income against outgo.
4. The troop draws up a budget for a year—and then forgets it.
5. The troop makes a short-term budget based on money already on hand in the treasury.
6. The troop makes a one-year budget, but concentrates more on expenditures than on income.
7. The troop has a budget for the whole year, planned and supported by all the members. The girls make the budget work by matching their plans to their money. At the end of the year, the troop's income and planned outgo are just about even.

---

1. Why, you haven't even begun to budget!
2. A little better, but not much. You're still in the baby-budgeting stage.
3. You're thinking in the right direction, but you're not doing a real job of budgeting yet.
4. What good is a budget if the troop doesn't use it?
5. This isn't really budgeting, just a short-term plan for spending money.
6. You're getting warmer! But you haven't learned that getting money *into the treasury* is just as important as spending it.
7. Hats off to your troop! You're doing a fine job of long-term budgeting, with everyone cooperating. At last, your troop is wise in the matter of money.

program starters

H ere is a chapterful of fun—games, recipes, fascinating things to make and do. If your troop is a new one, here are activities for meetings for the first few months. If you are a new member of a long-established troop, here are some of the things you will want to know. Even if you are not new to Girl Scouting, some of these activities may be new to you.

Take your choice. As Cadette Girl Scouts you and the other members of the troop plan your activities. Whether you choose to do one or try all, you're on your way to interesting badges and the Challenges.

Games To Play

1.
The Numbers Rhythm

Try this while waiting for the meeting to start or till the bus arrives.

The Game: Everyone sits in a circle on chairs or on the floor. One seat is named "the top" or No. 1, the next No. 2, and so on around the circle. The No. 1 player starts everyone off by explaining: "All together, now! Clap hands twice, slap your lap, snap your fingers!"

As everyone beats out the rhythm, No. 1 player shouts out a number in the circle, like this: Clap, clap, slap, snap, *"Four!"* At once, No. 4 replies in the same way: Clap, clap, slap, snap, "Four" (her own number), "Seven!" Immediately, No. 7, following the rhythm clap, clap, slap, snap, shouts, "Seven, Three!" Keep going until someone breaks the rhythm. This girl moves down to the last seat and everyone else moves up one seat.

Winner: The girl who moves into No. 1 seat and stays there the longest.

2.
Scavenger Hunt

Object: Find as many listed items as you possibly can in the given time.

Preparation: Each patrol gets a list (made by a committee of girls or the troop leader) of objects to collect within a given time and place. If it's an outdoor hunt, your list might include such things as a pine cone, oak leaf, maple seed, piece of quartz. Do not list any living thing. A list for indoors might read: a textbook, right overshoe, breadcrumb, elastic band. Include at least one hard-to-find item. The number of "hard" ones depends on your time limit. When time is up, all the patrols meet to display their collections.

Winner: The patrol which has collected the most items in the given time.

Variation: You can play a sit-down version by "hunting" specific things found in this handbook. Object? List the pages on which they appear.

3.
World-O Game

This absorbing game was developed by the World Association of Girl Guides and Girl Scouts. You may buy it at the Girl Scout Shop, order it from National Equipment Service, or perhaps borrow it from someone in your council. While you play, you'll find your Scouting vocabulary growing in two languages.

4.
Treasure Hunt

Object: Follow a trail of clues until you reach the treasure at the end.

Preparation: Two or three girls make up the clues and hide them, starting at the end of the trail and working backward. That way, they cover the course only once. Clues are in everyday prose, verse, code, riddles, as you like. Here are some sample clues:

o Up Main Street, left to 17 Hill Street, and look in the mailbox!

o Knights of old were mighty bold, But castles were icy, *water cold!*

o !ccrt kao kcalb eht ot emoC

The Game: Patrols start on the trail one after another at given intervals of five or ten minutes. Each patrol leaves the clues for the next team to find. The last patrol collects all the clues and brings them back.

The Treasure: Something delicious such as the ingredients for "Banana Boats," see page 76.

5.
World Association— "Thread the Needle"

The Game: Form two teams, each with the same number of players. Line up, clasp hands, and face the opposite team, with at least ten feet between lines. The girls number off and each number is given the name of a country in the World Association. For example, both No. 1's might be Australia, No. 2's Brazil, No. 3's Canada, etc. Each girl must remember her own country and the game leader should note the order of the countries named.

The game leader calls two adjacent countries like this: "Brazil and Canada!" The two girls called raise their clasped hands, forming the needle's "eye." The two end players on each team lead their lines through the "eye." Both ends may go through at the same time, but hands must stay clasped. The first team to come back to its original straight line wins a point.

Winner: The team with the most points after a specified playing time. The book *Games for Girl Scouts* has directions for many other games you will enjoy.

Party with a Purpose

"You are cordially invited . . ."

Party-going is fun, but party-giving is both fun and an accomplishment. Even if you've never been hostesses before, you and your troop can produce a wonderful party the first time if you go about it the right way.

First decide on an occasion. The beginning of the troop year is a perfect party occasion, particularly if your troop is new. Why not give a "Troop Launching"? You might invite your mothers or the members of the troop committee to come to the investiture or rededication ceremony.

If this is the first party your troop has given, you will be wise to keep it simple. As you gain experience, you will probably plan more elaborate occasions. The same basic planning is needed for a simple party as for an elaborate one. In either case, you will enjoy the pride of hospitality when your guests say, "Thank you, it was a delightful party."

Plan Your Party

What makes a good party? Pleasant people, tasty refreshments, pretty settings, and an interesting program. So first make your guest list.

Invitations should be mailed in advance so guests have time to answer. Be sure to give the date, hour and address of the party.

Decorations lend charm and color to room and table. A large bowl or basket heaped with fruit and vegetables makes an attractive centerpiece. Home-grown greenery, such as sweet potato vines, is pretty, too.

Refreshments should be delicious, but easy to prepare. Bake cookies or cakes from a mix, or something you've made before to be sure it will turn out well. Serve coffee or tea to adults; punch to the girls.

Service should be comfortable for both guests and hostesses. Decide if guests will help themselves at a buffet table, or if troop members will pass refreshments and pour. Lap-juggling is awkward, so use a large table, card tables, or snack trays, and remember napkins, cake forks, sugar, cream, and other accessories.

Financing the party is important. Estimate costs as you plan. Will the money come from the troop treasury? If not, where? Plan your party to fit your budget.

Activate the Plans

Invitations are out and everyone's coming! Now plans go into action.

Make a kaper chart covering "must" jobs: shopping for supplies, preparing food, decorating the room, hostessing the guests, cleaning up after the party is over. Assign a job to each patrol or double up on some jobs.

Rehearse party etiquette beforehand, practicing greeting guests and making proper introductions (see page 122). Remember, your manners reflect your troop and all Girl Scouts.

Entertainment for the party is based on troop program. At a "troop launching" the feature may be investiture. After the ceremony you might have some demonstrations; for example, show how to wear your uniform correctly.

A demonstration is an organized way to show how something is done and may be presented by one girl, a team of two or three, or even by a patrol. To give one, prepare equipment ahead of time and rehearse to be sure people can hear and see you well.

There are three parts to every demonstration. (1) Introduce yourself and preview what you plan to show. (2) Step by step give essential information, showing or clearly describing correct procedure. Use examples made beforehand to illustrate special points if necessary. End with the finished item if possible. (3) When finished, ask for questions, answer them, review important points briefly, and thank your audience for its attention. There is an endless number of things to demonstrate. Some ideas are: How to: folk dance, weave, give first aid, make a knapsack, paint a chair. Demonstrations can enliven your activities all year. Use them to show how you have met requirements for badges and to teach new skills to other troop members as well as to entertain parents and friends.

Postscript

Even after the party, cordiality goes on. Send thank-you notes to all who contributed to the success of the party. And write the girl who missed it a full, newsy report, so she feels she was there.

Look for more party ideas in Chapters 7 and 8. Read the Challenge of Social Dependability in Chapter 16.

Safety Spot Check

Safety measures are important, especially where many people gather. Safety also depends upon how you use and keep your meeting place. Recheck yours from time to time. Use this safety checklist.

Our Meeting Place Is:
- ☐ Clean
- ☐ Properly ventilated and heated
- ☐ Well lighted
- ☐ Easy and safe to enter and leave
- ☐ On the ground floor
- ☐ If not, are the stairways:
- __ uncluttered?
- __ well lighted?
- __ in good repair?
- __ provided with handrails?

Our Meeting Place Has:
- ☐ Safe drinking water
- ☐ Fire escapes and emergency exits
- ☐ Working fire-fighting equipment, such as: sprinkler system, approved extinguishers, fire alarm
- ☐ Electrical equipment in good order
- ☐ Sanitary toilets
- ☐ Hand-washing facilities
- ☐ Soap and paper towels
- ☐ Troop equipment in good order
- ☐ First aid kit

Ceremonies

Girl Scout ceremonies have a dignity that makes you feel proud to take part in them. They celebrate significant occasions in the life of your troop, such as the welcoming of new members, the presentation of badges, the troop's birthday. No wonder you are eager to join in!

Ceremonies present a fine opportunity for troop dramatics. Try producing your own versions. Build your ceremony around a pattern—a horseshoe, circle, or hollow square. The most successful troop ceremonies are brief and simple.

The Flag Ceremony

This is a tribute to the flag we honor as a symbol of our country. The ceremony should be well planned and performed smoothly and with dignity, for this is the spirit that helps to make it inspiring and memorable.

Occasions: A flag ceremony is often used to open or close a troop meeting and as part of the ceremony of an investiture, rededication, or Court of Awards. In camp, there is usually a flag ceremony every morning and evening. Cadette Scouts are sometimes asked to conduct the flag ceremony at meetings of other groups, such as school assembly or a P.T.A. meeting.

Pattern: Troop members stand in a horseshoe formation. At one end of the horseshoe, where she will best be able to see and direct the color guard, stands the person who will give the commands. Next to her, stand those taking special parts in the ceremony— for example, a reader or song leader.

In the weekly troop meeting, the members of the color guard may stand in the formation with the others. On special occasions or in larger groups, the color guard may be assigned a separate place outside the formation where they hold the flag in readiness.

The Ceremony: If the color guard is part of the formation, the person giv-

When only the United States flag is used, there are three in the color guard, the color bearer (who carries the flag) and two guards who walk on either side of her.
In a troop meeting where an additional flag is used, another color bearer is needed.
For larger events, plan on a bearer and two guards for each flag.

ing the commands calls, "Color guard, fall out!" At this, the color guard steps back out of the formation, circles the outside of the group and lines up facing the American flag. At a quiet signal from the color bearer, the guard gives the civilian salute in unison.

The color bearer steps forward and takes the American flag from its stand. She holds it with left hand supporting the pole at her side, right hand supporting it at shoulder height. Then she steps back into the color guard.

If there are other flags, such as the troop or World Association flags, the girls designated as their bearers then step forward, lift the flags from their stands, and step back. When there are two flags, the American flag is carried on the right. When there are three, it is carried in the center, and in front of the other two.

Wheeling to the right, the color guard marches to a place in front of the troop. During the rest of the ceremony, the color guard remains standing at attention, taking no part in the singing or speaking.

The person giving the commands says, "Girl Scouts, the flag of your country, pledge allegiance." Everyone gives the civilian salute and repeats the Pledge of Allegiance.

If "The Star-Spangled Banner" or another patriotic song is to be sung, the person giving the commands says, "We will now sing (number) stanzas of (name of song)." She then gives the pitch and starts the singing. Or, if there is a song leader, she steps forward to lead the singing.

At the close of the ceremony, the person in charge gives one of two commands. She may say, "Color guard, retire the colors!" In that case, the guard wheels to the right and takes the flags from the scene.

Or she may say, "Color guard, post the colors!" This means the flags are to be replaced in the stands in view of the audience. The guard wheels to the right, marches to the stands, and replaces the flags, with the American flag last in order. When all the flags are in their stands, the color guard salutes the American flag and returns to the formation.

The person in charge then dismisses the formation. The ceremony is ended.

Variations: A flag ceremony may include an inspirational reading, a brief story, or a group reading. You may wish to recite the Promise and Laws. However you vary it, practice the ceremony until you can perform it with the pride of complete confidence.

Sources of Inspiration for Ceremonies

Tell of Tradition: The founders of Girl Scouting and Guiding were energetic and resourceful people. Their lives will provide you with interesting anecdotes to tell the troop as part of a meeting opening or closing, or simply on your own. Pick two subjects to present in skits, charades, riddles, or guessing games, or write a short, original play.

Bring History to Life: Wherever you live, there is history all around you. Take some aspect of local history, turn it into a part of a troop ceremony. If you're from New England, for example, you probably know the story of Mary Lyon, one of the very first to work for the education of women and the founder of Mount Holyoke, the first women's college in the United States. You can learn more about her at your library or historical society. Can you think of ways for your patrol to dramatize events in the life of someone famous in your community?

Start a Quote File: In your reading you may come across a thought beautifully expressed in prose or poetry that has deep meaning for you. Add this to a file of quotations kept by the troop for use in ceremonies, for inspirational openings and closings of meetings, or at a Scouts' Own (see page 87). Here's an example:

> *Then deem it not an idle thing,*
> *A pleasant word to speak;*
> *The face you wear, the thoughts you bring,*
> *A heart may heal or break.*
>
> —DANIEL CLEMENT COLESWORTHY

You can buy a file box and cards or make one (from a shoebox, for instance) and cut cards to fit. Decide on the most efficient filing system for your use. You can file the quotations alphabetically under authors' names, first lines, or by subject. Or you might cross-file them under two of these headings. By contributing quotations to the file for future use, you help to make troop ceremonies richer, more beautiful.

Openings and Closings for Meetings

All troop meetings should have a definite beginning and ending but not necessarily always a ceremony.

The opening indicates that the meeting has officially begun. It is held as soon as all (or most) of the girls arrive and may be either informal or formal in tone.

An informal opening could be a song or perhaps a patrol demonstration. An example of a more formal opening is a flag ceremony.

The closing brings the troop meeting to an official end. Like the opening, it may be simple or more formal in spirit.

In an informal closing, the girls might sing a favorite song followed by "Taps," the traditional melody sung by both Boy Scouts and Girl Scouts to indicate "lights out!" Good songs for closing ceremonies are: "Now the Day Is Over," "Golden Slumbers," "All Is Silent," "Slumber, Slumber," "Good Night Round." All these are in *Sing Together—A Girl Scout Songbook.*

Another idea for an informal closing is the friendship circle. The girls form a circle. Then each girl crosses her right arm over her left and clasps the hand of both her neighbors. Hands are held during the goodnight song and the closing words. Then, everybody drops hands to stand at attention while "Taps" is sung. When you are part of a friendship circle you can feel its meaning—an unbroken chain of friendship. You might like to try this around the dying embers of a campfire.

"Goodnight, Scouts" are the words spoken by all while giving the Girl Scout sign. This is the signal that the meeting is over.

For more formal closings, a flag ceremony is often used.

Here is still another idea for a closing which your troop might enjoy. Divide the troop into two groups. As one group softly hums the music of "Taps," the other group reads or recites in unison words suitable to the closing. For example, as the first group hums, the second might read:

> *Not what we have,*
> > *But what we use,*
> *Not what we see,*
> > *But what we choose—*
> *These are the things*
> > *That mar or bless*
> *The sum of*
> > *Human happiness.*
>
> —C. URMY

After the recitation of the poem, both groups sing "Taps."

Openings and closings are always interesting when they are varied. Here are some suggestions which may be used for either openings or closings.

A Moment of Silence—for a brief period, no one speaks aloud as each girl thinks of her Promise and its meaning or concentrates on one particular Law which is hard for her to obey. If you are thinking of a Law, try to find one small way to help you improve and make a silent resolution to follow it.

Responsive Reading—this is a kind of choral or group reading of the Girl Scout Laws. One patrol starts off in unison: "A Girl Scout's honor ..." The Law is completed in unison by another patrol or by the entire troop: "...is to be trusted." Or each patrol, in turn, recites a Law, going from the first to the tenth Law in planned rotation.

End the ceremony with an inspirational song, sung by the entire troop. You will find appropriate songs in the Girl Scout songbooks.

Surprise!—each patrol, in turn, prepares an opening or closing, presenting it to the troop as a surprise. This could be a favorite game or a snack. Have you ever had a "Dessert Wrap"? Each girl brings to an evening meeting one serving of dessert, cake or fruit for example, imaginatively wrapped. After the mystery packages have been displayed, each girl chooses one, not her own. Off come the wrappings, the desserts are eaten, and the meeting begins.

One Wish—a subject is chosen, such as Juliette Low, or international friendship. After a moment for thought each girl (or each patrol, if the group is a large one) tells her special wish. For example: May the bond of friendship between Guides and Scouts help bring world peace.

Thought for the Day—after your patrol has practiced different openings and closings, why not plan *both* ceremonies around the same theme. Start by selecting an idea or thought that appeals to you. You will find inspiration in the Girl Scout Laws or in a character trait you admire. Find a quotation (In the Quote File?) or write something original to express this idea. Then, choose an appropriate song. Use the quotation for the opening and the song for the closing, or the other way 'round. Your entire patrol might read or sing together for dramatic effect.

A ceremony that mirrors a sense of true conviction and deep feeling is one way of demonstrating your understanding of the Girl Scout Promise. Such understanding is basic to each of the Challenges.

Holidays

A long time ago, holidays were "holy days," celebrated as religious observances. Today, we have all kinds of holidays; traditional ones like Thanksgiving, patriotic ones like Fourth of July, sentimental ones, like St. Valentine's Day, and universal ones, like New Year's Day.

Some holidays are observed in a way long determined by tradition and custom. Can you imagine Thanksgiving without a turkey, for instance? Or St. Valentine's Day without hearts, flowers, and cupids?

Learn something about a holiday of a religion or region different from yours and find out how it is observed. Along with other members of your patrol demonstrate what you have learned. Make a Christmas creche, for example, or show how candles are lit in the Menorah at Chanukah.

Make a holiday calendar that shows at least fifteen holidays that will fall in the next three months. Include a variety of days—patriotic, religious, and traditional. Plan to include celebrations of some of them in your troop program.

Of course, Girl Scouts have holidays all their own. Two favorite birthdays are those of Juliette Low (October 31) and of the Girl Scouts themselves (March 12), the day the first troop was started by Mrs. Low in Savannah, Georgia, in 1912. On one of these two birthdays, Girl Scouts often give their contributions to the Juliette Low World Friendship Fund and mark the days with special ceremonies, as well. Can you create any original ideas for holiday fun?

Wire Jewelry

The love of ornamentation is older than civilization. In fact, people made and wore jewelry before clothes were known. Some jewelry was worn to show rank or wealth, and some out of superstitious belief, to ward off evil or disease. Some of it was for practical use; clasps to fasten robes and buckles for belt closings. But most jewelry, whether of feathers and berries or beaten gold and precious gems, was worn for beauty. People have always loved to dress up—and still do.

You can have the pleasure of creating a lovely piece of jewelry and making it so well that it will have a finished, professional look. Here are instructions for making three simple wire ornaments: a "caged" stone, perhaps one you found on a hike; a graceful, free-form pin; and a pair of earrings. Why not make one as a gift?

"Caging" a Stone

Materials: A 6"-8" length of wire (18 or 20 gauge) and a pretty stone.

For simple wire jewelry, you need:
o Hammer
o Fine steel wool
o Needle file
o Polishing cloth
o Round-nose pliers
o Tin snips
o Wire (brass, copper or silver) in the correct gauge or measurement. Gauges are numbered (12,14,16, etc.). The higher the number, the finer the wire.
o A plan. Work out your design with paper and pencil or string before bending the wire. Too much bending will harden it.

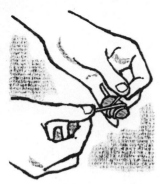
Wrapping stone with string.

Bending wire with pliers.

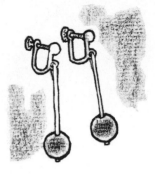
The finished earrings.

1. First experiment with string, wrapping it around the stone to see where the wire will be needed to hold the stone firmly.
2. Make a loop at one end of the wire. Hold stone and loop in one hand and with long wire in the other, follow your string pattern. Use pliers to guide bending and leave enough wire to wrap around loop a few times.

Earrings

Materials: A 6″ length of wire (18 or 20 gauge); earring backs with rings for dangles; 2 beads, ⅝″ in diameter.

1. Cut wire in half.
2. Smooth and round ends of the wire with file.
3. With pliers, bend a loop in one end of wire; slip through hole in earring back.
4. Put other end of wire through the bead. Bend 1/16″ of wire at right angle to hold on bead.
5. Polish with cloth.

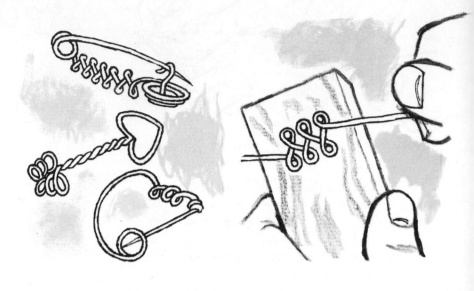

Wire Pin

Materials: A 4″-6″ length of wire (14 or 16 gauge); paper and pencil.

1. First, draw a few sketches to get an idea of the form you want your pin to take. Remember, simple designs are often the most beautiful. In reckoning the wire to be used, allow 1″ to 1½″ for pin prong.

2. Start with a small open loop at one end to serve as catch. Now, bend wire into the shape that pleases you. File the prong end to a point and bend back, as shown here.

3. You may add interest and variety to your design by flattening them lightly with the flat end of the hammer. Other sections are round.

Using a Jig: If you want your pin design to be evenly balanced, rather than free-form, make it on a jig. This is a simple device that will guide the wire into even circles and loops.

To make a jig, take a block of wood and mark your pattern on it with a pencil. Then drive nails into the wood at points where you want the wire to bend. By winding the wire around the nails, you will get your pattern.

Be sure to leave an extra length of wire to make the prong; file the end and bend it back.

After you have made several pins, you can use the same technique to make bracelets and necklaces.

Prints

What can you make with linoleum prints? A great many things, all useful and pretty; greeting cards and invitations, book jackets and book plates, giftwrap paper and (if you're really ambitious) wallpaper. A large print, on paper or fabric, can be matted and hung on the wall. You can also print dress or drapery fabric. And think of the stunning posters you could turn out!

Linoleum block printing is a form of relief printing. This means that you start with a flat surface and cut away the parts that are *not* to be printed. You can work this two ways. One is to cut out the design and ink just the background (as in the greeting card) and the other is to cut the background away and ink just the design (as in the overall pattern).

Materials needed are linoleum, cutting tools (bought at art or handcraft stores), carbon paper, tracing paper, soft pencil, block printing ink or printers' ink for paper, textile paint for fabric; a pane of glass, roller (brayer), spoon, printing paper, turpentine, rags. And now you are ready to begin!

Designing: For your first attempt, use a simple shape (fish, boat or flower). Keep it to two or three inches. Make several rough sketches of your design until you get one that you'd like to print. Remember, the *left* side of your design is the *right* side, when printed. If you don't want it this way, reverse it on the linoleum, as shown here. This is most important where lettering is used.

If you use your design as is, place a piece of carbon paper, shiny side down, over the linoleum. Put your design over it and trace the lines. To reverse the design, put tracing paper over the original drawing. With soft pencil, trace over it, pressing hard. Now, put the tracing paper on the linoleum, penciled side facing it. Rub the tracing with spoon or fingernail as hard as you can and you will transfer the drawing onto the linoleum in the position you wish.

Cutting: Linoleum cutting tools have interchangeable metal tips fitting into a wood handle. Broad tips are for cutting out large areas. Narrow tips are for cutting fine lines and details. Cut away the linoleum parts you do *not* want to print. Always keep the hand holding the linoleum behind the tool and cut *away* from yourself. That way, if the tool slips (and it often does), you won't be hurt.

Patience is necessary. Don't try to cut out too much at one time.

A simple forward motion on the tool cuts out a smooth, even sliver. Make small, shallow cuts because deep digging makes ragged edges. If there are little pieces in the areas not to be printed, don't worry. These "left-overs" add interest to your print. Besides, you can always cut away more after you've seen your first print.

Printing: Put some ink on the pane of glass and run the brayer over it. Then roll the inked brayer over the linoleum. Put a sheet of printing paper gently on top of the linoleum, holding it firmly so it won't slip. Rub the paper with the "heel" of the spoon, slowly and carefully, taking your time. Press down hard and be sure not to miss any spots. Now, lift a corner of the paper to see if the ink has printed clearly. If not, replace the paper and press some more. Lift the paper and you have your print. Color can be added to a finished print with another linoleum block or by hand.

Cleanup: When you've finished printing, use the rags and turpentine to clean the linoleum, roller, and pane of glass. Store the linoleum flat, especially if it is not mounted on a wood block. You will be able to use and reuse the design for years to come.

There are more suggestions for things to make in Chapter 5, "Try Something New." Look in the badge section, too.

Make Music

The world over, Girl Scouts and Guides enjoy music at meetings, camps, parties, hikes—wherever they go.

The world is full of songs, songs for marching and dancing, story-telling songs and songs that express moods and feelings. There are patri-otic songs and folk songs, art songs written by famous composers. Every country has its vocal music, which always sounds best sung in the native language.

Learn as many songs as you can. Take the vocal music of your region wherever you go—it will make an excellent "swap" with new friends you meet. If you know some songs in the language of the country you visit, it will help you feel at home. And by all means, learn the song of the World Association of Girl Guides and Girl Scouts. The words are on page 75.

Develop high musical standards by choosing songs with true feeling and meaning, traditional songs, timeless ones. Build a repertory, a stock of songs for all occasions, so you need never be at a loss for music.

Where do you start? Get your own copy of the *Girl Scout Pocket Songbook* and be sure the troop library has at least one copy of *Sing Together—A Girl Scout Songbook*.

I Want To Be a Farmer

American

I want to be a farm-er, a farm-er, a farm-er. I

want to be a farm-er and by my la-dy stand With a

pitch-fork on my shoul-der, my shoul-der, my shoul-der With a

pitch-fork on my shoul-der and a sick-le in my hand.

Bow, la-dies, bow; Gents, you know how;
All prom-e-nade; All prom-e-nade;

Swing that left hand la-dy 'round, All prom-e-nade.

FORMATION:

Single circle facing center; women are on their partner's right.

FIGURE 1: All join hands and circle to the left (measures 1-8). Everyone takes two steps toward center keeping hands joined. Each person puts his own right arm over his head resting his hand on his left shoulder; the circle continues to move clockwise (measures 9-14). Dancers bring own arms back to original position—unwinding the circle (measures 15-16).

FIGURE 2: Loose hands. Each person balances to partner—men step on right foot bringing left up to it, women step on left foot bringing right up to it (measures 17-18). Stepping on opposite feet each person balances to corner (measures 19-20). Men swing left hand lady twice around (measures 21-22). Men promenade with that left hand lady counter-clockwise, she being on the outside; hands are joined in skating position (measures 23-24 and 17-24 repeated).

Positions are resumed in the single circle with left hand lady on man's right and the action repeated as often as desired.

—*Contributed by R. Bruce Tom, Columbus, Ohio*

From *The Play Party Book.* Used by permission of the Cooperative Recreation Service, Delaware, Ohio.

In this way you can be certain you will be able to "join in the chorus" with Girl Scouts from all over the country. Another book you might want to own is *Chansons de Notre Chalet*, which has favorites of Girl Guides in other countries, many with words in two languages. Your National Equipment Service carries these songbooks; see the Bibliography.

Be a songwriter. For special troop or patrol occasions, you might write appropriate words to a well-known tune. A truly creative project would be the composition of an entirely original song, words *and* music. Some of the girls might work together with a music teacher or musical friend standing by to offer help.

Enjoyment of music is not limited to solo performers. If you have a fine voice, you have a talent and a gift to give. If not, sing anyway! Join the group around the piano or campfire and lift your voice. Another way to enjoy music is to listen to it on the stage, on records, on the radio or television. It will bring an added element of joy and appreciation into your life.

Still a third way to make the most of music for yourself and others is by sharing it, teaching what you know.

To teach a song, choose one you know well and like. First, tell something interesting about the song or composer. Then:

1. Sing the song through for the others to hear. If it is very long, sing only one or two stanzas to give the melody.
2. Now sing one phrase or line at a time. After each phrase, invite the group to repeat it softly, while you sing along.
3. Add a phrase at a time, until you have taught the complete song.
4. Repeat once or twice, but don't overdo it. Give the group a rest by singing old favorites. Try the new song some other day.
5. If you teach a round, have the group sing it through first as a straight song until it is note-perfect. Then try it in two parts. If this goes well, it is time to try the full number of parts. Be sure each group knows exactly when to come into the song and how many times the round is to be sung, so all parts finish correctly.

To lead a song sung by a small group, you need not indicate formal beats. Every one can feel the left-right, left-right of a hiking song, the vigorous beat of an action song, or the soft, swaying rhythm of a lullaby. Informal singing is best with an informal leader who keeps everyone together. For larger groups and important occasions, it is useful to know how to show the beat by hand or baton.

The right hand keeps the beat going and controls loudness and softness by larger and smaller gestures. The left hand indicates expression and signals entrance in part-singing. Practice these motions at a mirror. Then, try them out on a friend or two. When you can lead a few simple songs with authority, you are ready for your public.

Every musician should know that music and/or the words which are copyrighted may not be reproduced (written, printed, or mimeographed), sold, given away, posted on bulletin boards, or used in any public performance without permission of the copyright owner.

WORLD SONG

OF THE WORLD ASSOCIATION OF GIRL GUIDES AND GIRL SCOUTS *

Our way is clear as we march on
And see! Our flag on high
Is never furled throughout the world
For hope shall never die!
We must unite for what is right
In friendship true and strong,
Until the earth in its rebirth
Shall sing our song! Shall sing our song!

All those who loved the true and good,
Whose promises were kept,
With humble mind, whose acts were kind
Whose honour never slept.
These were the free! And we must be
Prepared like them to live
To give to all, both great and small,
All we can give! All we can give!

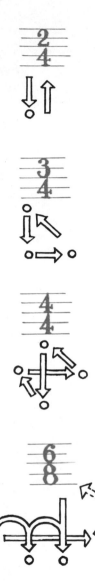

* The publisher and copyright owner will not permit us to print the music, written by Jan Sibelius. You may purchase it separately from the National Equipment Service.

Try It Outdoors

Practice the five steps in wood fire building till you're a never-fail fire builder.

Then try your hand at at least two of the following suggestions:

1. Make breadtwists on a green stick (*slowly*, over coals). Directions for this and other stick-cookery ideas are in *Cooking Out-of-Doors*, a Girl Scout cookbook.

2. Bake Banana Boats. Peel back a long strip of banana peel on the inside of the curve, leaving one end attached. Scoop out some of the banana and fill with chocolate chips and marshmallows. Replace strip of peel. Wrap tightly in aluminum foil and lay on hot coals for about ten minutes. (You'll need a spoon to eat this!)

3. Have a contest!
   o Who will be first to bring water to a boil?
   o Who will be first to burn through the string?
   o Can your patrol be first to light a fire using . . .
     wet kindling?
     only two matches?
     trench candles for a "starter"?

4. Build an outdoor ceremonial fire and have a ceremony to go with it.

Five Steps In Building a Wood Fire

1. MAKE A SAFE AND ADEQUATE SPACE.

Clear away leaves, grass, or anything burnable for at least 10 feet or in accordance with local regulations. Provide equipment for putting out the fire.

To control fire, use stones, bricks, logs, or trenches to keep fire in place. To hold pots, use grates or rods on stones or bricks.

2. GATHER TINDER, KINDLING, AND FUEL, ENOUGH TO SERVE YOUR PURPOSE.

Tinder—use shavings, twigs, pine cones, anything that will catch from a match. *Kindling*—wood up to thumbthick used to get fire going. Good tinder or kindling snaps when broken. Avoid crumbling sticks or those that just bend. *Fuel*—wood larger than kindling or charcoal. Make a wood pile for wood; keep charcoal in bag, placing it away from fire.

3. BUILD A FOUNDATION FIRE.

You will need: (a) a double handful of good tinder; (b) two double handfuls of kindling, graded in size, about length of pencil; (c) enough fuel on hand.

Make a small rack in an "A" shape to hold tinder off ground. Pile handful of tinder lightly, leaving space underneath for draft.

Light match, letting flame catch on wood of match stick. Then insert it under bar of "A" to light tinder. Add tinder carefully where flame takes hold. Blow gently if necessary.

As flame catches, add more tinder, then kindling. Keep fire compact, but with air spaces. Fire needs air and fuel to burn.

4. BUILD INTO KIND OF FIRE WANTED.

Tepee for quick cooking. Leaning tepee for a reflector. Criss-cross for coals. Quick fire to heat water. Keep fire going, use, and never leave it unattended.

5. PUT IT OUT AS SOON AS YOU ARE THROUGH USING IT.

Let fire burn down. With stick scatter fire, break up coals. Sprinkle with water; stir well. Add water, until you can press hand on any spot. If there is no water, use sand or dirt. Cover with rocks or dirt. *Check before you leave the site.*

Chile Con Carne

—a good one-pot meal

3 tablespoons shortening	½ teaspoon chili powder
¼ cup chopped green pepper	salt
½ cup chopped onion	pepper
2½ lbs. ground beef	2 (15-oz.) cans pinto
1 (1 lb.) can tomatoes	or red kidney beans.

Heat shortening in large skillet. Add the green pepper and onions and sauté until onion is transparent, stirring frequently. Add beef. Continue cooking and stirring until meat is well browned. Pour off fat. Add tomatoes and seasonings and simmer one-half hour, stirring occasionally. Add beans last to avoid mashing them. Add additional seasonings if desired. Reheat just to boiling and serve. This is especially good served over rice. Serves eight.

Ten Tips for Cooking with Charcoal Briquets

1. Place small twigs, tiny trench candles, or strips of cardboard milk cartons on the bottom of the fire box of your stove.
2. Place charcoal briquets on top of this.
3. Light the fire-starters, and gradually add a few more briquets as the first ones catch. (For safety, never use liquid fire-starters.)
4. Blow at the base of the fire if necessary.
5. Let the fire alone for 12 to 15 minutes. It should then be ready to use.
6. Charcoal will be grey-white in daylight, and red at night because it burns from the outside in.
7. During a long cooking period, use a stick or tongs to knock off white ash on outside of briquets.
8. When you finish cooking, dunk any leftover briquets in water. They can be dried out and used again.
9. Store briquets in a dry place between usings. Charcoal readily absorbs moisture from the air and kindles slowly when damp.
10. Heavy canvas or asbestos gloves are good protection to have when cooking.

Make and Use...

...Vagabond Stove

You will need: a pair of tin snips; heavy work gloves; a No. 10 tin can. Cut two openings as shown.

Make small wood fire within a circular mark made with the can and when it is burning well, place the stove over it; or use a Buddy burner. The top will heat immediately. Grease and wipe off with paper. Grease again and use top as frying pan. (Try pancakes, or eggs.) Work in teams of three—one to cook, one to keep the fire going, and one to eat.

...Tin-Can Charcoal Stove

Punch holes around base and top of a No. 10 tin can, using a punch-type can opener. Remove top of can with a roll-type opener. Attach a 24″ piece of wire for a bail. Force wire screen into the base above the punched holes to hold the charcoal and ensure a good draft. Make a grill of wire or coarse screening.

...Waterproof Matches

Dip "strike anywhere" wooden matches into nail polish or melted paraffin. Dry on double thick newspaper. Carry in covered metal box.

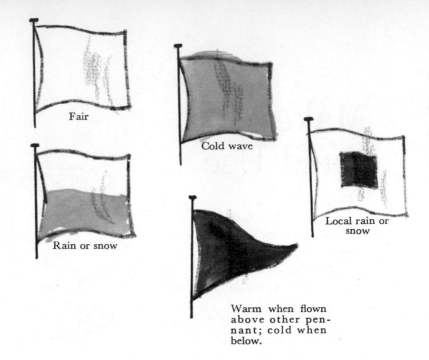

Fair

Cold wave

Rain or snow

Local rain or snow

Warm when flown above other pennant; cold when below.

Observe and Record

A fascinating outdoor world is waiting for you to explore it. Full of beauty, it offers many treasures for you to take. Your chief instruments of exploration are your own senses. Sharpen your vision, your observations. Record what you see for your pleasure and the enjoyment of others. In city or country, you may see:

The World of Birds: Build a bird feeding station, put it up and stock it with food. From your window, watch it 'round the calendar recording what you see. What kinds of birds visit your station? What do they like to eat? How? Watch the brash bluejays stand stock-still, gorging on sunflower seeds, while dainty chickadees carry off a seed at a time, cracking the shells between their toes to get at the meat.

The World of Trees: Take sketching equipment to the park or woods. Observe the various kinds of trees; those that shed their leaves and those that remain green all year 'round. Learn their names, their typical shapes, and the shapes of their leaves. Sketch the same trees at different seasons, bare, in bud, in full leaf, and gay with autumn colors.

The World of Stars: Can you recognize the five constellations that shine the year through, north of the Equator? Do you know how to find north by the North Star? Look at the stars at regular intervals during one evening. Observe them on several different evenings, too. Your newspaper may carry a "star map," showing where certain stars may be seen at certain hours. Study such a map. Then, make one of your own, reporting your observations to the troop. Include dates, hours, and locations.

The World of Weather: Forecasting weather in large areas is a complicated science but with keen observation and practice, you can become a good local weather prophet. To help you, make a piece of equipment, such as a wind vane, barometer, or rain gauge (see Bibliography and page 102). Then with a thermometer and an acquaintance with cloud forms and what they mean, you will be able to predict your local weather fairly well. Keep a daily weather log. If you are in camp, find a place to fly the weather flags shown on the opposite page. Perhaps you can find a place to fly them in the city, too.

There are many badges covering outdoor skills, and many more exciting activities suggested in the Challenge of Emergency Preparedness.

DAILY WEATHER LOG

DATE	TUES. AUG. 5	WED. AUG. 6	THURS AUG. 7
HOUR	8 A.M.	6 P.M.	9 A.M.
WIND DIRECTION	SW	SE	NW
VELOCITY	4 mph	5 mph	Strong
CLOUDS	CIRRO-STRATUS	CIRRUS and CIRRO-STRATUS	STRATUS
BAROMETER	RISING 29.8	RISING 30.0	FALLING
TEMPERATURE	84°	86°	90°
REMARKS	DEW HEAVY		NO DEW ON GRASS
FORECAST	FAIR: not much change in temperature	Continued FAIR tonight and tomorrow probably followed by showers THURS evening. Warmer FRIDAY.	Possibility of rain tonight. Warmer tomorrow.
AS IT WAS	TRUE	Until THURS A.M.	RAINED IN NIGHT.

A plain baggage tag, good for temporary trails, seasonal phenomena. Mark with pencil or felt ink marker and weatherproof with thin shellac.

A wooden peg to stick in the ground.

A tin-can label, enameled and lettered, to be suspended by wire or tacked to bark.

Offer Your Service

Find out for yourself!

An inquiring mind and helpful spirit can lead you into fine adventures of service. What do you know about your community? What is your community? It could be the street you live on, your neighborhood, village, or city. And whether you live north, east, south, or west, there are always needs for service waiting for willing hearts and hands.

Find out about your community. You can learn much from your newspaper, local radio, or even the classified telephone book. Social agencies, the chamber of commerce, government officials, your parents, your school, and your troop leader are fine sources of community information. Can you think of any others?

And while you're finding out

A wooden pulpit sign, easy to read, good for things close to the ground.

A hanging sign, a small wooden block with eyelets for hanging by wire or string.

A sheltered label of wood, to protect pictures and lettering from rain.

about your community, find out what services you can bring to it.

What can you do for your Girl Scout council? Your council's camp sites would appreciate any number of "out-of-door good turns." All the following things have been done by girls your age; many have been done with groups of boys: Plant seeds, bulbs, bushes, trees, or myrtle (do you know why myrtle is useful?). Clear or reroute streams. Repair footbridges. Cover exposed tree roots. Terrace eroded paths or hillsides. Paint the wound after limbs are cut off trees. Trim bushes to keep paths open. Post borders of site. Make and post signs asking the public to leave flowers for the next sightseers to enjoy. Bring a nature trail up to date, or make a new one. Here are some points to keep in mind.

1. Nature trail signs should be simple and clearly printed.
2. After the name, add an interesting fact to the nature sign.
3. Vary the types of signs along the trail.
4. Whether high or low, signs should be plainly visible.
5. It's better to have too many signs, rather than too few.
6. Some signs are permanent (for trees and rocks); others are seasonal (for flowers).
7. If you use wire, twist it loosely, never tightly around a tree.
8. Use small tacks on thick bark. Never use nails on trees.

A flannelgraph is a chart which is built up, one idea at a time, by placing cutout illustrations or lettering against a flannel backdrop. The cutouts are backed with flannel and will stick to the backdrop. They can be moved around at will.

There are other ways to help your Girl Scout council. Find out from your leader whether you can be of service by preparing signs, maps, flipcharts, or a flannelgraph for use in training courses.

Here's a service to the council that can be performed by any troop in any part of the country. Write a complete, lively report on one of your troop's projects or current activities and send it to your council. Your leader will know the kinds of information to be included in your account and the person to whom it should be sent. Several of you might write the report, each taking a different part of the activity.

The council may use your report as a basis for a newspaper story or radio program. Your account might become part of a bigger report to the Community Chest, or United Fund, or to Girl Scout national headquarters. It might be used in a training course for troop leaders, or as an idea-source for other troops. Though you may never see your story in print, your council will make good use of it.

If there's a bulletin board in your council office, or in your community center or school, you might prepare a display for it, arranging magazine clippings, snapshots, and original drawings to tell a story about Girl Scouting. You might even blockprint posters for a special message on soil and water conservation, trees, wildflowers, or wildlife.

Exhibits, too, can be designed and set up by you for use within your Girl Scout council. Choose a subject, such as the correct display and use of flags or the proper placement of insignia on the Girl Scout uniforms. Then, think up ways to demonstrate these subjects by using posters, models, or skits.

Sometimes, your council asks troops for help on a special occasion. You might be invited to:

o Make table decorations for a lunch or dinner meeting.
o Submit a design for the cover of a council bulletin.
o Make the flag of a member country of the World Association of Girl Guides and Girl Scouts for an international activity.
o Plan, prepare, and install an exhibit in a store window.

Your Girl Scout council may need different kinds of help but always find out first what you can do before you make elaborate plans.

What can you do for children in your community? Make sure your plans will be welcomed by those on the receiving end of your project. Here are some activities which have been carried out successfully by other Girl Scout troops:

o For a child care agency, such as a day nursery, collect, repair, and donate toys to the children.

o For a children's library, make a display and posters, mend books, read aloud during story hour.
o For a kindergarten, wash, iron and mend the doll family's wardrobe. Or design and sew a new one!
o For a children's hospital, make and donate "play kits" of small pieces of variously colored and textured papers, paste, coloring crayons, etc. Or write and illustrate a series of letters to a child hospitalized for a long time.
o Consider "Operation Deep Freeze."

"Operation Deep Freeze" is a way of providing institutions such as hospitals, convalescent homes, or orphanages with good things to eat for special occasions. Working alone or with members of your patrol, bake cookies, pastries, and birthday cakes to be delivered to the institutions and stored in their freezers for later ward parties, teas, and birthdays. Even though you will not be able to see the guests at these parties, the patrol responsible for delivery may be able to see how such party food is frozen and stored.

More ideas for exciting service projects are in Chapter 11. Service is a vital part of each Cadette Scout badge. And for still more ideas for opportunities for service, read The Challenge of Active Citizenship in Chapter 16.

Girl Scout Dictionary

Buddy Burner: A device for providing heat for frying or boiling (*not* good for toasting). To make, select a shallow can and insert a loosely fitting coil of cardboard the same height as the can. Pour melted paraffin to partially fill the can and let it harden. Never melt paraffin directly over a flame. Put container into a larger pot of hot water. Always have a lid handy to smother flame if vapors catch fire. Work with small quantities of paraffin and give the process your undivided attention.

Court of Awards: A special occasion at which Girl Scouts receive symbols of the badges they have earned.

Drip-o-wash: Temporary hand-washing facility for an outdoor event. To make, punch a hole near the bottom of a No. 10 tin can or tall juice can and insert a twig plug in the hole. Make a handle for the can by punching two holes under top rim and tying a rope through them. Fill can with water and hang from a branch of a convenient tree.

Nosebag: A bag or wrapping that contains everything for a meal for one person.

Quiet Signal: A quick way to get attention in any Girl Scout gathering. Raise your arm straight up over your head. When you see this signal, stop whatever you are doing and raise your hand, too.

Scouts Own: A special inspirational occasion which can take place during a troop meeting, an intertroop gathering, or in camp. Neither an entertainment nor a religious service, it is an occasion on which girls express their deepest feelings about their Girl Scout ideals.

"Sit-Upon": Something to sit upon in the out-of-doors, of course. Try making one from double layers of an old shower curtain or from several newspaper sheets folded between two layers of oilcloth. Add beltloops and snap-fasteners to yours, and it will never be accidentally left behind.

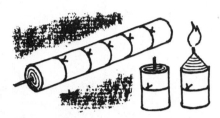

Trench Candle: An emergency fuel or kindling. To make, roll several thicknesses of newspaper into a long roll. Tie with a series of strings about three inches apart, leaving long string ends for dipping. With a saw, cut roll into pieces about half-way between each string tie. Soak the pieces well in a container partially filled with melted paraffin. (See safety precautions under Buddy burner.) Hang to dry. Use to kindle fire on a wet day. Make tiny ones to use under vagabond stove or to start charcoal fire.

Wide Game: An adventurous game with the fun of a contest, sporting event, and treasure hunt, all based on a special theme. It can last an hour or go on all day. It can range over one city block or one hundred acres of camp site. No wide game is exactly like any other wide game. Try one and see!

ook at your hands. Have you ever thought of the wonders they can do? They can make all sorts of things—delicious food, pretty things to wear, beautiful things to look at, practical things to use. All they need are the right materials, some knowledge of their use, and a creative spirit to give them inspiration.

A creative spirit goes questing and finds interest in everything from a shelf of cooking spices to a lump of clay waiting to be given shape and meaning. Here in this chapter are pots of paint and building tools, chemicals and skeins of yarn, inviting you to come try them. You need not be especially talented to do this.

try something new

Look through the ideas in this chapter and find the ones that appeal to you most. Here are activities in the arts, the home, and the outdoors. You need not be an expert to try any one of them or even all of them.

Approach your choice seriously, but joyously. Perfection does not count so much as what you, the individual, can accomplish. Whether you paint a picture or knit a sweater, you put your ideas, tastes, and skills into it. If the finished product is not quite what you had in mind that makes little difference. You will have had the fun of trying something new and challenging. Besides, you can try again. You will improve as you go, if you put forth your best effort.

What will you get out of it? So many things that they cannot all be said. You will enter a romantic realm of fascinating materials, textures, and colors. Your knowledge and skills will increase and, at the same time, you will advance in Scouting.

You will enjoy one of the most satisfying of human experiences—self-expression. And you will know the special pride of saying, "I made it myself."

The Artistic Needle

A little needle can do so much—sew garments, replace buttons, mend tears. But it can do more than homely tasks. It can lift ordinary things out of the commonplace, create beauty with cross-stitch precision or the intricacy of tapestry. It can use fabrics and threads in much the same way as a painter paints.

See what you can do with creative stitchery, using scraps and bits of cloth, threads and yarns in different colors and textures. Also, you will need fabric (monks cloth, decorator's burlap or unbleached muslin) as your background or "canvas." The scraps are your "paints," appliqued or sewed on to the background. With them, you create a design inspired by your interests and observations. For example, you can suggest birds, trees, and clouds by the way you apply fabric and colors.

Creative stitchery is a free, happy art. You can make wall hangings, pillows, aprons, and other charming things for the home or as gifts. The best way is to work directly with the materials. You might make a preliminary sketch, but do not spend much time on this. Keep your design simple and harmonious in shape and color. Use traditional stitches or invent your own.

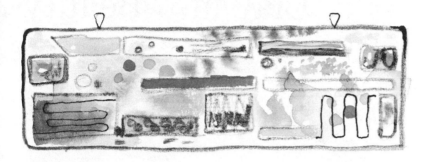

Ornaments of Glass

Slump glass is an unromantic name for an exciting art. By fusing bits of common, colored glass, you can create jewel-like decorations. Collect colored glass from empty soft drink bottles and medicine jars, broken vases or household containers. Never handle broken glass with bare hands. Wear gloves or use tweezers. To break large pieces, wrap completely in several layers of heavy cloth and tap carefully with a mallet. Small, flat pieces are cut with a glass cutter.

Make a free-form hanging ornament. Cut harmonious shapes of colored glass. Arrange them on a kiln tile or shelf which has been heavily coated with a layer of dry clay or kiln wash. For added decoration, use tweezers to place bits of broken glass, glass beads, or threads on top of these pieces and they will be fused together. Look at the picture on page 88.

Make a flat panel. The base is a piece of plain glass ⅟₁₆″ or ⅛″ thick. On this, place smaller glass pieces in a design, closely or widely spaced. These pieces, varying in sizes, shapes, and colors, may be fastened to the base with bits of transparent glue.

Finished designs are fired in a kiln at high temperatures, from 1250° to 1600°. Clear glass needs fiercer heat; reds, blues, and greens take lower ones. After the desired temperature has been reached, the kiln must cool for twenty-four hours before the door is opened and your brilliant fused-glass designs are revealed.

Clay into Beauty

1. Clay should be soft enough to bend without cracking, dry enough not to stick to hands.

2. Remove air bubbles by wedging the clay, slapping it hard on a table or squeezing it.

3. The lump of clay may be cut with a thin wire to test for the presence of bubbles.

In the country, you may find clay along a river bank or lake shore. In the city, you can buy it in moist or powdered form. Learn to shape this pliable material into things of beauty.

What can you make? A piece of sculpture or tiles for a mosaic. You can model jewelry or wall plaques by hand or press them into plaster molds of your own design. Experiment with color, learning about glazes and the handsome decorations called incising and graffito. Fired at high temperature in a kiln, your creations will be lastingly durable.

Creative Expression
...through Painting

You have probably "made pictures" ever since you were a child, feeling a deep enjoyment of the rainbow colors of crayons and chalks, the textures of charcoal and tempera paints.

Now your world is larger. There is more inside you to be expressed. This is a good time to explore new painting media; caseins, watercolors, oils. Try all kinds of colors, lines, and arrangements to express your moods, to free your imagination. That is the purpose of painting —to express something of yourself.

The chalk drawing on the opposite page was done by Mary Jane Adams, a twelve-year-old Girl Scout from New York City.

...through Words

The moving lines below, written by a 13-ycar-old girl, won a poetry award in the "By You" column in the *American Girl* magazine, published by Girl Scouts of the U.S.A. These poetic images were created by her out of her own mind and mood.

Language is a means of expression available to all. Though you may not think of yourself as a creative writer, you are. Whenever you write an original birthday greeting, a letter, you are expressing your ideas and feelings in words of your choice. True, you may not be a poet. You may be a playwright or storyteller. Try and see!

Loneliness

Loneliness is small and cold,
Diamond hard and eons old.
Loneliness is sharp and chill,
Like cold gray rain on a cold gray hill,
Like a tall black rock and a seagull's cry,
Like an empty land and a sea and a sky,
Like a weed-grown track and a broken fence
Long since left to the elements
Loneliness ...

—LUCY HORTON

Artistic—first comes the photographer's taste and judgment.
Mechanical—next comes the moment of taking the picture.
Chemical—finally, comes the skill of the darkroom.

Art Through a Shutter

Taking a picture may be your way of writing a poem, telling a story, expressing a mood. The camera lens may be your eye, through which you see and record your special world. For photography can be more than a mechanical matter of shutter-snapping. In the world of an artist, it is an art.

To appreciate this, you have only to look at pictures made by imaginative, contemporary photographers. Look for the work of such artists in your library or a museum. Then you will see what really creative photography can be.

How much do you have to know to take artistic pictures? Actually, a simple, inexpensive camera can make poetry for you if you turn it upon subjects that mean something to you. As you progress, you will be quicker to catch subjects, more sensitive to designs of light and shadow, traceries of trees, expressions of people.

The more you know about photography, the more you can do, the greater your satisfaction. Books and magazines can help you learn. Most manufacturers of photographic supplies publish books to guide you through the mechanics of lenses, depth of field, exposures, filters, flashbulbs, and so on. You may advance to color slides and movies, or learn printing and developing techniques.

But your greatest satisfaction will come when you take pictures with a sense of artistry and deep feeling.

Weaving

Weaving is an art form that dates back into unrecorded time and is essentially the process of interlacing fibers. The inkle loom can be made of inexpensive and easily acquired materials.

Fibers for warps must be strong such as: carpet warp, pearl cotton, linen threads, jute, nylon parachute cords, fish cords. Here are some materials you might start collecting to inspire you in your weaving adventures: cotton rug yarns, nubby and boucle yarns, gift wrap ties, package twines, raffia, chenille, burlap or fur fabrics cut into narrow strips, leather or felt strips, soutache and flat braids, single strings of sequins, beads, or seeds, twisted or folded cellophane. Also experiment with natural fibers—broom cornstalks, seed stems and heads, cattail leaves, reeds, honeysuckle, unpeeled cornhusks, beach grass, long pine needles.

Try making belts or bands for decoration, place mats, wall hangings, book covers, purses, scarves, rugs.

Inkle Loom Weaving

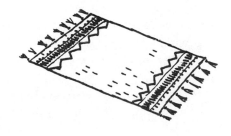
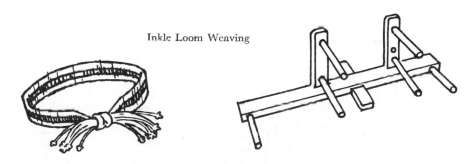

Two-Harness Table Loom Weaving

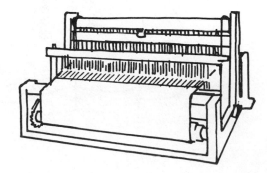

Patternless Skirt

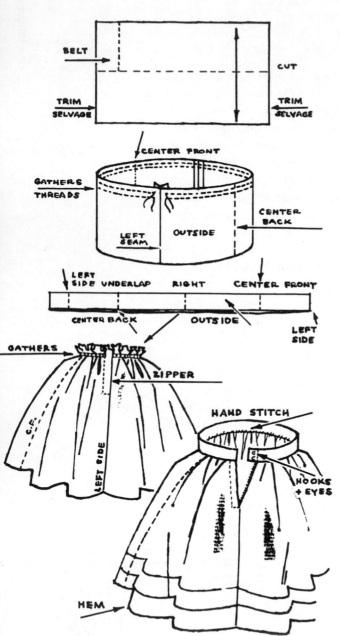

To buy the right length of fabric, measure your own skirt length, double it, and add 9 inches. To prepare fabric for sewing, shrink it and cut off selvages.

For the belt, cut a strip lengthwise of the fabric, 4″ wide and 2½″ longer than your waist measure.

Make markings at center front, sides, and back of skirt and belt, leaving overlap extra. Stitch skirt side seams, using #6 machine stitch for length of placket area. Press seams open. Insert zipper, following directions on packet.

To gather waist, sew two rows of #6 stitch (with buttonhole thread bobbin) or two rows of small running stitch by hand, placing them ⅜″ and ⅝″ from fabric edge and ending them within ¾″ of left side seam. Knot one end of each row and pull gathering threads in to your waist measure.

To attach belt, fold lengthwise right sides together and stitch short ends; turn and press. Turn both long, raw edges under ½″ and press. Pin outside of belt to outside skirt front, matching markings. Stitch and press. Hand blindstitch inside belt edge to inside of skirt.

To finish skirt, sew hooks and eyes on belt. Hem, and trim as you like.

A Toy for a Child

This is great fun and good experience, too. When you choose a toy to make, consider the child. Is the toy right for his age and abilities? Is it safe and sturdy? Will it help to develop his imagination, muscle control, habits of neatness? Here are three ideas for toys to make. Can you invent more?

Make a "store-more" by painting or papering a storage chest, egg carton, or cigar box to hold all kinds of childhood treasure.

Publish a book. Write an original children's story, bind it into a book or notebook, and leave room for your young friend to "illustrate" it.

Paint spools in many colors for many uses. (Children chew on toys so choose paint that does not contain lead.) Make them into dolls, glue them into miniature furniture, string them like giant beads.

Trefoil Sweater

This heavy outdoor sweater is adapted from a Norwegian-type cardigan. The directions are slightly different from many sweaters you have knit. There is a 3-inch ribbing with the opening in the front, then the sweater is put on circular needles and you knit continuously to the top. You end up with a long cylinder which is cut apart for front opening and sleeves.

Body of Sweater: With straight needles cast on 156 stitches (172-188) of main color. Work three K stitches then K2, P2 across to last 3 stitches and K to end of row. Work ribbing for 3 inches, keeping border stitches plain. Slipping first stitch, knit on to 28-inch round needle. Increase 2 stitches at each side seam 39 (43-47) stitches from front edge and again 78 (86-94) stitches later every 7th row until there are 196 (212-228) stitches. Continue knitting until the sweater measures 10½ inches or desired length to underarm. Work Border I pattern (53 rows) making sure to twist yarns when changing colors to prevent a hole. Carry unused color loosely across wrong side of work. Bind off.

If you make a slight mistake in the pattern it may be corrected later by embroidering with cross-stitch.

Sleeves: With straight needles cast on 52 (52-56) stitches and work K2, P2 for 3 inches. Change to shorter round needle. Increase 6 stitches while knitting 1st row. Increase 2 stitches at underarm every 7th row until there are 104 (104-110) stitches. Continue knitting until desired length for sleeve. Bind off.

Collar: Cast on 80 stitches with main color on shorter round needle, knit 1 row then work Border II. Continue knitting for 16 rows in main color and bind off loosely. This will form facing to make turn about collar.

Strips: Cast on 6 stitches: K1, P1 for 3 inches, continue in stockinette stitch (knit one row, purl one row)

Materials: Four-ply knitting worsted 16 oz. main color; 3 oz. contrasting color. Straight needles No. 4; two No. 5 circular needles, 16 and 28 inches long. 8 buttons less than 1-inch wide.

Gauge: 6 stitches equal 1 inch—7 rows equal 1 inch.

the length of the sweater, including the collar. Make second strip, working buttonholes as follows: 1st buttonhole 6th row from bottom (in ribbing) K1, bind off 4 stitches, K1. On 7th row, K1, cast on 4, K1. Work 8 buttonholes up to neckline about 3 inches apart. Reinforce buttonholes with yarn.

Finishing: Block all parts of the sweater. Tie all threads. With a basting stitch, mark the center front of the cylinder from bottom to top, starting at the opening in the ribbing. Make sure it is a straight line by following the stitches. Place the front section in the sewing machine and put sewing machine regulator on 12 or 13. Stitch twice ¼ inch on each side of the basting stitch. Mark off a point at the side seams equal to depth of your sleeves. Put one thickness in the machine and stitch down to mark and up again, leaving about ½ inch between. Weave the shoulder seams together, or with right sides facing, sew loosely with yarn in back stitch. Weave or sew the collar onto the sweater, with front edge on center front basting line. Cut between the stitches for the armhole opening, sew on sleeves, sew collar facing down. Cut front opening and sew on strips, buttonholes on right side. Sew on buttons.

BORDER I

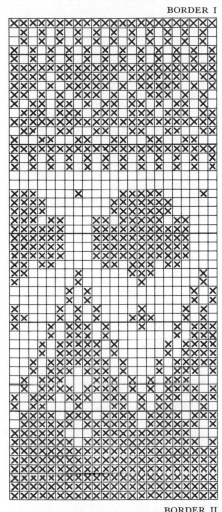

BORDER II

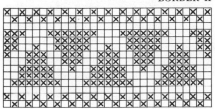

Adventures in Cooking

Be a kitchen traveler—in time and place! Make something you've never made before. Food from faraway regions or different eras can be romantic, as well as delicious. The recipe for "Creole Kisses," for example, is a modern version of one of Juliette Low's own favorites. You will find others in the *Girl Scout Centennial Receipt Book*.

Consider what sister Girl Guides may be eating tonight. Try making one dish that is common fare in India, Norway, or any other country in the World Association of Girl Guides and Girl Scouts. For more ideas, see Chapter 8 and the Bibliography.

And you need not stay in the kitchen. Try new methods outdoors. The portable charcoal stove is an excellent piece of patrol equipment you can make. With it you can lay the fire before you leave home and light it when you reach the site. Or you can cook without a stove; start with the Bacon-and-Egg-wich. Look for more recipes and methods in *Cooking Out-of-Doors*.

Bacon-and-Egg-wich on a Rock

Select a thin flat rock and heat thoroughly in your fire. (Avoid rocks which appear to have been put together in layers. These may be shale, slate, or schist, inside which moisture collects. When these rocks are heated, moisture produces steam which causes the rocks to explode.) Remove hot rock from fire with tongs, a forked stick, or asbestos gloves. Brush off any loose dirt. Cut two slices of bacon in half and cook on one side, on the hot rock. Tear a hole in the center of a slice of bread, and place it over two of the pieces of bacon, crisp side up. Drop an egg in the hole, cover egg with two remaining pieces of bacon, crisp side down. When done on one side, turn and continue cooking to your taste.

Creole Kisses

Whites of 2 eggs, beaten stiff

1 cup sugar

1 teaspoon baking powder

1 teaspoon vanilla

1 cup broken or chopped pecans

or 2½ cups of cornflakes

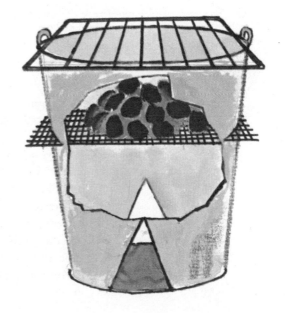

Beat eggs until stiff enough to hold peaks, but not dry. Combine sugar and baking powder and add slowly to egg whites, folding in gently. Fold in vanilla, then the nuts or cornflakes. Drop mixture from a teaspoon on an oiled cookie sheet. Bake in slow oven (250°F.) until partly dry and firm enough to retain shape. Remove from cookie sheet while still hot.

Portable Charcoal Stove

Materials: A 12-quart galvanized pail, a square of ¼ inch mesh heavy grade hardware cloth, grill, or cake rack, heavy work gloves, heavy screwdriver, large hammer.

With hammer and screwdriver, make two cuts 4 inches below and parallel to top of pail. Insert hardware cloth. Make three draft holes about 2 inches high. Place grill or rack on top of the pail for cooking surface.

To use: Push crumpled paper through draft holes. Cover hardware cloth with layer of crumpled paper or trench candle starters, add a layer of kindling, and top with charcoal briquets. Light paper through draft holes. Broil on grill or use it to support a pot.

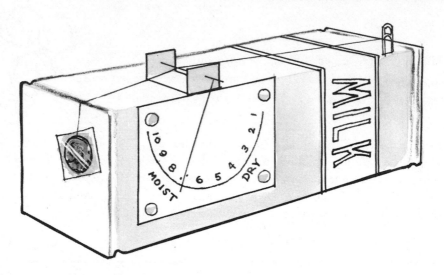

Weather Telling

You can make a hair hygrometer to measure the humidity, or moisture, of the air. It can help you forecast the approach of a warm or cold front. Humid air stretches the hair; dry air shrinks it. Although the change in length of the hair is very slight, attaching it to needle and broom straw magnifies the change. When the hair shrinks a hundredth of an inch the tip of the straw will move 1¼ inches. This is a magnification of 125 to 1.

Materials Needed: Clean milk carton, sewing needle, 3-inch broom straw, transparent tape, glue, a human hair at least 9 inches long, 4 thumbtacks, sharp knife, blank card, paper clip, a penny.

To Make a Hygrometer
1. Wash hair with soapy water, rinse in clear water, put aside to dry.
2. Make an H cut on one side of carton, about one half inch less than needle length. Fold back tabs and punch hole in each with needle. Twist needle in holes until it will turn freely.
3. Push broom straw through eye of needle; fasten them together with glue and let dry.
4. Cut narrow slit at far end of carton and push paper clip half way in.

5. Mark card with half circle; print "dry" and "moist" as shown and numbers 1 to 10 equidistant along the half-circle. Fasten to carton with thumbtacks.
6. Using transparent tape, fasten one end of hair to penny. Try not to touch rest of the hair because oil on your skin stops the hair from absorbing moisture.
7. With penny at left end of carton, put hair under needle, then around and under needle again. Slip free end into paper clip and fasten with glue. The penny should hang about an inch over the end of carton.
8. To adjust hygrometer for use, put in bathroom, run hot water until mirror clouds up. Because air is 100 per cent humid, the broom straw will move as the hair stretches. When it finally stops, move straw so it points to number 10. Carefully carry hygrometer from bathroom to shaded, protected spot outdoors where you plan to use it.

To Use a Hygrometer

Keep hygrometer in place protected from sunlight. Before taking a reading, tap carton *gently* two or three times. In order to use it to forecast weather, take your readings at the same time every day. In general you will find that humidity of the air increases before rain and decreases afterward. The table below shows humidity changes in relation to fronts.

	BEFORE	DURING	AFTER
Warm Front	increasing	very moist	slight decrease
Cold Front	steady	very moist	rapid decrease

With permission of Whittlesey House a division of McGraw-Hill Book Co., Inc., from *Everyday Weather and How It Works*. Copyright 1951, by Herman Schneider and Jeanne Bendick.

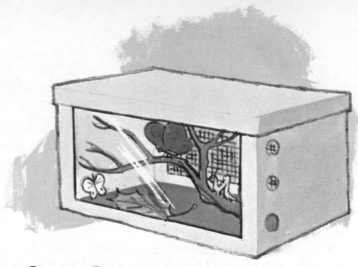

Bring Outdoors In

Insect Inn

Make an "Insect Inn," a temporary lodging for insects or small animals whose habits you wish to observe. Supply your guests with food and furnishings like those in the place you found them. After a short time, give them their freedom.

Magic Firelight

Imagine a fireplace leaping with rainbow colors! This magical effect is produced by pine cones and other native materials treated with certain chemicals. To make them, you need:

o Pinecones, clean and dry, or native materials such as driftwood, knots, goldenrod galls.

o Chemicals, available in commercial form from drug or farm supply stores:

Green—Barium chloride
Orange—Calcium chloride
Lavender—Potassium chloride
Yellow—Sodium carbonate (washing soda) or Sodium chloide (common salt) or Sodium bicarbonate (baking soda)

Warning! Nitrates and chlorates are highly inflammable. Do not use them. Be sure to ask for the chemicals exactly as listed.

1. Dissolve each chemical in a separate container. Use wood or glass (*not metal*). Use 1 pound chemical to 1 gallon water.

2. Soak cones or other materials in solution for a few minutes, drain, and dry. Quantities may be dipped in a mesh or burlap bag and hung to dry.

Flowers All-Year-'Round!

Make dried flowers out of real live ones. Experiment with the flowers and plants that grow in your locality. Depending upon the season of the year and the climate, some varieties will dry when hung upside down for a few days or weeks in a cool, dry, dark place.

Sturdy varieties, such as zinnias, marigolds, can be dried in sand. You will need: fine, clean, perfectly dry sand; a number of small cardboard boxes; trays (or cookie sheets or convenient shelves).

Arrange the boxes on trays and pour a thin layer of sand on the bottom of each box. Put several flowers on top of the sand, face down and not touching each other. Slowly and carefully cover the flowers with more sand. Do not replace the box covers.

Keep the boxes from being shaken or becoming damp and, in three to four weeks, pour the sand off gently. If you have worked carefully the flowers will have kept their shape and much of their original color.

A Roomier Room

Do you have a room to yourself or do you share your quarters? Either way, you can make living in it prettier and more practical in a number of ways. Here are some ideas.

Bricks stacked one-atop-another support painted boards, making sturdy, inexpensive book and storage shelves. Easy to assemble, move, rearrange.

A sheet of painted or varnished plywood across two file cabinets or painted crates makes a fine desk. Skirt coverings convert the desk into a dressing table.

Use walls and doors for storage and display. Shelves, magazine racks, bulletin boards (make your own of felt in a frame), and pegboards are smart.

For extra storage space, use under-bed boxes or chests with well-fitting lids. Conceal them by means of a dust ruffle or a floor-length bedspread.

New Plans

What is a badge? It is a symbol of accomplishment, earned and worn proudly by you—a symbol that you are ready and able to give service. Every badge on your sash tells something about you.

A badge means you have increased your skill and knowledge in a particular subject; that you have had the fun and satisfaction of learning to do something well. It means that you are a true Scout, willing to give time, thought, and work to a worthwhile activity and to service for others. Every activity, fits into some badge or other. How do you decide which ones to choose?

First, consider the excitement and fun of an activity that you have never done before. Perhaps you never before had any interest in it. Try a really different one to see!

Look through the badge section in this book. List the badges you would like to try. Ask yourself, "Am I really interested in this activity? Will I enjoy working on it with my patrol, my troop, and by myself? Will it help provide a needed service to someone else?"

Now, while you are learning to make something new—make room on your badge sash.

a more attractive you

In the busy world of family and friends, home and school, sports and hobbies, troop meetings, parties, and boys, every girl longs to be as attractive as she can be. Some girls spend hours fussing with hairdos and nails, wavering between this dress and that one. All this interest is quite natural, but it is only a small part of the beauty story. For there is really only one way to be truly attractive.

The real secret of loveliness is being lovely.

What does this mean? It means that too many girls concentrate on *looking* a certain way, rather than *being* a certain way. Often, they pick something specific, an imperfect nose, perhaps, or hair that won't hold a curl, and bemoan the fate that made them unattractive.

But this is not what attractiveness is all about. It is a combination of a great many things, some of them are visible, most of them are not. It is the total of all your qualities, your inner self, as well as those that show. It is the kind of person you are. That is why this chapter is about so many things that make up the picture of you, those things that are on the surface and those shining through.

Beauty Sleeping and Waking

Every morning, miracles happen. The sun rises, night vanishes, and you open your eyes to a new day.

How do you wake up? Are you bright and energetic? Or do you drag yourself reluctantly from bed? Much of your good looks and vivacity depends on your sleeping pattern. This is not just theory, but scientific fact.

Sleep is like food, air, and water. You must have all of them. The rules for health-and-beauty sleep are short and simple, but basic to well-being.

Sleep nine hours a night, every single night, in a comfortable, well-ventilated place. Give your body time to rest, relax, and grow into beauty.

Now you are out of bed and starting your day. Wash the sleep away with plenty of mild soap lather and thorough rinsings with clear, lukewarm water. Make sure to dry hands and face well, blotting with a spotless towel until all dampness is gone.

You brush your teeth, of course. This is one of the most important functions you perform for your beauty and health, so do it properly. There is a correct method of brushing teeth and a correct type of brush for you. If you are not sure of these, ask your dentist for a lesson in toothbrush technique.

Good looks and good feelings come from regular health and grooming habits. These include a dental checkup twice a year and conscientious daily care. This is not too much to give in exchange for one of the greatest assets you can have, a lovely smile.

The Girl in the Mirror

Take a long, critical look at yourself in the mirror. What do you see? Can you put a checkmark after each of these points to show you pass the test?

Hair: Clean, well-brushed, neatly arranged in a style becoming to you.

Skin: Clean, cared-for, with make-up applied sparingly for glowing natural radiance.

Teeth: Well-brushed, in sound health, under good dental care.

Hands and nails: Hands always immaculate, nails smoothly filed to medium length.

Feet: Comfortably shod, with toe-nails cut short and straight across.

The basis of good looks is good health. Have a regular health examination (by your family doctor, school health service, or free neighborhood clinic) every year. You must have a yearly health examination to take part in swimming, camping, or other strenuous activities in Girl Scouting.

Thorough cleanliness is vital to health and charm. Bathe daily. Wash your hands well before eating and after using the toilet. Remember, the ten most common disease carriers—your own fingers. Do not borrow or lend comb, brush, towels, lipstick.

Now turn from the mirror and look not at yourself, but *into* yourself. Are you an interesting person? Can you think of others rather than only of yourself? Do you enjoy life's gifts—literature, music, the fine arts? The beauty you absorb becomes part of your charm and individuality, gives you a fuller life.

Come to Breakfast!

Sometimes, you see an advertisement for a skin cream that is said to "feed the skin." This is not so. It is wise to learn to judge advertising claims, so you are not misled by long scientific words or false claims.

The only way to feed your skin (and all the rest of you) is to feed yourself. Eat foods that nourish your body. That is the finest beauty treatment you can have.

Scientists have found that a balanced daily diet includes food from each group in "the Basic Four." You need them all, working together, to convert their elements into strong bones, clear skin, glossy hair, and sparkling eyes and energy. Vitamin pills should be taken only on doctors' orders. They supplement but are not substitutes for essential foods. If you eat the foods you need for health and energy, you will be eating for good looks, too.

One of the surest signs of "grownupness" is the ability to make a sensible decision and keep to it. This is true in every aspect of life. Your food habits are no exception. So, though mother may be the household dietitian and cook, it is also up to you to choose the foods that will contribute to your health and beauty whether you are at home, at school, or at the soda fountain. If you do this, your body will reward you by responding to your wisdom.

Whether you are planning snacks for your troop meeting, refreshment for your troop party, or three meals a day for a weekend troop camp, you should follow these same basic principles. By the time you are the chief food planner as wife and mother in your own home these principles will be second nature to you.

Are you strong enough to give yourself good advice—and follow it?

Milk Group   Fruit and Vegetable Group

Meat Group   Bread and Cereal Group

IF YOU WANT TO LOSE WEIGHT:

o Don't go on a drastic diet. Your growing body needs nourishment. Be sure to ask your doctor to help you make your own plan of how to eat well and shed pounds.

o Eat slowly. Relax at meals.

o Eat three balanced meals a day.

o Avoid fatty, starchy, salty foods, or preparation methods.

o For snacks, have fresh fruits and vegetables, skim milk, and juices.

o Learn to count calories. This helps you choose low-caloried food with high nutrition value.

o Get plenty of exercise and sleep.

o Take time to develop regular elimination habits.

IF YOU WANT TO GAIN WEIGHT:

o Be sure to talk first with your doctor.

o Enjoy three full meals every day.

o Build up your appetite with a brisk walk before mealtime.

o Take a short rest after every meal.

o Help provide a pleasant atmosphere by your actions and conversation during meals.

o Substitute cream or part-cream for milk.

o Eat nourishing, nonfilling snacks between meals and at bedtime. Try milk and crackers, fruit and cookies.

o Drink 8 glasses of water daily.

o Sleep 9 hours every night and learn how to relax when you can.

"She Walks in Beauty"

Is there a full-length mirror in your house? If not, try this experiment next time you're at the department store. Face your top-to-toe reflection and slump. Let your shoulders sag, your chest cave in, your arms droop at your sides. The image will show you a mournful Raggedy Ann, her figure awkward and sagging, her face sad and spiritless.

Now, think of your body as an engine in smooth working order. When one part moves correctly, the others follow in natural, rhythmic order.

Walking: Let your walk reflect good spirits. Head high, shoulders relaxed, step with a smooth, rhythmic gait. To walk faster or slower, change speed, not length of strides.

Sitting down: With the weight of your body on the balls of both feet, lower yourself diagonally into the seat.

Desk sitting: Lean forward from the hips, not the waist. Keep shoulders high, head straight. It's less tiring than a droop and more becoming.

Lift your head up, up out of your shoulders. Hold it high with natural ease, not stiffly. Keep your chin parallel to the floor, not tilted up toward the ceiling.

Now straighten your shoulders, making sure they are relaxed, not pressing backward or forward. Breathe deeply, filling your lungs, and your chest moves into the right position. As you breathe in, pull your waist up tall, tighten your stomach, tuck your buttocks under you. Point your feet straight ahead, not toed-in or toed-out.

See what happens to Raggedy Ann. She acquires a real figure, fine bearing. Spirit comes into her face. She looks capable, confident, and much prettier.

Good posture and exercise are health and beauty aids for every girl. Proper carriage gives your body organs room to function properly. Exercise, walks, and games in the fresh air and sunshine, give your muscles firmness and tone. Give your body good posture and activity, a chance to work. Your total appearance will have bounce and sparkle.

Car-exiting: Slide to door near sidewalk. Step out with foot next to door, head and shoulders following, keeping in sideways position. Bring out the other foot. Do an about-face and you are gracefully, neatly out of the car.

Stair-climbing: Flex knees. Transfer your weight from ball of one foot to the other, lifting your body for each step. Move smoothly without swaying.

Choosing a Wardrobe

Have a "Fashion Show-How!"

Which colors suit you best? What is the most flattering skirt length for you? Should you wear smooth or nubby fabrics? Plaids or solids? Does your wardrobe have a planned, coordinated look?

It takes taste, judgment, and knowledge to select the best clothes for you. A good way to improve your fashion sense is to have a "Fashion Show-How" with the girls in your patrol or troop. Ask several girls to volunteer to bring three outfits—dress-up, school, and sports—and model them as the others make their comments, considering these and other questions: "Is her hemline at the most becoming length?" "Does that nubby texture add needed roundness?" "Is that the prettiest neckline for the shape of her face and neck?"

Discuss these comments and study them. If, for example, most of the girls agree you would look shapelier in a flared, rather than a straight skirt, try one the next time you go shopping.

Have an "Accessories-Swap!"

Collect items of different sizes, shapes, colors—scarves, beads, gloves, purses, hats, jackets—and let each girl experiment with the shapes and colors assembled. Discover the different effects created by shades and intensities of color, by size of purse and hat brim. You will find you look smarter, more "gotten together," with a few well-chosen accessories, rather than a clutter.

Make large collars by cutting a round hole in colored paper about 18"x24" and slitting the paper for an opening. Which color becomes you best? Try at a mirror and see.

If you are interested in fashion design as a career, study the history of costume. You might make watercolor or tempera sketches of your own design, collect and classify textile samples, learn all you can about how clothing is made and worn to the best effect.

Have a Quiz

When you shop for clothes try to resist the temptation of a fad or the desire to buy something, anything, just to go home with something. A good wardrobe is planned, not picked at whim. Before buying, ask yourself, "Is this for me?" And ask some more, such as:

o Is it becoming to my face and figure?
o Will I get good use from it?
o Is the price within my budget?
o Will it go with things I already own?
o Does it fit properly?
o Can it be laundered? Is it pre-shrunk?
o Is the style right for my age and usual activities?
o Will I like it a month from now?
o Can it be worn for more than one season of the year?

Base your purchases on the kind of life you lead. Learn to read labels and know what they mean. Shop in reliable stores where clothes of good quality though not necessarily expensive are sold.

Your clothes are a means of expressing your personality and tastes. They tell a great deal about you. What would you like them to say?

Ready To Wear

Girls often complain that they have nothing to wear, either for a special occasion or just in general. There are two ways to make sure this does not happen to you. The first is to think out your wardrobe so it is well balanced, with the right things for school, sports, and dress-up. The second is to keep your belongings in tip-top, ready-to-wear shape.

To achieve this, you must develop regular habits of clothes care and storage. That way, you need never worry about safety-pinned straps, hems too long or too short, or spots and stains that ruin the appearance of the prettiest clothes.

If you become known as a Girl Scout who always has her uniform in a ready-to-go condition, you may be pleasantly surprised at the opportunities that come your way. Here are some general rules to help you keep your things in order.

Shoes must fit properly and always be in good repair. Regular brushing and polishing preserves leathers. Shoetrees or crumpled tissue paper preserves shape and fit when not in use.

Hose and socks should be washed after each wearing. Towel-dry them after rinsing. Have several pairs of one color to make them go further, smooth hands and nails to prevent snags.

Underwear should be changed and washed daily. Smooth straps with your fingers.

Dresses and skirts need brushing after wearing; keep well-pressed. Close zippers and buttons before hanging. Launder or dry-clean regularly.

Knitted things will keep shape if neatly folded in a drawer.

Coats should be brushed and hung with buttons closed to keep them clean and shapely. Treat them well; they are costly.

Hats ought to be brushed well after wearing, stuffed with tissue paper, and kept in boxes.

Gloves keep their shape if pulled gently after wearing. Dry washable ones on a glove form or towel.

Raingear should be allowed to dry thoroughly before storing.

Everything has its place. Hang clothes neatly in clean closets on good hangers. Organize drawers so you can find things without hunting and scrambling.

Cleaning and repairs should be attended to as soon as possible. This means straps are tacked, buttons are replaced, rips and tears are mended.

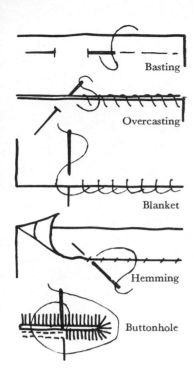

Basting

Overcasting

Blanket

Hemming

Buttonhole

A special tip for Cadettes: On your uniform blouse, sew one side of a snap fastener on the top of the right shoulder seam close to the neckline under the collar. Sew the other side of the snap to the under side of the top of your badge sash. Use the buttonhole stitch for the neatest and most durable method. Never sew a snap on a single thickness of material.

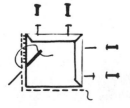

Sew a Fine Seam

A nimble needle will help you make useful things for yourself and others. Equip a sewing box or, perhaps, a basket you have woven with needles, thimble, thread, pins, scissors, darning cotton, tape measure. Master the five basic stitches and you are on your way to becoming a skilled seamstress.

The hemmed patch is sturdy, covers holes in things that are washed often. Made right, it looks almost the same on both sides.

1. Cut edges along warp and filling threads to make hole rectangular.
2. Make diagonal cuts, about ¼", at four corners. Crease or press edges back to the wrong side.
3. Prepare patch fabric by washing and, if needed, fading. Take fabric from hem or facing if unused fabric is not at hand. Allow ample material for seams. Pin and baste patch under hole, matching fabric design and grain. On right side, hem patch to creased edges by hand or machine.
4. On wrong side, trim patch to extend ¼" beyond hemming stitches. Turn edges under, cut away corner bulk. Then pin, baste, and hem patch down.

Decorative patches are colorful, striking, and often practical. With them, you may cover worn spots or add gaiety to a garment. To make, cut a paper pattern in the shape you want. Secure the pattern to fabric with transparent tape or pins, trace around it, and cut ⅛″ beyond tracing line. Machine-stitch on this line. Clip the ⅛″ margin at close intervals to make it easy to turn under and flatten edges. Press the patch. Sew it over worn spot with blanket or blind stitch or by machine. For an original decorative patch, use your initial in the International Flag Code. Make a small flag of fabric scraps. This becomes a handsome pocket on a solid-colored skirt or a smart monogram on back or sleeve of your jacket or pajamas.

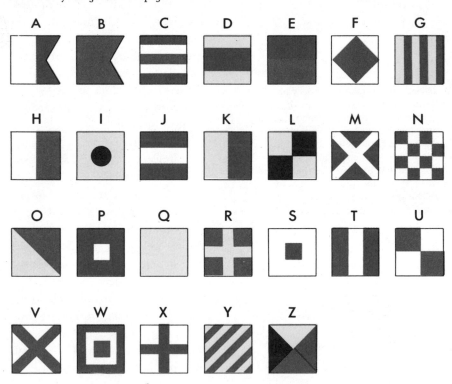

A Busy Darning Needle

With a darning needle you can make smooth, nearly invisible repairs of tears and snags, strengthen worn spots, and fill in holes in fabrics and hose. Darning is similar to weaving. Always use threads that blend in color and texture with the article to be darned.

For woolens, use ravelings from the fabric itself or preshrink matching darning wool.

For cottons, use fine cotton thread.

For nylon, silk, or rayon, use fabric ravelings, a single ply from a split silk thread, or nylon thread.

Darning Small Holes

1. Trim off jagged edges around hole.
2. Fill in broken lengthwise threads with matching yarn, weaving needle under and over a few yarns at one edge of hole, then across to opposite edge, weaving under and over again. Do not pull yarn tight. When darning hosiery, use darning ball to hold work smooth.
3. Fill in crosswise yarns by weaving under and over each lengthwise thread.

Darning Tears

1. Lay material to be darned wrong-side up. Bring torn edges together with transparent tape. If cloth is weak or ravels easily, do not use tape, but baste a piece of thin cloth (net, gauze, etc.) in matching color under place to be darned.
2. Beginning at one end of tear, insert needle. Following grain of fabric, make short running stitches across tear. Make each row a different length to avoid a bumpy ridge. Make sure to catch the edges of the tear and do not pull thread tight. Steam and press flat.

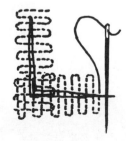

1 Present a younger person to an older one.
"*Mrs. Blake, this is my friend, Jane Cooper.*"

2 Introducing your troop leader to your mother.
"*Mother, may I present Mrs. Murphy?*"

"She Has a

Not too many years ago, this was one of the finest compliments a lady could inspire. Today, it is still true, for it describes one of the most delightful feminine traits, a combination of graceful carriage, unfidgety repose, a voice soft and clear, and kind consideration of others. It is poise—without pose.

Do you have these qualities? Do you stand without drooping, sit without fussing, feel easy with other people, and make them feel the same with you?

If you do, your manner creates a pleasant impression wherever you go. If you do not, cultivate these qualities. It is not difficult. Remind yourself to walk tall, but not stiffly, to sit serenely, to speak pleasantly. Soon it will be second nature. For now that you are a young lady, your manner should show it.

Who are the people in your life?

3 In a boy-to-girl introduction, the girl's name comes first. *"Jane, this is Edward Stone."*

4 Presenting yourself to a new troop member. *"Hello, I'm Sue Smith."*

Queenly Bearing."

You probably think at once of your family, the girls in your troop, your best friend, perhaps a boy or two. But your circle is much bigger than that. It includes everyone in your world—neighbors, troop leaders, clerks in shops, bus drivers, strangers who may pass you on the street, and more. You move among them daily. How do they see you?

That depends on the way you behave, on your manners. Often, a girl does not mean to be rude and loud. She may simply be thoughtless or in a silly mood, and so, she forgets herself, and behaves in an unattractive way.

All good manners are based on remembering yourself.

If you respect the person you are, you will respect other people too, and will not act in an unbecoming way. Your manners reflect your attitudes and reveal the kind of person you are.

Good manners are also based on rules of behavior that are considered correct and pleasant. If you are unsure of yourself in a social situation, the best thing is to act naturally and honestly. Think of ways to put others at ease, too. Later, consult a good etiquette book, so you will know what to say and do next time. These rules are more than automatic formalities, for they help to clear away awkwardness. When you know the appropriate things to do, you are more relaxed, your manner is lovelier.

Here are some guides to graciousness, to a friendlier social life. Start where many nice things begin—the first introductions.

Good Manners Are Good Taste

They belong in every area of your life. In public, your behavior should be inconspicuous. It is unfair to spoil other people's comfort by boisterousness, an unattractive quality except in a puppy.

Courtesy should be extended to everyone. Wait your turn on the bus line, at the store counter, at a patrol discussion, at the dinner table.

Respect other people's rights and property as you would your own. At home, wherever you go, leave things as tidy as you found them (or tidier). This is a good thing to remember when you go visiting. A considerate guest is always welcome, appreciated, and asked to come calling again.

Have you ever waited for a friend who was late for an appointment? It is one of life's most annoying experiences. Remember this when you make a date. Be on time.

Real friendliness is one proof of good manners. Welcome new troop members and new neighbors, with cordiality. It is an attractive trait.

Daintiness, too, is pretty to see. Let your eating habits be neat. Learn to handle utensils properly, gracefully. Avoid mannerisms, exaggerated gestures, affectations. Make frequent use of two of the most charming expressions of courtesy, "Please" and "Thank you."

So many "do's" and "don't's" may be somewhat disheartening. Don't be dismayed. The rules of attractive behavior fall quite naturally into your life as you go along. First, be aware of them. Then, practice them.

A very good place to begin is in your own home with your own family. Here you are part of a small world in which everyone has an important role. Have you ever thought of your family in quite this way?

What roles do your parents play? They provide you with food, clothes, a place to sleep. But just as important, they give you themselves. They care for you and about you.

When you realize this, you understand other things, too. Since they are concerned for you, they want to know about you: what you do, where you go, who your friends are. This is not prying into your privacy for the sake of inquisitiveness. It is their wish to offer you attention, encouragement, love, and understanding.

Your brothers and sisters, too, are in this family world with you. Together, you form a unit, a haven of familiarity and common interests. You must view each family member as a person in his own right, entitled to family privileges but also to his rights as an individual.

Each of you makes special contributions to the circle. What are yours?

SARAH JOSEPHA HALE was one of the first career women in the United States. Born on a New Hampshire farm in 1788, she grew up and married, had five children, and lived a quiet domestic life for many years. Then, her husband died, leaving her with their large family to support.

Mrs. Hale turned to writing as a means of making money. Her verses and novel attracted some attention. In 1837, she became editor of *Godey's Lady's Book*, the forerunner of every women's magazine since printed. Famous for its fashion news, *Godey's* had tremendous impact in other ways. In it, Mrs. Hale advocated higher education for women and the need for their services as teachers. She had the taste to buy and publish the work of the young Edgar Allan Poe. A practical woman, she believed all women could and should be given opportunities to work and serve. Though born in the 18th century, Sarah Hale may well be considered a thoroughly modern woman.

Your Family Fortune

Rich, poor, or middling, your family has a wealth of love and experience to share. Family get-togethers to make plans and decisions are one way of sharing. If you have a special problem, talk it out in the family circle.

Remember that parents have problems, too. They have many responsibilities—jobs, housework, meals, the health and well-being of the whole family. Now that you have more skills, you can help out in many ways.

Is your disposition good-humored, affectionate? That is a way to be an appreciated member of your family.

If you are the sort of girl who demands things your parents cannot afford and expects mother to tidy up after you, you are being babyish. A daughter wins respect and greater freedom by showing she can do things well, keep her possessions neat, lend a hand with mop and dustcloth, join in family chores and family cheer.

She believes everyone in her family is important and treats each one with courtesy. She does not consider the TV set and telephone her exclusive property, nor does she monopolize the phone for endless chitchat.

Respecting the rights of others, she limits her calls to brief exchanges. She keeps a list of emergency numbers near the phone for use in a crisis.

She thinks of her family as people to love and be proud of. Do you?

Finer Than Finery...

. . . is the spirit that shines in your eyes, your attitudes, your personality. Clothes are important, but they are only clues to the person inside. If you want to be attractive to others, don't depend on things that show. Be a real person, not an imitation of girls around you.

Open your mind to new ideas. If you take a real interest in a variety of things, people will be more interested in you. Do you seize every opportunity to enjoy literature and poetry, music, drama, and dance? Do you merely look or really see the beauty in painting, sculpture, folk art, industrial art, interior design. Do you do things and make things? Are you willing to try new activities suggested by other girls in your patrol or troop?

When you are having a good time, do you show it? Enthusiasm can light up your face and your life. It is brightness that kindles enthusiasm in others, building fun and good spirits.

Are you genuine in your attitudes and beliefs? If you are insincere, other people will sense it. If you believe in what you say and do, they will sense that, too, and respect you for it.

Is your character all that you want it to be? If you are uncertain about this, give serious thought to the Promise and Laws. They are guides that can lead you straight to the kind of girl you admire. Even though you may not be aware of it, younger girls look up to you. Do you offer a fine example for them to follow?

Do you care about other people? This question is not so simple as it may seem. You may answer, "Yes, I want to win their interest and admiration." This is not really caring about others, it is caring about what others think of *you*. Are you prepared to give the attention you wish to receive?

So you see, attractiveness is a great many things. It is vigorous health, cleanliness, grooming. It is a confident, gracious manner and a pleasant voice, a cheerful disposition and an interest in life. It is courtesy and character, a sense of humor about yourself, as well as others. It is everything about you.

If you can achieve all this, and you can, you had better be prepared to receive many compliments in your lifetime. Learn to accept them gracefully with an appreciative smile and a modest "Thank you."

let's have a party

When you give a party, you are chef, artist, and diplomat rolled into one. The more roles you can play well, the better the party.

You have fun, of course. But behind the gaiety is the solid experience of making a workable plan. This is a fine place to use the "Steps in Planning" and kaper charts in Chapter 3. You can learn to give a well-planned party, one that is thoroughly organized yet with a relaxed atmosphere. You can acquire the quality of graciousness.

There is satisfaction in practicing the feminine skills as a hostess, while

making other people glad they came to your party. These experiences become part of you forever, so when you give a party, give a good one!

As a Cadette you will be taking another step toward First Class if you combine a service project with your social event. Here are a few kinds of parties to start you thinking.

Cookout: Might also include a "How-To" session (photography, ceramics) or special program (jungle breakfast, sunrise hike).

Work Party: Fun and food after a job like planting trees, chopping wood.

Father-Daughter Event: A luncheon, buffet, or dinner to honor dad.

Mother-Daughter Event: A daintier version, perhaps a tea.

Special Theme Party: Based on regional, national, or world interest, such as international Scouting or a "Know Your State" party.

Special Day Party: Rededication, investiture, "Last Day of Camp."

Service Project Party: For children (Brownies or at a nursery), for older people (troop sponsors, P.T.A.)

Activity Party: Talk, eat, and bowl, skate, swim, play ping-pong, folk dance, social dance, or pull taffy.

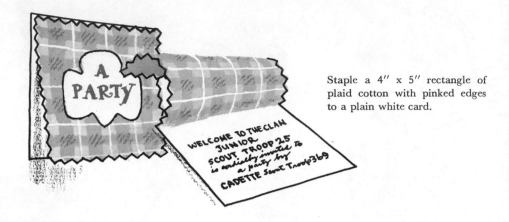

Staple a 4″ x 5″ rectangle of plaid cotton with pinked edges to a plain white card.

WELCOME TO THE CLAN
JUNIOR
SCOUT TROOP 25
is cordially invited to
a party by
CADETTE Scout Troop 369

A PARTY

Of plain, heavy paper, make a folder measuring 1½″ x 2½″. Make a miniature Christmas tree ornament of felt, decorate with ricrac, sequins, and a gilt cord. Staple or tie cord to inner crease of folder. Write inside.

you're invited

GIRL SCOUT

TROOP 369 invites

EXPLORER POST 79

TO A BARN DANCE

Make a haystack cutout of yellow construction paper.

Informal invitations may be phoned and formal ones written as directed by a book of etiquette. But the best invitations create a party mood, giving basic information (see page 57) and a hint of fun to come. Use paper, tinsel, paints, shells, unexpected materials from your sewing and knitting boxes, to create invitations that reflect the party theme and your skill. Match your invitations to your plan, mail them out, and get down to the basic party-giving details.

Who Are the Guests?

Your party may start with an occasion you wish to celebrate or a list of people you wish to ask. If, for example, it is a Juliette Low Birthday party, you might invite guests who have been helpful to your troop. If you start with the people, draw up a list of those you want to ask and plan the party accordingly.

In other words, either plan your guest list for the party you want, or plan your party for the guests you wish to invite.

What Shall You Serve?

Party menus should be special. This does not mean that refreshments need be expensive. They should be inviting, a little different from daily fare, and appropriate to the guests, the occasion, and the season.

If your guests are boys, remember that they are always hungry. Look for novel ways of preparing familiar foods. Frankfurters, for example, can be filled with melted cheese or wrapped in bacon and heaped with relish. Try a self-service sundae bar stocked with several flavors of bulk ice cream, a scoop for dipping, and a variety of nut, sauce, and fruit toppings. A party for women would suggest a different menu; a platter of pretty finger-length sandwiches or a beautifully arranged fruit salad.

Plan a menu that is appropriate for the kind of party you are giving and it will be sure to be successful.

Shall We Go Shopping?

Before party day, list everything you will need to buy, keeping an eye on the budget. Have a plan. If a patrol is shopping, you might divide the list according to the way foods are grouped in the market to save time. Or, if more convenient, the list may be divided among individual girls, depending on where they live.

Know your stores and markets. Choose those that are clean, economical, and offer good variety and service. Know your foods, too. Study the different can sizes, study labels for information on grade, quality, and sometimes, number of servings in the package.

Learn to judge the quantities you need for the number of guests. It is embarrassing to have too little and wasteful to have too much. Be sure there is proper storage space for your purchases. Is there room in the refrigerator, freezer, breadbox?

Are You Prepared?

To be a calm, relaxed hostess, do as much advance preparation as you can. Salad greens may be washed, dried, and refrigerated the day before the party. Casserole dishes are often assembled and refrigerated, all ready for the oven. Hamburger patties may be shaped, put between layers of wax papers, and refrigerated. Cakes and cookies baked and kept in airtight containers.

Apply the same idea to decor and service. Count out dishes and utensils in advance, making sure you have the right number. Prepare coat hangers, guest towels, umbrella stand. Clear breakables away. If it's to be a dance, roll back the rug. Try to envision what has to be done. Then do as much as you can, in planned order, before party day. Things will run more smoothly if you do.

The type of service you choose depends on the kind of party you are giving and the facilities you have. For a spur-of-the-moment gathering, you need only a few refreshment platters placed conveniently around for guests to help themselves. Buffet service is a collective method, with tableware, napkins, utensils, and refreshments arranged on one surface, from which each guest serves himself. An individual sit-down service is more formal. Here, a complete setting is laid out for each guest. Before you decide on the type of service you want, consider the number of people expected. Are there enough tables and chairs for a sit-down service? If not, a buffet would be the choice. If you decide on a sit-down service, consult a reliable book of etiquette for correct serving procedure. Whatever you decide, keep the service simple and pleasing to the eye. Use flowers, pretty colors; polish dishes and glassware till they sparkle. Be prepared for cleanup too, include it in your kaper chart.

How Was the Party?

How did things go? Plan a post-party discussion to judge your accomplishments. Did your plans work well? Could you improve them? Did you make any mistakes? If you did, don't worry. You won't make them the next time you plan to give a party.

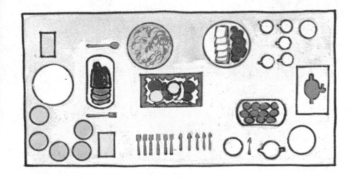

Buffet Service

Individual Service

Tasteful Tables

You can bring these outlines to life with color, taste, imagination, and a dash of ingenuity.

Suppose you give a sit-down treat of ice cream and cookies to young children. How about a circus theme? Sew or staple animal cutouts around a plain white cloth (so they may be removed later), use brightly-colored coated paper plates and smooth-edged plastic spoons. Your centerpiece? A clown puppet or stuffed lion. For more fun, tie a balloon to each chair.

You could give a pink tea by using a pink-striped sheet as a cloth, potted pink geraniums as a centerpiece, and cookies with strawberry icing for dessert. For extra effect, tie a pink ribbon in a bow around each napkin.

See what you can dream up when you set a party table. Think first: "What kind of party is it?" The theme will inspire you. Keep things simple, convenient, appropriate, and consistent. It is best, for example, not to mix paperware with fine china. Each belongs to a different kind of party.

You need not follow the settings exactly as shown, but may vary them according to preference. Shop for ideas in store windows, chinaware departments, magazines. Experience the feminine glow of pride of being effective with things you have or can make with your own hands.

Family dinner: Arrangements should be low, for comfortable conversation.

Buffet service: Arrangement may be tall, but should not interfere with setting.

Tray setting: Small flower arrangement (3″ to 6″), must not clutter tray.

The Art of Flower Arranging

Materials for harmonious, graceful flower compositions are simple. You will need: a container; holder (needle or chicken wire); plastite, plasticine, or a form of clay to keep holder firmly in container.

Starter arrangement: Holder is placed off-center in flat container. There are three basic lines; tallest at the back, shorter at one side, lowest in front, slanting forward. Fill in flowers, following these basic lines.

Color: Choose flowers that blend or contrast, containers that enhance them: white daisies in a sunny yellow pitcher, pink roses in a leaf-green vase. Relate colors to your table setting.

Balance: Decide on a basic contour or shape, symmetrical or asymmetrical. Study the finished effect. Then add or remove flowers to fit your plan.

Harmony: Flowers, leaves, containers complement each other. Rough textures (zinnias, marigolds) look good in baskets, containers of wood, copper, brass; smooth fragile flowers (roses, sweet peas) are enhanced by silver, glass, delicate china containers.

Some Basic Rules

o Smaller flowers to the top
o Combine round and spiked materials
o Heavier the flower, shorter the stem
o Never crowd
o Foundation must appear solid
o Strip all leaves below water level
o Cut flower stems on a slant
o Aim for simplicity

Join the Dance

The music starts and you're off to the smooth rhythms of a ball-room dance or the gay swinging patterns of a square dance. Learning the steps is not hard. Invite a troop member or adult (troop leader, dance consultant) to teach you. While learning, you might have a "practice prance" trying out new steps with a group of boys who are beginners, too.

Dancing is a great personal pleasure, as well as a social asset. If you have special talents, you might explore ballet or interpretive dancing. You might evolve original dance movements for a pageant or other production. Even without special talent you can attend recitals, watch TV performances, and dance for the joy of it.

Nearly everyone enjoys folk dances. That is why, for generations, they have been handed down like precious heirlooms, from parents to children all over the world. Dances from different countries tell you something about their peoples. When you see a slow-moving, languid dance, you may guess that it comes from a country where the climate is too hot for the energetic movements of cold-weather lands.

Singing games, the simplest form of folk dancing, can be learned from books (see Bibliography). You may sing, play records, or call on the musicians in your troop for accompaniment.

Good folk dancers love to teach others. Once you learn, you will want to share the fun at picnics and parties. You may even have a chance to teach American dances to people from foreign lands. To be a good teacher:

o Choose your dances carefully, taking into consideration age and capabilities of the people you are teaching.

o To avoid perplexities, practice the pattern in advance, using the instruction book. You may work it out with friends.

o Have a picture of every figure clearly in your mind, so you won't need the book when you are teaching.

o Teach a dance step by step. Give instructions clearly and simply, so you need never touch or push any of your pupils.

o Enjoy yourself! Everyone else will have fun, too.

Square dance calls and patterns may vary. Here are some basic terms.

Square dance: Four couples stand, forming a hollow square about eight feet across. Boys have partners on their right.

Allemande left: Boys join left hands with girls on their left and all turn counterclockwise. Dancers return to their places.

Balance: Couples face, holding right hands. Step on right foot, swing left over; step on left, swing right over.

Cast-off: Partners face top of room in two rows, boys left, girls right. They separate. Each goes down outside of his (her) line to meet at other end.

Do-si-do: Couples face, then pass around each other back-to-back, with right shoulders leading.

Grand right and left: Partners face, clasp right hands, pass each other on right. Left hand is given to next dancer, who passes left. Next one passes right, and so on, right and left around circle until original partners meet. Also called "Grand Chair."

Honor or address: Partners or corners face. Boys bow, girls curtsey.

Promenade: Couples join hands in double handclasp, walk or skip in circle, counterclockwise, girls on outside.

Reel: Partners hook right elbows, circle in clockwise direction.

Slip-step or sashay: A sideways gallop.

Swing your partner: Hold partner as in ballroom dancing. Swing swiftly around once or twice, pivoting on right foot and pushing with left.

Komarno

(a town in Hungary)

Bohemian

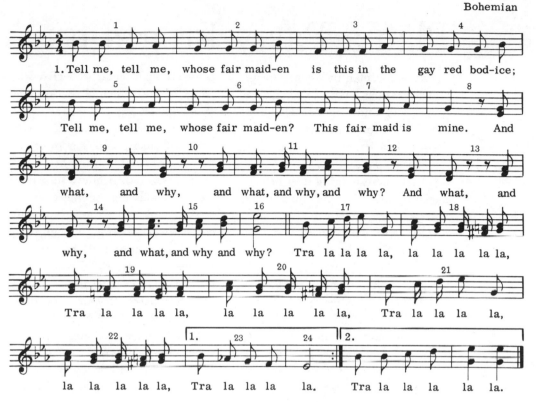

1. Tell me, tell me, whose fair maid-en is this in the gay red bod-ice;
Tell me, tell me, whose fair maid-en? This fair maid is mine. And
what, and why, and what, and why, and why? And what, and
why, and what, and why and why? Tra la la la la, la la la la la,
Tra la la la la, la la la la la, Tra la la la la,
la la la la la, Tra la la la la. Tra la la la la la.

FORMATION:

Couples in a single circle, or about the room as in social dancing. Partners face each other and join crossed hands.

FIGURE 1:   Beginning with the left foot the woman dances eight polka steps (skip, run, run) backward, while the man begins with the right foot and dances forward. They move to the right round the room (measures 1—8).

FIGURE 2:   Still retaining their hold they dance "cutting steps" in place as follows:—spring so as to throw feet alternately forward, (starting with the right foot,) pointing on the ground, as words "what" and "why" occur (measures 9—16).

FIGURE 3:   Partners clap on the first beat of measure 17 and linking right arms turn with eight running steps (measures 17—20). Clap and turn with left arms linked (measures 21—24). Repeat whole figure.

Plan a Party Program

Just as you plan the theme, menu, and decorations, so should you plan a program of things to do. This is a sure way to avoid awkward party lags.

Music is a happy party-goer. For an informal dance, try a "Record Relay." Ask guests to bring their newest dance records. (Remind them to initial the labels, so that the right ones go home with their owners.)

Give a "Listen and Learn" party. Here, each guest brings one interesting piece of information about a specified composer. After discussing his life, personality, and times, listen to some of his compositions.

Do any of your guests play musical instruments? Do you? You might present a concert, with a program made out in advance. Another time you might have an impromptu songfest.

Games are popular, especially with active boys or younger children. For outdoor parties, have sack races, horseshoes, or a scavenger hunt (see Chapter 4). For a change of pace, play quiet games—Twenty Questions, Charades, Ghost. A wise hostess has a new game or activity ready when the moment seems to call for it.

Dramatics offer many chances for entertainment. Have you ever acted out a ballad, a simple, story-telling poem? It is particularly effective with voice or instrumental background. (See Bibliography.)

Puppets and marionettes can be star performers, and shadowgraphs (cardboard cutouts or live actors casting their shadows behind a suspended sheet) make fascinating entertainment.

Skits and stunts are perfect for campfire parties. Or, if your troop is really ambitious, try writing, costuming, and staging a play for an orphanage in your locality.

Have a Dance: If your troop is giving a dance, form committees to:

Learn dance floor etiquette from consultants or books. Explain it to the rest of the troop by demonstrations or with wall posters. Inquire whether your school, community center or "Y" would like to have a set of posters for display.

Teach basic steps (two-step, three-step, glide) to nondancers, with friendly encouragement for shy people.

Select a variety of records that appeal to all tastes—some fast, some slow, and a few specialties.

Plan "mixers," group dances all can enjoy, to get the dancing started.

Talent on Tap Roster: List the talented troop members—musicians, actors, dancers—you can ask to perform.

You're Welcome

A warm welcome feeling is a gift imparted by a hostess to her guests. From the moment you greet them with "I'm so glad you're here" to your cordial "Come back again," you set the tone of the party. So be prepared.

Before the event, spend parts of one or two troop meetings discussing manners, introductions, and party procedures customary in your locality. Learn how to make everyone feel part of the party. Plan games that all can play. If you are dancing, change partners often, so that no one feels left out. If you spot a shy guest, give him something to do. A boy cooking kabobs over charcoal will soon forget his shyness.

Learn how to start a conversation. "We're talking about hobbies. What's yours?" or "I noticed your smooth back dive. Where did you learn it? At school or at Boy Scout camp?" Hospitality is really thoughtfulness. To find the key, you need go no further than the Girl Scout Promise and Laws.

DOLLY MADISON was a blue-eyed beauty whose face radiated charm, vivacity, and great liking for people and gaiety. As James Madison's wife, she enjoyed the glittering balls and receptions of Washington society. When her husband became fourth President of the United States, Dolly became First Lady and first hostess of the land. She gave wonderful parties. Her taste and tact united rival statesmen, rough frontiersmen, polished diplomats, and elegant ladies. An original hostess, she introduced ice cream to the New World. She helped the children of the city celebrate Easter by inventing a novel egg-rolling party on the White House lawn.

Dolly had courage. In 1814, when the British attacked Washington, she escaped disguised as a farm woman. That night, from across the Potomac, she saw her city in flames. But she had fled with two treasures—the original Declaration of Independence and Gilbert Stuart's portrait of George Washington.

What Every Good Hostess Knows

Certain party situations call for direct action. Will any of the guests need transportation? How will people know the right time to leave? Who shall we invite as chaperons?

The right time to end the party is established by you. You may do so in your invitations, by writing: "From 5:00 to 7:00." Or you may tactfully tell a few friends when you expect the party to end and they will start the leave-takings. Or you may post signs, reading "Open until 10:30." Whatever the parting hour, abide by it, even if the merriment is still going strong. It is better to end on a note of fun than a fizzle.

Chaperons are good to have. Think of them as adult hosts, just as eager for your party's success as you are. It is gracious to bring your friends of different ages together. Furthermore, in case of crisis, an adult's presence in the background is a great help.

What Every Good Guest Knows

If you are going to a party (instead of giving one), be a happy addition to the group. Start with the right attitude. You are going to have a good time, so join heartily in whatever party activities are provided. Greet your hostess and chaperon when you arrive, thank them for a lovely time when you leave. Be friendly and courteous to everyone, younger children, older relatives, household help. Don't criticize or make comparisons with other parties. And if, by chance, you cause some breakage or damage, offer to replace it if you can. Make sincere apologies to your hostess, just once. Don't dwell on it.

Remember . . . parties can be fun for everybody.

Invitation To Accept
the Challenge

Are you ready to meet the Challenge of Social Dependability? Now is the time to check on your progress. There are badges to be earned in many fascinating areas: in personal development, family living, and party giving. Read the requirements for the Chef, Homemaker, and Hostess badges. Activities in such badges as these will help you fulfill the purpose of this Challenge: to show that you have the understanding and skills to get along well with others and to carry a full share of the responsibility in successful social situations.

If you have been working on good health habits, better grooming, and a lovelier manner, you have taken beginning steps toward meeting this Challenge.

If you have had several chances to practice the art of social ease and grace as a hostess and as a guest, you have taken more strides along the way.

If you have taken the Girl Scout Promise and Laws to heart and are turning them into daily action, you may be ready to meet the Challenge of Social Dependability.

What are the next steps?

Carefully check yourself against the Challenge Preps for this Challenge in Chapter 16. Learn and practice those things which you do not know. If you and the other members of your group decide that you now measure up, tell your leader that you feel you are ready to accept the Challenge. If she agrees with you, start planning your party now.

Happily, there is no single or "best" way to do things. Much depends upon your taste, judgment, and skills. The Challenge of Social Dependability gives you a chance to make the most of you.

world of holidays

There's something different in the air, a feeling that today is going to be special. If you have ever awakened with this tingle of anticipation, you will recognize the holiday feeling.

By now, you have come to know and love the holidays that glorify your life—the solemnity of religious observances, the pride of patriotic days, the fun of Girl Scout celebrations. They are part of your life as an American girl. They are your holidays.

Now, send your imagination on a trip around the world. Wherever you go, there are girls like you, awakening with the same tingle of holiday anticipation. In Malaya, they welcome the New Year with candles and new clothes to wear. In Liberia, they celebrate Flag Day with banners to wave at parades. In Switzerland, they light huge bonfires on the mountainsides to salute their National Day. On the Day of the Indian Child in Mexico, there are special exhibits of the arts of talented Indian children to commemorate the birthday of Mexico's hero, Benito Juarez. And in Turkey there is a holiday called Children's Day, because the Turkish people believe the future of their country depends on their boys and girls. A world full of holidays.

Different in Place

Of course you can't travel to all these countries to take part in the celebration, but you might do it right here. Our country is a land filled with people who came from other countries and who observe the holiday customs and traditions of their homelands. Who do you know that celebrates holidays differently from your family?

If you ever meet a Girl Guide, or if you have a Guide pen pal, ask her about holiday celebrations in her country. In this way you could share in the holiday fun and spirit of your sister Scouts in far lands.

Different in Time

Most holidays commemorate something that happened in days long past. So as you celebrate you are traveling in time. Does your state have a special event it remembers? For example, April 19 is Patriots Day in Maine and Massachusetts. In Texas, San Jacinto Day is a holiday. You could plan a celebration around the day your state was admitted to the Union.

Ways of celebrating change, too. It would be interesting to find out what people did on the Fourth of July in your town twenty years ago, or fifty, or even one hundred.

ETHEL BARRYMORE was a remarkable beauty and, for many years, one of the leading actresses on the stage, in the movies, and in television. Educated at the Convent of Notre Dame in Philadelphia, she was in private life Mrs. Russell Griswold Colt and the mother of three children.

As some people inherit wealth, Ethel Barrymore inherited a great acting tradition. Both the Barrymores, on her father's side, and the Drews, on her mother's side, were world-famous performers. She did not accept this inheritance as her rightful due, but worked to earn and keep her fine reputation as an actress and her position as a star in the world of theater.

As she traveled about the world, she added to her knowledge of sports, music, books, politics, and history of the places she visited. She attracted good friends and kept them through the wit of her speech and the strength of her beliefs. When she died in 1959, she had lived eighty full years of glamor and work.

Girl Scout Holidays

Here in the United States, Girl Scout Week is celebrated each year during the week of March 12, the anniversary of the first troop meeting. Plans are usually made by the whole troop, but may be carried out by the troop, by patrols, or by individuals. Traditionally there are Seven Service Days, each emphasizing a particular Scouting activity.

On *Girl Scout Sunday or Sabbath*, plan to demonstrate your understanding of the first part of your Girl Scout Promise—Duty to God.

Monday is *Homemaking Day*. Teach a homemaking skill to a younger girl. (Try the recipe on page 100. It can also be made in a frying pan indoors.)

Tuesday is *Citizenship Day*. Your experiences as a Cadette Girl Scout citizen would be a good subject for a writing project, such as a theme assigned in school or an entry in the *American Girl's* "By You" department.

Health and Safety Day falls on Wednesday. In a store window, a school, or a community center put up an exhibit that demonstrates a good safety practice.

On Thursday, *International Friendship Day*, visit a museum, attend a concert, learn a song, or make something which will add to your knowledge and appreciation of other cultures.

Plan to share your new knowledge with your troopmates, younger Scouts, or other girls on Friday, which is *The Arts Day*.

Saturday is *Out-of-Doors Day*. Arrange a way for someone who rarely has a chance to do anything out-of-doors—a homebound older person, a handicapped child, or a busy mother of young children—to experience some of the awe and wonder of the outdoors.

Girl Scout Week is a time to take a good look at what the troop has done during the winter; to plan for the coming spring and summer months. It is also an excellent occasion for a special rededication ceremony or a Scouts' Own.

February is *International Month* wherever there are members of the Girl Scouts. Read *Trefoil Around the World* to learn about Scouting in over fifty countries; find a way to send greetings to Girl Guides in another country on Thinking Day, February 22. During this month, too, many troops include people of different cultural backgrounds in their activities. Girl Scouts not only respect ways that are different from their own but are eager to learn more about them.

Festive Folk Art

Throughout the world, people love their holidays. Each holiday has deep meaning to the people who observe it, just as your holiday observances have importance to you.

All sorts of folk arts have been inspired by holidays and festivals. Pantomimes and plays, pageants and ceremonies, legends and stories were often developed for such celebrations, and special designs in the hand arts were created for festive days.

In our Girl Scout books there are many examples of songs and dances used on holidays in our own and other countries. In *Sing Together*, look for "Skye Boat Song" which is sung at festivals in Scotland. In *The Ditty Bag*, you will find the "Swedish Christmas Polka," and "Las Mañanitas," sung at Latin American birthdays. Try dancing "The Cornish May Dance" found in *Promenade All*. "Auld Lang Syne," which we sing on New Year's Eve, is sung in various versions and tongues almost all over the world.

Nothing bespeaks a holiday more than the decorations, and paper sculpture is exciting holiday decor. Fanciful shapes, brilliant colors, and airy designs turn everyday places like schoolrooms and living rooms into festive fairylands.

In many countries, paper has long been used in folk art. Mexico flies paper banners and makes piñatas; Sweden produces charming Christmas ornaments; Switzerland and India turn out lovely products of paper crafts.

This is how the Japanese fold a paper square into a crane, symbol of hope and happiness. Follow the steps, using paper slightly heavier than tissue paper. Be sure to press each fold firmly. You will enjoy this ancient art, which is called *origami*.

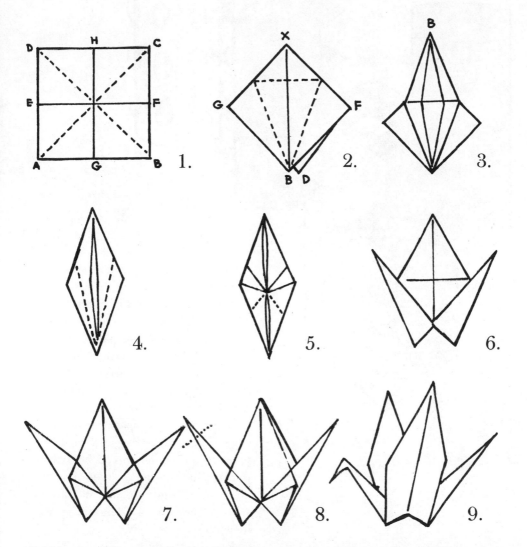

1. Fold square as shown; solid lines form peaks, dotted lines form valleys. **2.** Bring ABCD together to form small square. Bring F and G to center fold. Repeat on other side. Fold down top to form triangle. **3.** Unfold to small square. Pull B up over center point X, pulling in G and F. Repeat with D on other side. **4.** Fold outside points to center on dotted line. Repeat on other side. **5.** Make diagonal creases on neck and tail. **6.** Fold up neck and tail. **7.** Unfold tail. Push into wing, reversing center fold at the same time. Repeat for neck. **8.** Fold head on dotted line. Push into neck, again reversing center fold. **9.** Spread wings gently, holding bottom and pushing down on X.

To make paper decorations you will need: newsprint to sketch out your design; some kind of stiff paper, such as bond mimeograph, butcher, Kraft, poster or construction paper, metallic paper, bristol or tag board; chipboard for a cutting surface; a knife, scissors, or single-edged razor blade; a dull kitchen knife for scoring; transparent tape, library paste, or rubber cement; staples, brads, paper clips, or pins; spring clothespins to hold the paper while you work. Try to express your taste through choice of paper, shapes, and designs. Here are some ideas to start you off.

Paper cylinders make charming decorations to hang, to stand on floor, table, or mantel, or to use as gala lampshades. Decorate them with cutout designs, folds, or splits. If you cut your design, lay paper flat on a piece

of chipboard to protect cutting surface and absorb pressure of knife or
cutting tool as you cut.

Paper strips become graceful, harmonious shapes when folded, curled,
looped, or bent into figures like these.
Use combinations of papers—white,
colored, and metallic—joining strips
with paste or staples. Suspended by
yarn or ribbons, taped to wall or
window, these gay forms make
original, attractive party and holiday
decorations.

Flat cuts are fun as holiday decor
and also interesting as part of a table-
top display or exhibition. First the
design is planned on flat paper. Then
cuts are made in it. The cut forms are
raised almost to a right angle, so that
they stand upright, like scenery on a
stage, while the basic sheet of paper
rests flat on the table top.

If a man be gracious and courteous to strangers, it shows he is a citizen of the world, and that his heart is no island cut off from other lands but is a continent that joins them.

— Francis Bacon.

The same human feelings—joy, devotion, gratitude—prompt celebrations of holidays and festivals all over the world regardless of geographic location, racial origin, or religious belief. For example, people everywhere give thanks for their blessings in some special way. Some show their gratitude by sharing with those less fortunate, others by refraining from eating certain foods to remind themselves of their blessings. Some people do not eat on certain days, others eat only during certain hours. Still others invite poor strangers as guests of honor at a feast, while others plan a special menu for a family gathering.

If you were the guest of Girl Guides in Lebanon or Egypt or the Sudan, you might find them expressing gratitude for their blessings by enjoying a very large and varied midday meal after not having eaten during daylight hours for a long time. The meal would be quite different from an American one. While we generally serve one large main dish and a few side dishes, people in the Middle East prefer a great many courses served in small quantities.

At the table of a wealthy family in the Middle East you might find: peppers stuffed with lamb, parsley, and onions; a macaroni dish; cous cous, which is a base of fine cereal, steamed and served with a meat and vegetable stew. You might find almond pastries and baklava, made of honey and ground nuts, and fresh fruits served in bowls of cold water. Possibly, one dish would be *brik belatham*, a delicious lamb pastry.

The name of this dish is spelled *brik belatham*, a transliteration from Arabic script. (The word "transliteration" means the phonetic re-spelling of a word from one alphabet into another, when the two alphabets have no symbols in common.) When your family or guests ask you to pronounce it, say: *brreek bell-éh-thim*.

brik belatham

FOR FILLING	½ cup fresh parsley, finely chopped
1½ cups finely diced lamb, such as inexpensive stew meat or shank	6 eggs
8 small scallions, sliced fine	FOR PASTRY
2 teaspoons salt	2 cups sifted flour
½ teaspoon pepper	¼ cup shortening
1 tablespoon olive oil	2 teaspoons salt
	7 tablespoons cold water

To make filling, boil the first five ingredients in about two inches of water until meat is tender and water cooked almost dry. Add parsley and mix.

To make pastry, blend flour, salt, and shortening thoroughly. Gradually add water, kneading constantly until dough is elastic. Divide into six balls. With dry rolling pin, roll each ball about 8 inches in diameter and thin enough to see through. Fold round edges to make a square. Leaving about 1 inch space around edge, make a ring of meat mixture (using 5 teaspoonsful) around the middle of square. Break egg into the center. The meat mixture will hold the egg in. Quickly fold a corner of the square to its opposite corner and seal edges firmly, making a triangle. Gently place in frying pan of hot shortening. Fry until lightly brown. Turn once. The egg white should be firm, yolk soft. Serves 6.

Each holiday, in every part of the world, at home or abroad tells you something of the people who celebrate it. This greater under-standing brings you closer together in spirit, and may start you on the road toward international friendship.

let's explore the out-of-doors

The whole wood-world is one full peal of praise.
—ALFRED, LORD TENNYSON

Praise the green that shades, the soft, brown earth that springs underfoot, the golden sunlight and dancing rain. Praise dewy mornings filled with birdsong, nighttime skies blazing with stars. Praise the glory of being alive in the outdoors.

Whether you're off on a one-hour hike or a weekend troop camp, you will feel comfortably at home with nature if you know the skills of camping and can put them to work. Here, at this primitive camp, the girls have provided for all their needs. There is the sleeping area, with sleeping bags arranged in a congenial circle. If it rains, that won't dampen the fun. They've pitched a shelter tent nearby. They are even ready for a violent storm because they pitched camp near a barn. They use the shelter tent to store most of their gear, too.

Over there is the kitchen area, with storage places for equipment, dry and perishable foods, and wood for cooking. Not far away is the work area, with surfaces for food preparation, a dish-washing arrangement, a waste-water disposal system, a "dining room." In another direction is a latrine with leaves and branches for privacy. These girls are all set for outdoor living. Are you?

Go All-out for Fun!

Walk out for a part of a meeting. In your town, can you see a monument, a gabled roof, a stained glass window?

Meet out in good weather. Do you know some games, arts, songs, and dances that can be enjoyed outdoors?

Hike out to an interesting place and take a sketchbook along. Hike for the joy of it, and to see what you can see. Look for starfish or spiders, cactus or cattails.

Cook out for the satisfying taste of food in the open, for the pride of building a good fire, learning new ways to cook outdoors.

Sleep out under the stars in camp or your own backyard. Practice tying knots, making a neat bedroll, or pitching a shelter.

Camp out for more fun than you can imagine, for days filled with activities you can't do in town. Do you love sports? You can learn to swim really well, to paddle a canoe down a winding stream, or perhaps to sail a boat. Do you love nature? It is all around you, offering miracles of beauty and science.

There is friendship in camping, a kind you never forget. You share with other girls—planning hikes, games, skits, nature trails, and surprises. You talk about the many things that interest you. Together, you sing well-loved songs around the campfires.

Girl Scouting offers many types of camping. Troop camping is planned and carried out by girls and leaders at a cabin or a primitive or established site. Or the troop may plan an itinerant adventure; travel by day and set up camp for the night.

Day camps, run by the councils, welcome girls from many troops with a variety of activities and a trained staff to help. Experienced campers may sometimes stay overnight.

Established camping means two weeks at a camp equipped with all facilities and a staff. Many councils have these camps, but not all.

For you, a Cadette Scout, camping is a way of coming into your own. You can use the skills you learned when you were younger, perhaps teach them to girls less experienced. You can undertake more advanced skills and, with your patrol, plan things you want most to do. While doing them, you meet badge requirements, fulfill Challenge preps, and come closer to specialized Senior activities. Also, you're preparing for the fun of advanced camping in inter-council camps and national and international events.

Inside Outing

Every outing needs planning to make it a success. First refer to the "Steps in Planning" on page 34. Then use this chart as a checklist to organize your outing before it starts, while it's going on, even after it's over. Try to pick out jobs for your finance, transportation, commissary, equipment, and health and safety managers, and your recorder, too.

BEFORE an Outing

ARRANGEMENTS

Decide where, when and how to go, to return.

Discuss rules of safety and sanitation.

Get permissions needed:—use of property, fire permit, parents permission.

Estimate cost, if any to troop treasury or girls.

Get health examination if needed.

Make provisions for rainy weather.

FOOD

Plan menu and make shopping list:
- How much will it cost?
- Who will shop?
- Who will pay?
- What will each girl bring?

Plan transportation, packing, carrying.

GEAR

What equipment will you need for site? For cooking? For program?
What will each girl bring? Each patrol?
How will it be packed and carried?
How can we go even lighter?

PROGRAM PLANS

Plan what to do, to see, enjoy.
List jobs to be done, and assign to one person or group.
Review, practice, or learn skills needed for the outing.

DURING an Outing

FUN

Plan games, activities, coming and going.

At the site arrange: games, hikes, nature activities, trail-making, mapping, campfires, construction, art activities.

And remember outdoor good turns!

SITE

Be prepared to take care of:
- Storage of gear.
- Fireplaces
- Shelter
- Possible emergencies

Follow rules of sanitation and safety.

Divide the jobs. Give everyone a chance.
When you strike camp, leave site clean.

MEALS

Know your:
- Fire building and fire safety
- Food storage
- Cooking
- Cleanup

AFTER an Outing

Back at home, remember to take care of leftover food, money (if any) and put equipment in shape.

At your next meeting, talk it over. How was it? What will you do, or not do, next time? Remember thank-you notes.

The Art of Campcraft

Campcraft is an art composed of many skills. The more skills you have, the more comfortable and confident you will be in the out-of-doors.

Imagine this scene. Your patrol arrives at a camp site. There are things to be done: tents must be pitched, water supply assured, firewood chopped, fireplace made. And you're starving!

Will the work go speedily and well? Will tents rise under hands trained to tie trim, secure knots? Will you know how to make certain the water is safe to drink? Can you handle an axe correctly? Can you build a fire you know will light? Can you cook things that look good, taste delicious, and pack plenty of nutrition?

These skills (and more) should be at your fingertips. You can learn to do them so capably that jobs are done well in a twinkling.

One of the most rewarding campcraft skills is cookery. If you can cook at home, you can cook outdoors. Actually, the chief difference between under-roof and under-sky cooking is the fire you build and your cooking technique, so you will want to know as many cooking methods as you can.

Modern food preparation and packaging are wonderful helps to the outdoor cook. Learn to use mixes, concentrates, canned foods. Of course, not everything you prepare will be cooked. You will be serving raw vegetables, fruits, bread and butter, always making sure your daily menu is balanced to include the Basic Four (see page 113).

An outdoor table need not be a table at all. If you have bought or made a picnic table, you will probably use it. Sometimes plan to eat at a sit-down spot on the ground, out of the way of foot traffic. Whether you use a conventional table or a "ground table," set it neatly, with attractive added touches. Each girl may bring her own mess kit, or use paper service if you wish.

Make things comfortable. Away with soggy sandwiches, grit in the gravy, ants in the dessert, and oft-repeated picnic menus. You have passed the beginner's stage and are ready and able to serve something scrumptious.

When It's Time To Eat

Here are some ideas for fitting food to the occasion. Try some of them and add your own. Perhaps the troop could keep a file of the most popular menus to use when an opportunity to go out comes up suddenly. This will save time. Recipes are all in *Cooking Out-of-Doors*.

TROOP MEETING SNACKS

Various toasts—try pineapple on raisin bread. All sorts of things cooked in aluminum foil. Raw vegetables. Dried fruit. Herb tca (black birch, sassafras, or wintergreen).

HIKE COOKOUT

One-pot pocket stew (everyone brings a "pocketful" of vegetables; bacon, hamburger or tuna fish is bought with troop treasury money). Serve with crackers. Fresh fruit.

BACKYARD OR PARK PATROL COOKOUT

Simple dishes: One-pot chili or kabobs. Snow-on-the-mountain.

More advanced dishes: Fish-in-a-paper bag or scalloped ham with potatoes and onions. Carrot sticks. Banana fritters with orange sauce.

COOKOUT PARTY WITH BOYS

Hamburgers or frankfurters with cheese or bacon, cooked in aluminum foil or on grill. Baked beans. Raw celery. Frozen cookies reflector baked, apple charlotte, candied apples, or cake with hot fudge sauce. Milk in warm weather, cocoa in cold.

MENUS FOR WEEKEND OUTINGS

Be sure you know what facilities there are to keep perishable foods refrigerated and to store dry foods and what method of cooking you will use at your camp site.

First supper: Chowder or arroz con pollo. Cabbage, raisin and apple salad. Mock angel food cake.

First breakfast: Bananas. Dry cereal. Biscuits with ham, or French toast. Milk.

First lunch: Individual foil lunch (meat, potato, onions). Sliced tomato or carrot sticks. Bread twists and jam.

Second breakfast: Fruit or fruit juice. Pancakes with syrup. Toast and jam. Cocoa.

Second lunch: Sandwiches. Fruit— canned, fresh or dried. Cookies. Milk.

Second supper: Barbecued chicken or lamb. Potatoes baked in sand or foil. Green tossed salad. Reflector cake or gingerbread (bake while meat is cooking). Fresh fruit.

Wheelbarrow—a fine fire-place in yard or driveway.

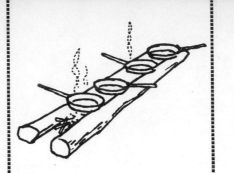

Hunter Fire—for kettle or skillet.

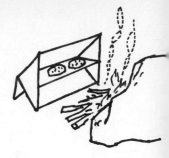

Reflector Fire—gives high steady heat for use with reflector oven or plank.

Toasting: To brown by heat. Best over good coals for an even, golden brown texture. If necessary to use a flaming fire, hold food to one side of the flame, not in or over it.

Baking: There are several methods: (1) on the end of a green stick, as for bread twists (2) in a reflector oven (3) in a Dutch oven (4) in heavy weight aluminum foil.

Frying: To cook in hot fat: (1) directly on top of a vagabond stove, (2) in a skillet, (3) in the bottom of the kettle in which you plan to make your chowder.

Broiling: To cook by direct exposure to heat. Good for tender meat cuts (chops or steak) place on a green stick, a green stick broiler, or wire rack or broiler. Best when turned often and slowly over coals, rather than flames, which will smoke the food.

Barbecues: A long-term roasting of large pieces of meat over coals, with a special sauce for basting and flavoring.

One-pot meals: A main dish cooked in one kettle, such as all the ingredients of a chowder or stew. Just add dessert and beverage for a complete meal.

Nonutensil meals: No pots, no pans, no kettles! Make your own implements (broilers, toasting sticks, etc.) with the skillful use of your jackknife.

For quick heating: use a tepee fire, a small steady fire with heat concentrated under bottom of pot. Keep heat high by replenishing firewood often.

Cook over coals whenever possible; the heat is even and there is less chance of burning; kettles stay cleaner, too. Be sure to allow time for flames to die down and coals to form before cooking.

Crane and Pothook—useful for hanging kettles over a fire.

Trench Fire—good on a windy or very hot day.

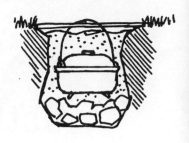

Bean Hole—for pit cooking. Clambakes and imus are large-scale versions.

Altitude affects cooking. Lighter air at high levels lets the water boil sooner and at a lower temperature. Over 2,500 feet experiment to find out how to adjust cooking time and recipe.

Doing the dishes, outdoor style, is a fast, efficient process when you:

o Remember to put water on to heat while eating.

o Wipe plates and utensils clean with paper napkins.

o Wash in hot, sudsy water.

o Rinse in clear, hot water.

o Place in dunking bag, dip in boiling water, hang bag on rack or bush. No need to dry with towel.

If each girl is washing her own, divide the big pieces (platter, serving bowl, etc.) among you, each girl doing one according to plan.

Pots and pans come clean faster if you have coated their outsides with soap or detergent before cooking. To wash them, wipe out with paper napkins and fill with water or rinse as soon as you have finished cooking. This will "pre-wash" the pot, soaking the inside for easier scouring. Pour greasy water (if any) in water drain or carefully at edge of fire. Never pour hot grease into a drain; allow it to cool and harden before disposing of it with the garbage.

Dispose of disposables with system. Burn papers, cardboard cartons, as soon after cooking as possible. If you burn garbage, see that it is drained as dry as can be. Otherwise, drain, wrap in newspaper or put in container, and place in covered receptacle if there is one. If not, take it home along with cans, jars, or foil. Save space by removing ends of cans, placing them inside and flattening the can. Never bury any refuse.

Gather Your Gear

Hiking and camp gear includes everything you need for comfort and efficiency when you are living out-of-doors. Clothing, equipment, tools, and accessories should be chosen to fit your camping plans.

When choosing clothes, take into account the season, the expected weather, the site, and the kinds of activities you will be enjoying. Once you have hiked on a rugged country road, you will always remember that your socks must be free from holes or rough darns, your shoes well-fitting and sturdy.

All your clothes should fit you well. Two or three light sweaters, worn one over the other, protect you from the cold, let you peel off as it gets warmer. A ski cap (winter) or crew hat (summer) protects your hair from sun and wind, keeps it tidy. A long-sleeved shirt prevents sunburn. Jeans or slacks of smooth fabrics keep brambles from scratching legs. In wet or snowy weather, a raincoat or poncho keeps you snug and dry.

Let common sense guide you. Old, comfortable clothes are appropriate for out-of-door fun.

The kind of basic gear you will need depends on where you live and what you have a chance to do. Some things you may borrow or buy, others you can make. Be sure to put your name on your own things.

Take pride in your gear. Keep it in good repair, always clean and ready to go. Learn to make it right, make it light, and pack it tight! Check this list. Which of these will you need for your next outdoor adventure?

o Hike kit, knapsack or pack basket
o Eating utensils (plate, bowl, cup, knife, fork, spoon)
o Knife and sharpening stone
o Hanked rope
o Bandana to use as a kerchief, potholder, bandage, signal flag, trail marker, nosebag
o Sleeping bag or bedroll and groundcloth
o Flashlight
o Compass
o Sit-upon
o Canteen
o Hand axe

The Girl Scout Equipment Service carries a wide variety of outdoor equipment. Study the catalog and visit the nearest official Girl Scout Equipment Agency.

Patrol or troop gear should be planned for multiple use and to fit your particular outdoor activities. Consider making your own knapsacks, charcoal stoves, reflector ovens, food and gear bags, and lightweight tents. You may be able to borrow other kinds of tents and such large tools as a saw, two-handed axe, wooden mallet, and shovel, if you need them. Depending upon what equipment is provided at the camp site and what activities you have planned, you may also need to consider other cooking and eating equipment, and small tools such as a hammer and tin shears. See page 188 for contents to include in your first aid kit, which is an essential part of your troop gear.

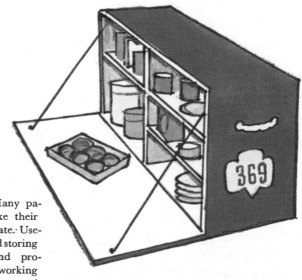

Build a chuckbox. Many patrols design and make their own, simple or elaborate. Useful for transporting and storing food, equipment, and program supplies, or as a working surface, it is an all-around piece of gear. Make yours light enough for two girls to carry, even when fully packed.

Pitch a Wall Tent

Find corners, A, B, C, D. Peg down with sides, front, and back straight, flaps tied. This makes a rectangle or square. If tent has floor, stretch and peg corners.

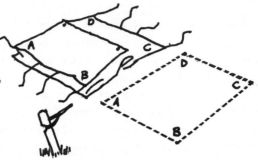

Assemble poles, if jointed. Insert top pins through grommets (H) at center front and back of ridge.

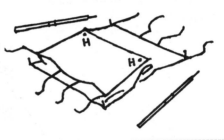

Two girls raise poles and tent, hold in place, poles in center of front and back, at right angles to ground.

Other girls, one at each corner, stretch corner guy ropes (see Step 5). Pound in pegs and place ropes, first tying taut-line hitch. Pull evenly, so tent is trim.

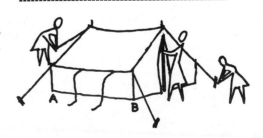

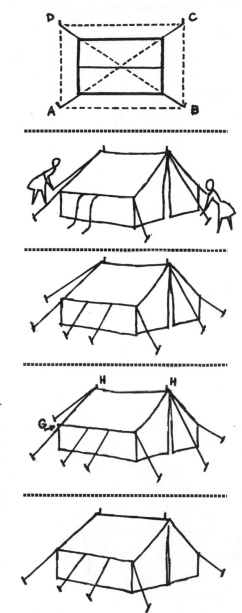

Imaginary lines from A-C and B-D cross at middle of ridge, straight from one corner peg to its opposite. The four pegs should make a rectangle on the ground.

Place pegs for front and back guy ropes. Look through tent. Front and back pegs and both uprights should be in a line.

Put in side pegs in line with front and back corner pegs. Place guy ropes. Adjust all ropes, so tent is "square" and smooth. Someone stand in front to advise and check.

Knots to use:
Bowline at H.
Overhand at grommets (G).
Taut-line hitches at all pegs. Adjust as needed. Whip *all* rope-ends.
Roll flaps and walls *inside*, tie tapes with square knots.

When using a ridge pole:
Place it inside tent, holes matching grommets when on ground (Step 1). Insert pins of uprights through ridge and grommets (Step 2).
No front and back guy ropes needed with ridge pole.

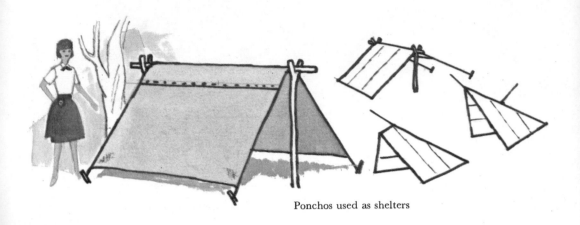

Ponchos used as shelters

Choose a tent to fit your ability, taste, budget, and camping plans. Whatever type your tent, learn to keep it looking trim. Canvas and ropes shrink when wet, so loosen guy ropes during wet weather and tighten afterward. Secure all parts so that nothing flaps in the wind. Touching the roof when it is wet breaks the air seal which keeps the canvas waterproof. Hands off, or there will be a leak. Tents should be taken down as carefully and systematically as they are put up. Be sure your tent is completely dry inside and out before striking, otherwise you invite mildew. Brush off all dirt, cobwebs, and so forth, and fold smoothly on seams. Care of tents is every camper's responsibility.

Baker tent

Toolcraft

The proper use and care of tools is an important outdoor skill. Without it, you cannot improvise utensils from tin cans, fashion a crane for a kettle, drive tent pegs into the ground. A good camper is known by the way she handles tools. She knows what each is for and how to use it. She can clean, oil, sharpen implements to keep them at tip-top performance. She wields them skillfully and safely, stores them away carefully when they are not in use. She uses tools for constructive purposes only, never to deface woodland beauty or the property of others. She values each tool for its helpfulness and practices to perfect its use.

Sod removal is sometimes necessary when grass is growing where you want to build a fire or make a drain. To prevent a grass fire, to protect and preserve the grass, and to leave the site as you found it, remove the sod in this way.

Cut a twelve-inch square straight up and down with a straight-edge shovel. Cut deeply enough to lift out whole sod in one piece, cutting underneath if necessary. Keep number of sods removed to a minimum.

Remove sods to shade, grass-side up. Keep them separated and water regularly. Before you leave, replace sods, fill in cracks with dirt, and water thoroughly.

The Handy Hand Axe

This tool is for light chopping. The flat end of the head can be used as a hammer. *Handle with care.* When not in use, it is sheathed, left in a chopping block, or hung on two nails. Never leave it in or on the ground or stuck in a tree.

Wear axe on belt. To carry, hold with blade down and turned away from your body. Pass to someone else *handle first.* To receive it, grasp handle near the head to control heaviest part.

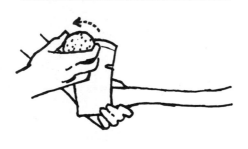

To sharpen, hold axe-head in one hand, a rather coarse sharpening stone in the other hand. Move stone in circular motions, flat against blade. Turn axe, repeat. To finish, use a fine stone, lightly wet to reduce friction.

To use, grasp end of handle firmly, thumb around fingers, raise by arm and wrist motion. Strike sharp, firm blows, taking your time. Stand and hold axe so that glancing or missing blows cannot strike you in any part of your body.

To cut across a stick, strike on edge of block. Hold at least two feet away from the striking point. Make diagonal cuts. Do not try to cut square across a stick.

To cut a sapling, clear away brush around it. For safety, first take a practice swing to make sure you have room to swing a full arc. Make sharp diagonal cuts on the trunk. Repeat, making cuts larger as you progress.

To point a stick, hold it at an angle on chopping block. Strike at an angle, turning the stick to make a point.

To split a stick, place axe as shown. Raise both stick and axe together; bring down on edge of block. Repeat if needed. Or, lay stick flat on block, do not hold. Bring axe down sharply at stick center. Or lean stick against log and strike in center, where it touches log.

For safety, stand so axe will not touch any part of body should it slip. Make sure nothing can catch and deflect axe overhead or at sides when you swing. Be sure bystanders are far away from you, at your side or in back of you, rather than in front.

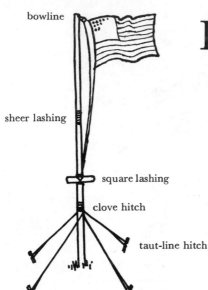

bowline

sheer lashing

square lashing

clove hitch

taut-line hitch

Knots and Their Uses

Knowing how to tie good, secure knots is part of good campcraft. Different knots are used to do different jobs. Learn the knot to do each job. Good knots can be tied easily, will hold fast, will not jam, and can be untied easily. Have a practice rope about 6 feet long and 3/8 inches thick. Keep the ends whipped and carry it hanked. There are different ways to tie the same knot. Perhaps when you were a Junior Scout you learned to tie the clove hitch and the bowline. Now learn the alternate ways.

The clove hitch is used to start most lashings, and to secure end of rope to a post. Make two loops as shown. Move right hand loop in front of left hand loop and place together. Slip over post. Tighten by pulling ropes away from center, loosen by pushing toward center.

The bowline forms a loop that never jams or slips. Here is a quick way to tie it. Cross end over standing part at place knot is wanted.

Twist end of rope down into loop and up as shown, forming a smaller loop with end inside. Pass end in back of standing part, then forward and down into loop. Draw up tight. Use it for hoisting, lifesaving, or mooring a boat to a ring or post.

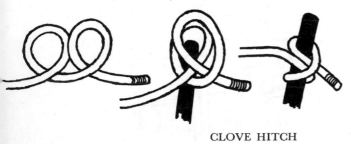

CLOVE HITCH

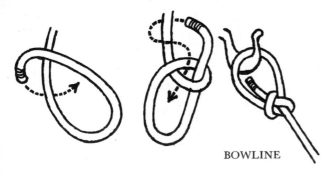

BOWLINE

The *fisherman's knot* is used to join twine or light ropes. Lay the two ends together, each pointing in the opposite direction. Then tie an overhand knot in the end of each, *around* the other rope. Pull ropes in opposite directions, pulling the knots together.

The *taut-line hitch* forms a loop which slides. Make loop with short end over long. Twist short end inside loop twice. Carry end up above twist and secure with half hitch. Use on tent ropes.

The *highwayman's hitch* holds tight but unties with one jerk. Double one end of the rope; place loop in back of the bar. Holding the two ends with one hand, reach through the loop (1) from back. Pick up a bit of the longer rope, pulling a new loop (2) up and through (1). Pull down on the short end and pull (2) firmly back above the bar. Reach through (2), picking up a loop of the shorter end; pulling it up and through (2). Tighten by pulling the long rope.

To untie, jerk on the short end. Use it to tie your cache or dunking bag to a branch, so weight is on long rope.

Books on ropecraft are widely available. Learn to splice a rope and make a carrick bend belt, as advanced steps.

FISHERMAN'S KNOT

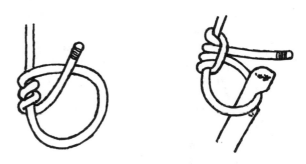

TAUT-LINE HITCH

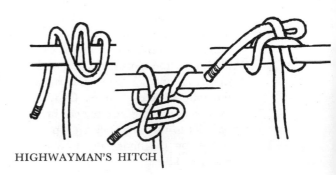

HIGHWAYMAN'S HITCH

Learn To Lash

Lashing is used to fasten sticks or poles together with binder twine, rather than with nails. It is safe to use on trees and is easily taken apart. Good lashing is neat and attractive and holds securely.

Square lashing: With one end of cord make a clove hitch around vertical stick. Bind sticks together firmly as shown, then tighten with a *frapping* (winding the cord between the two sticks). Finish the lashing with a square knot.

Diagonal lashing: Make a clove hitch around two sticks as shown Make three or four turns around one fork, then three or four turns around the other, pulling tightly. Frap and end as in square lashing.

Sheer lashing: Make a clove hitch around one of the sticks. Take several turns around both sticks. Frap and end as above.

Continuous lashing: Starting at center of cord, make a clove hitch at one end of the long stick. Roll ends of cord into two balls to prevent a tangle. Bring the balls from the clove hitch over the short sticks and under the long one, crossing underneath the long stick each time. Continue as shown, making sure the cord runs parallel to the long stick on top and crosses on the underside. End with a square knot.

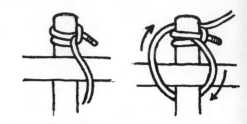

SQUARE LASHING

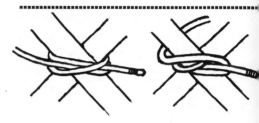

DIAGONAL LASHING

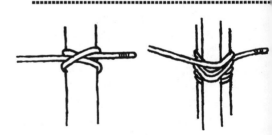

SHEER LASHING

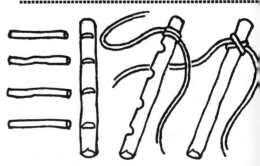

CONTINUOUS LASHING

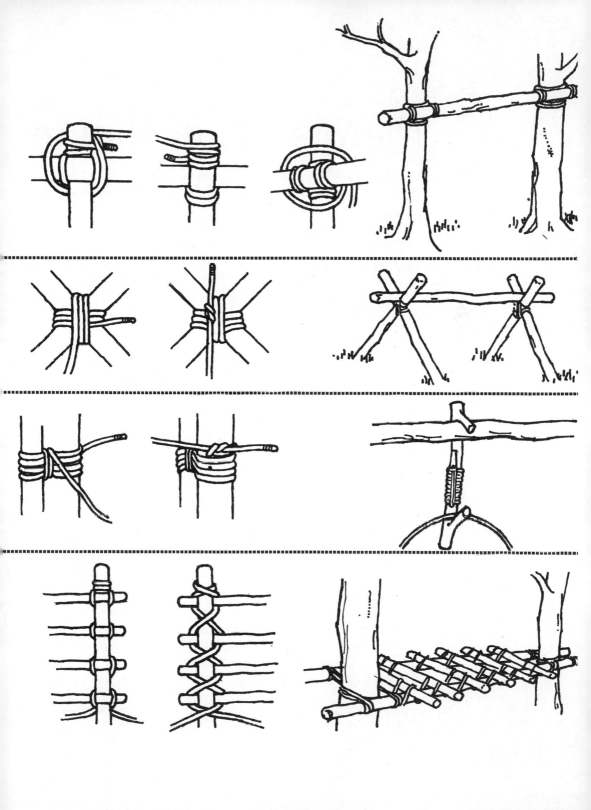

The Wisdom of Nature

"How smoothly nature's vast machine whirs on with all the big and little cogs revolving in their places. Each seed and bird and flower and fly, in its apparently haphazard existence, plays its part in the output of the seasons."*

The three kingdoms of the natural world—animal, vegetable, and mineral—are vital to each other. Without one, the others could not survive. From the soil, watered by rain and rivers, enriched by minerals, come the plants—grains and cereals, fruits and vegetables, nuts and berries, food for wildlife and for us. From green plants come the sugar we need, the oxygen we breathe.

Below the earth's surface, the root systems of plants and trees "tie down" the soil, lest it be washed away by flood or swept away by wind. On the earth's surface, move the members of the animal kingdom. Some are plant-eaters, while others, the predators, eat the animals that eat the plants.

But, unlike the other animals, man can think and understand. That is why it is our obligation to understand and protect the balance of nature. If we destroy any single element in wildlife, we harm all life. Our job is to protect, conserve, and enjoy. This is one way to live up to your Girl Scout Promise. Think of nature's world as your birthright, an open-handed gift of endless beauty and use. Now is the time to take or renew the Conservation Pledge: *I give my pledge as an American to save and faithfully defend from waste the natural resources of my country—its soil and minerals, its forests, waters, and wildlife.*

Are you a city mouse? You need not go to the country to explore nature. Cities have green places—parks and squares, greenhouses and florist shops — museums, and exhibits where you may learn about the growth of trees and grasses, the habits of birds, the cycle of the seasons. Every tree that grows on a city street has a name, belongs to a species, gives shelter to birds. Have you ever looked at

*Used by permission of Dodd, Mead & Company publisher of *Circle of the Seasons* by Edwin Way Teale. Copyright 1953 by Edwin Way Teale.

the common weeds that spring up so bravely in lots and sidewalk crevices? Many are as pretty and intricate as cultivated flowers. They are simply waiting to be discovered by you.

Whether you live in city or country, start by observing (see Chapter 4) and then develop your interest. Before you know it, you will want to know more, to see more. There are many inexpensive books on special subjects in nature—from fresh-water turtles to deep-sea shellfish, from bird migrations to possible life on the moon. In the badge section, you will see how many areas there are for you to explore. As you progress, your troop leader, nature consultant or camp counselor will help you. Try a patrol or troop project to share with others your interest and knowledge.

The enjoyment of nature can be experienced almost anywhere, without elaborate equipment, alone or in a crowd. Here is an interest for a lifetime—one that can be developed as a hobby or as a vocation.

LOU HENRY HOOVER lived the Girl Scout Promise. She was a true outdoor enthusiast and an ardent, resourceful camper. As wife and mother, she established homes in many far corners of the world—Japan, England, Australia. Mrs. Herbert Hoover was admired as a gracious First Lady and popular White House hostess during the years her husband was President of the United States of America. And, she gave much of her time and energy to the service of others—particularly to Girl Scouting.

As a troop leader, she took the girls camping, leading storytelling around the fire at night and birdwalks before breakfast. As National President of Girl Scouts of the U.S.A., she helped make it possible for more girls to learn about and enjoy the outdoors. Girl Scouts today honor her memory through a conservation project, whereby Lou Henry Hoover Memorial Forest and Wildlife Sanctuaries may be established by any council that meets the requirements.

Blueprint for Wide Games

You have probably enjoyed playing wide games on many different occasions. As Cadette Scouts, your patrol or troop may be asked to organize one. Here are the directions.

Decide time and area limits. Will it last one hour, all afternoon, or all day? Will it take place within one building, cover a city block, or range over the eastern end of the village, or the entire camp site?

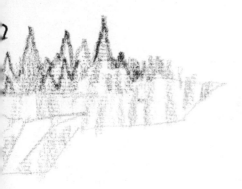

List all the skills and stunts, the techniques and knowledge that you hope to test or teach. Do you want the players to tie the taut-line hitch, teach a square dance, draw a map or read one, surface dive to retrieve an object from the bottom of the swimming pool? You might ask them to produce a skit, bandage a sprained ankle, complete two rows of knitting while balancing cups of water on their heads, or give directions in a language other than English. Estimate how long it will take to do each one.

With the limits and the skills in front of you, think up a theme—the story line. Here is a chance to be wildly imaginative. Usually it is easier for a group, such as a patrol, to list many suggestions, and then choose two or three girls to weave the story and plot the game from the ideas collected.

Collect the necessary equipment and recruit any helpers needed. Troop committee members, perhaps, or camp staff members will be strategically stationed to help the organizers test or check the players. You may need costumes to lend reality to the situations.

Lay out the game. Determine the place for each test. Write the directions, plant the clues, hide the messages, bury the treasure, or whatever.

Explain the rules clearly to the players just before they start. Players may start from the same place after set intervals of time or from different spots at the same time. Be sure everyone understands the time limits, the geographical area and other rules. For example, must each skill be demonstrated by every girl in each patrol? Or by each patrol as a whole? Will the winner be the patrol that finishes first, or the group with the highest score?

There are examples of wide games in *Games for Girl Scouts,* which is a fine book for your troop library.

Come Spend a Day at Camp!

Just before sunrise, all is still. The sky is a lavender-blue, the leaves a pattern of dark lace. A moment later, you hear the morning song of a bird. Then another and another. Bands of pink light up the heavens as the sun moves up majestically, bringing glory to the day. Now the birds are in full chorus. Bright-eyed and curious, they comment on the bustle below. The girls are waking up, adding girl-song to the morning's sounds.

You open your eyes to a world new-bathed in dew. Your first thought is, "Who said it was going to rain? It's a perfect day." Your second thought is, "What's for breakfast? I'm starved."

A delicious fragrance answers, "Pancakes." The girls on the "cooks' tour" have mixed the batter with blueberries, the ones you picked the day before. Nothing ever tasted so good as those pancakes, with a cup of cool, refreshing milk.

Now come the kapers. Dishes are done, tents cleaned, beds made, all in a twinkling. Everyone knows the Court of Honor has prepared an exciting program for the day, so why dawdle?

Everyone out for a wide game! It's been planned to last all morning and to take you to all sorts of thrilling, wonderful places: a grove of birch trees, a stream where a family of ducks has settled, an ancient oak tree with clues in a trunk hollow.

The theme of the wide game is science in the out-of-doors and the final clue directs you to "where green and blue meet and mingle." The beach, of course!

Patrol by patrol, the girls follow the clue. Into the inviting water you go, to splash, swim and enjoy water sports until lunch is ready.

How can a girl get so hungry in one short morning? Luckily, there's no waiting for lunch. The Beaver Patrol has fixed hearty sandwiches, a crisp, green salad, cookies and milk. Just right!

But look! The sky is turning gray. It's going to...it *is* raining!

You were going canoeing, but never mind. The alternate plan is just as much fun.

All patrols go into secret planning sessions for tonight's entertainment. Bursts of laughter are heard from each group. The Skylarks are writing a list of superstitions to be acted out in pantomime. The Revelers are devising strange costumes. One of them, the smallest, is completely enclosed in a paper cylinder. She holds a branch over her head. Later, you will learn that she is playing the oak tree you visited in the wide game. Her patrol is writing a skit on what the oak tree thought of the girls.

Dinnertime already? How the rainy afternoon has flown! You're broiling Surpriseburgers, hamburgers filled with cheese, relish, and other surprises. These go with a platter of raw vegetables. Dessert is blueberry pie (proving you can't pick too many blueberries) baked in the reflector oven and served with hot chocolate.

As night falls, the sky clears. Millions of stars blaze above as you gather around the campfire. Now come the surprise skits and stunts, each more hilarious than the one before.

Someone starts a song. One by one, you join in, your voices blending in harmony. Then, suddenly, it's bedtime.

It's been a wonderful day. Goodnight.

If there were an emergency in your home or camp today, would you know what to do?

There are two things to do about all emergencies. The first is to prevent them from happening whenever possible. The second is to know how to deal with them swiftly and effectively when they do happen. That is what this chapter is about.

Emergencies happen all of a sudden and call for immediate action. There's no time to stand around won-

in an emergency

dering what to do and how to do it. Delays may cost severe injury, loss of property, even loss of life. The real heroine in an emergency is the girl who reacts quickly with a sure knowledge of what to do.

So far in your Scouting career, you have learned a great many emergency methods: how to find your way by using a compass or by studying the sun or stars for direction; how to judge time and distance by various methods; how to make and read a sketch map. You know the value of using your personal measurements for judging. (Reminder: Since you have probably grown in the last year or so, it is time to review your measurements and bring them up to date.) Now you are ready for more advanced emergency measures, both indoors and out. Learn them thoroughly; practice them until you are expert.

Which Direction?

A topographical map is highly detailed, showing not only directions and distances but the heights and depths of an area. These are called the contours of the land. Map lines which connect points of equal height are contour lines.

Both the details and contours make this type of map especially useful to hikers. You can plan time better with such a map, for you can make allowance for hill-climbing and rugged terrain. To understand contours, place half an apple or potato, flat-side down, to represent a hill. To get the different heights or levels, slice the "hill" across at regular intervals.

With a pencil, outline the bottom slice on paper. Now, outline the next slice inside the first outline, and so on until all are done. The result is a series of rings, one inside the other, shaped like the "hill." The steeper it is, the closer the lines.

To use a map, first orient it. Either align "north" on the map with the magnetic needle of your compass, or locate the road where you stand and turn the map until it runs the same way as the road. Once your map is oriented, you can follow it cross-country.

To determine distance between two points on your map, check the map scale. This tells you how many feet or miles are covered by one inch on that particular map.

A map mounted on muslin can be folded without cracking, carried easily, and used for a long time. To mount a map:

o Fold it to desired carrying size.
o Open and cut in sections along folds.
o Glue sections on unbleached muslin, leaving a small space between cut edges to accommodate the fold.
o Spray with clear plastic on both sides to make waterproof.

Giving directions well is an emergency skill. Use landmarks and well-known routes: "Go north on Main St. to the fire house. Turn right. Go past the post office to the movies. Turn left on Oak St. and walk one block.

Play "Armchair Routes." One patrol gives directions from the meeting place to a public building, without naming the building. The other patrols follow the directions mentally to guess the destination.

Play "Place Problems." Example: Pretend a driver asks how to get to the highway or a lady asks directions to the park. Patrols might challenge each other to see which gives the easiest directions to follow.

Getting lost, like most emergencies, can be prevented with proper care and forethought. Here are two ways to avoid this experience.

If you are hiking in unfamiliar territory, know the "lay of the land" in general and make sure to start for home well before dark.

If you are with a group, don't stray out of voice or signaling range. Have pre-arranged signals—special shouts or whistle blasts—to notify the others if you lose sight of them. If, however, you should get lost, the first thing to remember is this: Do not panic. Use your head, not your legs. Here are three ways to help yourself out of the predicament. Try them in the order given.

First, stay put and don't wander. Call out or blow a whistle at regular intervals. Your group will follow your signals. When you hear the searchers, repeat the signals often.

Second, try to figure out where you are and where you have come from, using the compass or the sun for direction. Go back in the direction from which you came.

Lastly, follow a river bank, an overgrown trail, a ridge of hills, or cross-country power lines, which are usually strung along the shortest distance between two towns. If you are unsure of the direction, go downhill or downstream. These are most likely to lead to a town.

Repeat: Don't panic. Don't run about, worrying and tiring yourself. Use your skills to find your way back.

Survival skills will help make you comfortable in many kinds of emergencies. The primary ones are the campcraft skills in Chapter 9, particularly how to use your axe; how to build a safe fire and keep it going; how to improvise shelter.

Safe drinking water is an essential. No matter how clear and inviting water may appear, do not drink it unless you know it has been tested. Always carry water in your canteen or get it from an approved supply. If you have any question whatever about the safety of the water you are about to drink, purify it by one of these methods:

1. Boil it for ten minutes, cool, then aerate by pouring back and forth in two clean vessels.

2. Dissolve purification tablets containing iodine or chlorine available at drug or sporting goods stores. Follow label directions.

Outdoor Emergencies

HOW TO PREVENT THEM...

Water

1. Have a medical checkup to make sure you are fit for swimming.
2. Even if you are a good swimmer, never go swimming alone.
3. Check water for proper depth, freedom from dangers such as rocks, holes, strong currents, or undertow.
4. A properly equipped and trained lifeguard should be on duty.
5. Do not go swimming for 1½ hours after meals.
6. Do not overtire yourself, show off, or try to exceed your ability.

Ice

1. Know how to tell when ice is firmly frozen, strong enough for the weight of your group.
2. Know how to ice skate, swim, and keep afloat.
3. Never go skating alone.
4. Be prepared with a lifeline, plank, or ladder near at hand.

Fire Out-of-Doors

1. Always observe the rules of fire safety.
2. Consult local fire authorities before building an outdoor fire.
3. Have fire-fighting equipment handy, and know how to use it.
4. State and Federal Conservation Departments have pamphlets on this subject. Write your state bureau of information at your state capital.

"Throw, Row, Go"

1. If someone is in trouble, try to reach her with your hand, a branch, or an oar and pull her in.
2. If she is out of reach, try to push some floating material (boat, board) to her. She can hang on and stay afloat till rescue comes.
3. Or throw a long rope with a bowline knot loop for her to grasp. The heavy loop makes the rope easier to throw and catch, while a straight end might slip away. If the loop is big enough, she may be able to slip it under her armpits so she can be pulled in.
4. If she is too far away for this, row out to her in a boat or paddle out in a canoe to get her.
5. Swim to her only as a last resort and only if you yourself are qualified as a trained lifesaver.

1. If someone falls through, keep calm.
2. If possible, extend a plank, pole, or ladder to her.
3. Or throw her a rope with something tied at the end for her to grasp: a piece of wood, bowline knot, or ring buoy. Hold your end firmly. Keep the rope taut, so she can get her head above water or crawl out.
4. If you must go to her, tie a rope under your armpits. Someone on shore or on skates holds the free end. Lie flat, distribute your weight evenly as you slide toward her. Near the hole, crawl slowly. Grasp her and pull her out. Both of you must lie flat as you slide back to firm ice.
5. After rescue, keep her warm with vigorous exercise or skating. If necessary, give artificial respiration and send for a doctor.

1. Keep calm. Take constructive action.
2. Send someone or go to notify fire department. Large fires need experienced firefighters and proper equipment.
3. Put out small fires before they grow. Smother with sand or dirt or sprinkle water directly on the flames.
4. Push a small spreading fire toward its origin with a garden rake. Take care your clothing does not catch on fire.
5. Use shovels to dig a trench around fire.

Quick Measures for Indoor and Outdoor Emergencies

Severe Bleeding

1. Stop it as quickly as possible. Apply constant *firm* pressure directly over wound with sterile gauze or clean cloth dressing.
2. If possible, get someone to call a doctor.
3. When bleeding has stopped, tie dressing firmly in place. If you have no bandage, fold your bandana or some other garment into

Mouth-to-Mouth Method of Artificial Respiration

1. Place person on her back. Turn her head to one side and quickly wipe out any visible foreign matter (food, blood, etc.) in mouth with your fingers or with a cloth wrapped around your fingers.
2. Tilt head back so chin points upward. Pull or push jaw into a jutting-out position to get tongue away from air passage of throat.
3. Open your mouth wide. Place it tightly over victim's mouth. (If you wish, put a cloth between you. The air will come through.) Pinch person's nostrils shut or close them with the pressure of your cheek. Blow into person's mouth. Even if the teeth are clenched, the air will get through.
4. Remove your mouth, turning your head to listen for the outrush of air that means you are getting air exchange. Repeat blowing.

Internal Poisoning

1. Prevention is all important. Keep medicines, household cleaners and garden supplies, insecticides, and so forth, out of the reach of children. Label all poisons plainly: LYE, TURPENTINE, KEROSENE, INSECTICIDE.
2. Caution older children about the dangers of poison. Stress the

This is a brief outline. For further details, study the *American Red Cross First Aid Textbook.*

one. Do not remove dressing if it gets bloody. Press another dressing over the first and tie that one down firmly, too.

4. If an extremity is wounded, elevate it.

5. If the doctor cannot come to you, get the patient to him or to the nearest hospital as soon as you can.

For adult victims, blow vigorously at about 12 breaths per minute. For children, take relatively shallow breaths, appropriate for child's size at the rate of about 20 breaths per minute.

5. If you are not getting air exchange, indicated by visible expansions and contractions of the chest, quickly recheck and, if necessary, correct position of head and jaw. If you still get no air exchange, quickly turn patient on side and slap sharply, several times, between shoulder blades, to dislodge foreign matter. Again, wipe mouth free of foreign matter. Resume breathing into mouth.

6. Keep it up until a doctor tells you to stop. When person is breathing normally, wrap her warmly in blankets.

importance of reading labels. Keep children from gnawing on any painted toy or surface.

3. In most cases of poisoning, quickly dilute the swallowed poison by giving the patient as much water or milk as she can possibly drink.

4. Obtain medical advice by telephone as quickly as possible.

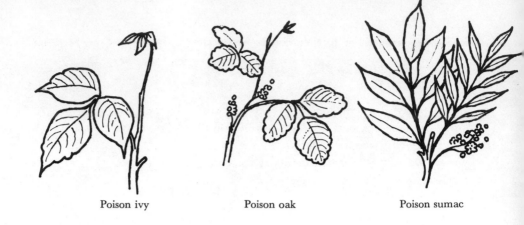

Poison ivy   Poison oak   Poison sumac

An Ounce of Prevention

The best way to deal with hazards is to avoid them. Protect yourself, in advance, from:

Sunburn: A severe case can be serious, as well as painful. Avoid prolonged exposure to sun, especially at the outset. Set a daily time limit, from 10 to 15 minutes, at the beginning. Gradually increase the time. If your skin is sensitive, cover up.

Poison plants: Study the pictures on this page. Learn the shapes and colors, so you can recognize and avoid contact with them. All three are common in parts of the United States. They produce an irritant poisonous to the skin. This may cause anything from an itching rash to severe skin eruption. If you have touched one of these plants (or think you have), wash skin thoroughly with soap and water. Then apply rubbing alcohol, followed by calamine ointment or lotion. If rash persists or gets worse, see a doctor.

Poisonous snakes: Like all nature's creatures, snakes are interesting, shedding their skins as they grow and getting new ones, "hearing" through body vibrations, sleeping with open eyes. Most snakes are harmless and their bites are cleaned and dressed like an ordinary wound. But the bite of a poisonous snake is serious and demands immediate medical attention. Take no chances. Wear protective leg and foot coverings if you are going into poisonous snake territory. Know their habitats, learn to recognize them at sight...and stay away. Learn what to do in case of poisonous bite.

Storm Lashing

Storm lashing protects tents and kitchen flys from the flapping action of a continuous breeze, and helps prevent them from being blown down during high winds.

To storm lash a 9'x9' wall tent you will need: four 16" metal tent stakes; two pieces of hemp rope ⅜" thick and at least 32' long. The length of rope needed for tents of other sizes can be determined by measuring the tents. After the tent is pitched:

1. Take one 32' rope and run it from one front corner (A) to the pin of the back upright (B). Loop it around the pin and run it to other front corner (C).

2. Next, run the second 32' rope from one back corner (X) to the pin of the front upright (Y). Loop it around the pin and run it to the other back corner (Z).

3. Now set one 16" stake at each corner of the tent, so that the ropes lie as snugly as possible against the rope of the tent (or fly) and take an equal strain. Keep ropes taut at all times.

For more stability, especially for kitchen flys, add guy ropes anchored by stakes directly in front and back (see illustration).

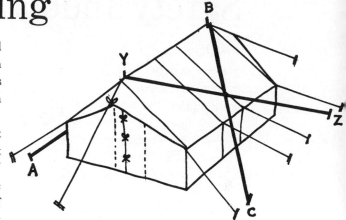

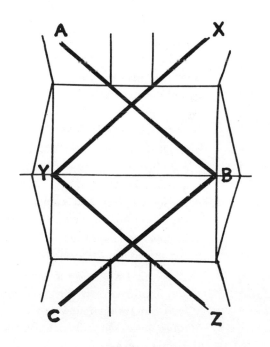

Safety Indoors

Some Ways To Prevent Fire

o Keep matches in closed glass or metal container.
o Extinguish matches under faucet.
o Keep flour in kitchen to smother grease fire. Never use water or other liquid on a grease fire.
o Read labels on electric appliances and follow directions on them.
o Disconnect electric appliances before answering the door or telephone.

If a Building Is on Fire

o Keep calm.
o Walk, don't run, to exit.
o Warn others as you go.
o Call fire department.

Some Escape Rules To Remember

o Close doors and windows. Feel a door before opening it. If it is hot, do not open it.
o If excessive heat and smoke, wrap wet towel around head, stay close to floor, and crawl to exit.
o Get out as fast as possible.

A first aid kit for home or camp may be a plastic or wooden box and should contain the following:

1″-compresses on adhesive in individual packages.*

sterile gauze squares (about 3″x3″) in individual packages.*
2 triangular bandages.*
sterile gauze (about 1 square yard) in sealed package.
1 tube sterile petroleum jelly.*
1 bottle of antiseptic.*
1 tube of calamine ointment.
1 bottle aromatic spirits of ammonia.*
1 box bicarbonate of soda
1 box salt
1 box sterile cotton.*
3″ splinter forceps (or tweezers)
1″ and 2″ roller bandages.
1 box of applicators.*
1 box of tongue depressors
scissors
paper cups
2 thin board splints
hot water bag
ice bag
2 teaspoons

Small quantities of the starred (*) items plus correct change for a possible phone call, 2 needles, and 1 pkg. matches, would make a first aid kit suitable for a patrol expedition.

Scientists develop new drugs and new treatments every year, so discuss this list with your local medical advisers before assembling your kit. The Girl Scout National Equipment Service also carries first aid kits.

When You're the Nurse

Home nursing is the gentle art of keeping a patient comfortable and cheerful, while obeying doctor's orders.

Make sure the sickroom is well ventilated, near the bathroom, and within calling or bell-ringing sound. If you can place the bed or chair near a window, the view may help provide diversion. Little touches help—a bedside table, reading light, drinking water, a bell (or glass and spoon) to summon help, tissues, a waste bag pinned to the mattress near the headboard. Nice extras are a basket or shopping bag for toys, reading, writing, or handcraft materials, and a radio.

Is the mattress firm? If not, put a bedboard (or sheet of plywood the size of the mattress) on the bedsprings. Pillows, hard and soft, can be arranged to support and relieve the patient. If you lack certain supplies, improvise. A suitcase or cardboard carton makes a satisfactory backrest. A bed cradle to hold bed covers above a sensitive part of the body can be made from rolled pillows, a light wooden box or carton (minus bottom and two sides), or barrel hoops cut in half and joined by wooden strips.

Make a bed tray or table from a light wooden box, painted or covered with oilcloth. A card table with legs sawed down will give a child plenty of surface for cutouts, paper, crayons, and toys.

Meals should be prepared according to doctor's orders and served attractively. Small portions, at proper temperature, are best. Use a bowl inverted over food to keep it warm. Dishes and mugs should not slide about. A toy, flower, or small plant is a cheerer-upper.

Mercury is a liquid metallic element that expands as heated and so rises in tube to indicate temperature.

To read, find silver mercury ribbon by looking into ridge of center canal. Degree of temperature is recorded where ribbon ends. For most people, normal oral temperature, indicated by a small arrow on the tube, is 98.6°F.

Before any nursing procedure, wash hands thoroughly with lots of soap lather. Rinse well and dry.

To take a temperature: (1) Hold thermometer firmly at top. Shake quickly with wrist loose, until thermometer registers under 95°. Dip in cool, clean water. (2) Place bulb end under patient's tongue, slightly to one side. Patient must keep mouth closed (without biting thermometer) and breathe through nose. (3) Remove after three minutes. Wipe with dry cotton. Read in good light. Cleanse thoroughly with pieces of cotton soaped and dipped in cool water. Record temperature and time taken for the doctor's reference.

LILLIAN WALD was a fighter. She fought ignorance, disease, dirt, and despair with all the weapons she could muster. Her ammunition came from two sources; her training and skill as a nurse and her fine courage. In 1893, she worked among the poverty-ridden, crowded tenement dwellers of New York City. She held classes to teach the need for fresh air, sun, and cleanliness. She visited and healed the sick. In dingy rooms, she improvised what was needed, heating tubs of water to scrub floors, walls, and children.

She organized a visiting nurse service that was the beginning of the Henry Street Settlement House, the first of its kind in the city. Here, people could bring their problems, learn skills, meet neighbors, leave children to be cared for. From this beginning, great things grew. Public health services, playgrounds, laws to protect children, sprang from Lillian Wald's great-hearted desire and determination to help and to set wrongs right.

Around the House

Every house has devices which turn the supplies of water, gas, and electricity on and off. Your father or local handyman will show you where each one is and how it works. Make a list of the turnoffs and post it in some part of the house where you know where it is. The fuse box or circuit breaker controls the amount of electrical current that flows into your house. Find out where it is and make a diagram showing which rooms are controlled by which fuses or circuit breakers. Paste this diagram inside the fuse box door, so you will know which fuse to replace if the electricity fails in some part of the house. Fuses do not get used up or wear out. When one blows, it is a signal that something is wrong—a faulty wire or an overload.

To change a fuse: Before replacing fuse, unplug all the affected appliances until you find out what is wrong, otherwise the new fuse may blow as soon as you put it in. Make sure your hands are bone dry. Turn off the main current. Never stand on a wet or damp surface. Know the correct amperage or number of the fuse and use only that number. Unscrew the faulty fuse and put in a good one. Turn current back on. Fuse boxes are often in dark places, so keep a flashlight handy.

To find out how to replace an electric plug: Instructions for this simple, but detailed, procedure are available in government and other booklets. Warning: Never try to fix anything that is not unplugged from the wall. Never try to repair heavy appliances. A poor job will not do, as it could cause serious injury or fire.

To unstop a clogged drain: The key is to prevent drains from clogging in the first place. Never pour grease down a drain. Don't comb hair over sink or throw other clogging material into drain. Use a flushing agent regularly and carefully. If a drain clogs, try pumping a plunger up and down over it. If that doesn't work, learn to use an augar or snake, an inexpensive tool that works into the pipe to push debris along.

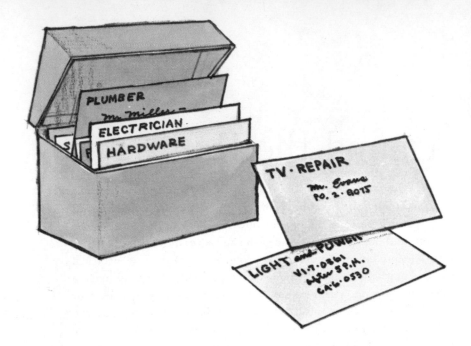

A *"Fix-it File"* is a great household convenience. Use a file box or small cardboard box to keep fix-it information for ready reference. For example, have cards labeled "electrician," "plumber," "glazier," with their names, addresses, and phone numbers plainly printed in case of emergency.

If you have painted something, record the brand of paint, the color you used, the place you bought it. You may need to do some touching-up sometime.

Other helpful information to have on file: guarantees on appliances and the directions that usually come with them; practical household hints; notations of materials you have used before and may want to replace or use again.

When you've finished a job, clean up. A professional worker leaves no unsightly traces of the job. Restore order systematically: in your home, your troop meeting place, or in camp.

o Check to make sure you've finished.
o Clean tools and brushes carefully.
o Put everything back where it belongs, for ready accessibility the next time a job has to be done.
o Clear away any debris, newspapers, bits of plaster, old nails, etc. Sweep or vacuum, if necessary.
o Before putting cans, bottles, and tubes away, cap them tightly.
o Wipe away any marks you may have made, such as fingerprints.
o Make a note of supplies that should be replaced.
o Now, wash your hands and face, comb your hair—and take a bow!

Emergency light. A tin-can lantern burns outdoors, even in a breeze. Make crosscut on can as shown. Bend flaps inside can for a candle-sized opening. Attach wire or rope handle. Stick candle up through opening. As it burns, push it further into can.

Emergency fuel. Learn to make a Buddy burner. Instructions are on page 86.

Emergency heat. Fill metal canteen with hot water. Or pour heated salt or sand into a bag. Wrap in a protective covering and use as a substitute hot water bottle.

An emergency kit is assembled for use in a situation where a special kind of emergency might happen. A good example is the provision your father makes *in advance* for an automobile mishap. If there should be a blowout, he carries in his car a spare tire, a jack to raise the car up off the ground, and tools for tire changing. In winter, he probably carries a set of tire chains.

Since situations vary, it is up to you to decide what should go into an emergency kit for a special situation. If you are going berry-picking in a brambly region, you will include tweezers for thorns, antiseptic and dressings for possible scratches. If it is swampy where you are going, you will take insect repellent to fend off mosquitoes. For cold weather, you may need extra socks and a chapping preventative.

Learn to anticipate what *might* happen and pack your emergency kit accordingly. This is good planning.

Emergency light, fuel, and heat are sometimes needed in a hurry. Here are three ways of providing these necessities quickly. Become an expert, so you can produce them without delay or difficulty whenever they are needed.

Communicate!

A .—
B —...
C —.—.
D —..
E .
F ..—.
G ——.
H ....
I ..
J .———
K —.—
L .—..
M ——
N —.
O ———
P .——.
Q ——.—
R .—.
S ...
T —
U ..—
V ...—
W .——
X —..—
Y —.——
Z ——..

In emergencies, it is often urgent to send a message in a hurry. Saving time may save the situation. Keep a "quick list" of emergency phone numbers near the phone.

A troop "Telephone Tree" is a time-and-worry saver. Suppose the meeting time has been changed at the last minute. By a pre-arranged system, one girl calls, takes, or sends a message to two others. Each of these girls calls two others, who continue to spread the word until all are alerted.

Signaling may be a lifesaver when no phone is available. In addition to a flag you can also signal by:

o *Lantern:* Lifted to the right of the sender means a dot; left, a dash. Lantern in front of sender is "position." Lowering once, end of word; twice, end of sentence; dark, end of message.

o *Flashlight:* Short flash is dot: long is dash. A 3-dot pause separates letters; 5-dot pause separates words. Longer pause, end of sentence. Dark for 60 seconds; end of message.

o *Whistle or buzzer:* Short sounds are dots; long ones, dashes. Separate words, sentences, and end messages same as by flashlight.

The idea of helping runs like a golden thread through the Girl Scout Promise and Laws. One of the fine things about growing up as a Scout is your increasing ability to help not only yourself but others. Now you can turn the principle into practice.

Emergencies happen on large scales, as well as small. Electric power has been known to fail in entire cities. In some regions, families are flooded from their homes. In others, tornados rip across the land, wrecking property, driving people into cold, hunger and, worst of all, fear.

It is a human privilege to help people in need. As a Girl Scout, you may work hand-in-hand with the American Red Cross or other agencies whose purpose is to bring comfort to stricken people. Well-organized squads of girls like you have done this. They have cooked meals and served them to large groups of people, taken care of children and animals, set up play centers, acted as messengers, sorted clothes, packed and unpacked relief supplies.

Every citizen is part of the Civil Defense system. Learn your community plan for emergency action. Do you know what CONELRAD is? It is the name of the national system of emergency radio broadcasting, used in case of air attack. The letters stand for "control of electromagnetic radiations." At such times, all regular radio stations go off the air, and only the two CONELRAD stations function to give information and instructions. These stations operate on two frequencies, 640 or 1240 on your standard (A.M.) radio dial. Mark the dials of your radio at these positions.

Emergency preparedness methods, from removing a splinter to working in a disaster area, is knowledge that will be of use to you all your life. In your Cadette Girl Scout career, there are badges to be earned in this area. And, when you are truly ready, the Challenge of Emergency Preparedness to meet (see Chapter 16). Resolve to accept it and meet it. You will find it a stimulating, worthwhile experience for now and the future.

Y ou have the power and means to give one of the most valuable gifts in the world — the gift of service.

While material things are necessary, and often nice to have, human beings need more than possessions. They often need sympathy and understanding. They need friends who care enough about them to show it by doing something in practical, helpful ways.

Whether the service you offer is big or small, it is an act of kindness. It is a translation of understanding

service
starts at home

into action. It is one of the most valuable gifts you can give because it is something of yourself.

Of course, the idea of service is not new to you. As a Girl Scout, you have always found ways "to help other people at all times." You know how good it feels, how happy it makes you to give help and comfort, freely and unselfishly.

Now you have grown up enough to look back a few years in your life and to appreciate the help and encouragement you have received from other people. You have grown up enough to know more, to do more. Best of all, you have grown up enough to realize that the beauty of service is this: the more you give, the more you get out of it.

Service begins at home. Your home is a place for you and your family to enjoy. Helping to care for your home is a fine service, not only to your family but to yourself.

Housecraft

Do you envision a day when you will have your own house or apartment? Then you can't do better than begin right now. One of the best ways to learn is by doing with energy and good will. A well-organized, attractive home provides a background which enhances you, now and in your future. Like campcraft, "housecraft" is many skills in one. Start practicing these skills now.

"*Think-ahead cleaning*" is a kind of preventive approach to housework. If you don't track dirt in, you won't have to work to get it out. Use the doormat. Leave wet rain gear outside or in a special place inside. Replace jar and bottle lids firmly, so they won't come off if the bottle falls on the floor. This kind of forethought is plain common sense. Can you think of other ways to keep mess and clutter from happening?

"*Go-along cleaning*" includes the things you do every day to keep your house tidy. Clean up as you go along. If you spill something, wipe it up at once. If you see a spot or stain, remove it. Make a spot-removal chart or get one from the U.S. Department of Agriculture or a manufacturer, and post it for convenient reference.

If you have been working on your hobby or doing lessons, put the materials away when you have finished. Put soiled things in the hamper, books on the bookshelf, towels on the towel rack. Keep things where they belong and your house will have a serene, orderly appearance.

Develop a system. That way, everything gets done when it should get done, and things don't pile up in hopeless confusion. Divide cleaning jobs into those you do everyday, weekly, and occasionally.

Everyday jobs: In your bedroom, straighten the room, hang clothes away, put shoes and slippers in place, and organize your belongings for the next day's activities before going to bed. Air your bed as soon as you get up in the morning and make it when you have finished dressing.

In the bathroom, "cooperation" is the slogan. Wipe up any spatters you may have made. After using tub or washbowl, clean it with a cloth or sponge and cleanser. If the mirror is filmed, wipe it shiny.

In the kitchen, see how quickly and efficiently you can do the dishes. Soak pots and pans, scrape and stack dishes. Wash in sudsy hot water; rinse in hottest water possible. Allow them to drip dry.

Keep the kitchen attractive and safe by wiping up spills on floor, spatters on stove, refrigerator, counters. Do small jobs at once, rather than letting them pile up. If you see a stained utensil, polish it at once.

These daily jobs may seem demanding and time-consuming. Actually, each takes only a few minutes and keeps your house fresh and bright.

Weekly jobs: Again, start with your bedroom. You will want to change the bed linens at least once a week. This is a convenient time to dust side, head, and footboards, springs, and other parts of the bed that are usually covered.

Once a week, brighten the bathroom with cleansers or detergents, removing stains and rings and polishing the fixtures and mirrors. Give the floor a real cleaning, too.

The kitchen floor needs once-a-week attention. Clean it thoroughly and wax, if needed. There are good dirt-and-wax removers on the market. Self-polishing wax works well on most floor coverings.

Follow the manufacturer's instructions for defrosting the refrigerator. Wash it inside and out. Wash all shelves and trays, and go over the inside with a mixture of one half teaspoon of baking soda to one quart of water.

The stove and oven should be wiped up after every use, but only after it is cold. In your weekly check, remove shelves and scrub them with a brush. Wipe out the inside with a solution of detergent. Rinse with clear water and let dry. If there are baked-on deposits, scrape them off with plastic or nylon scouring pads. Hint: The night before, leave an open bowl with a half-cup of ammonia inside the oven. The fumes will help to loosen particles, making your job easier.

Occasional jobs: These jobs are the big ones. Every so often, take dishes off shelves, wash them, replace shelf lining paper or wash shelves. Curtains should be washed and rehung, floors waxed. Clean and arrange clothes closets in the spring and fall, when your wardrobe, like the seasons, is changing.

A cleaning caddy will help you to make short work of the "now-and-then" accidents—fingerprints on the woodwork, a spill or splatter on the upholstery, a splash on the floor. It is best to clean these up at once. Dirt comes off more easily when it is not given time to sink in, dry, and harden. You can make one of these convenient household accessories for yourself. Get a shallow basket or box with a sturdy handle. Paint it with bright enamel and stock it with cleaning supplies, such as spot remover, furniture polish, woodwork cleaner, cloths, sponges. Buy supplies in containers small enough to keep your caddy light. Keep the caddy out of children's reach and always in the same place so you can find it quickly.

A lifetime appliance—that is you, of course. Use your body correctly when you work (see Chapter 6). Save your back by bending from the hips. Bend the knees to pick up something. Use long-handled equipment to avoid bending, a footstool or box to raise yourself if a work surface is too high. Remember to stand erect, sit to work whenever you can, and keep things within easy reach.

Cookery

Food is a necessity, but when it is well and tastily prepared, it becomes one of the joys of life. A girl who cooks well has, at her fingertips, one of the most basic (and popular) homemaking arts. What better way to learn than to join in the preparation and cooking of the family's meals?

By now, you know how to make a number of simple dishes. Why not branch out into more advanced cookery? With a good cookbook to guide you, you will find you are capable of wonders. Next time you are at the library or in a bookshop, glance through the cookbook section. You will see all varieties of recipes from simple to elaborate, familiar to exotic, from "quick" dishes to those requiring long preparation. All you need is the ability to follow directions accurately and methodically.

Cooking has a special vocabulary. When a recipe tells you to "stir," for example, that is not the same as "beat." Do you know the difference between "simmer" and "boil" or "sauté" and "fry"? To get the results you want, you must understand cookery terms. Otherwise, your dishes will not come out quite as you expect.

Modern science has entered the kitchen. There are new methods of cleaning, prepackaging, and precooking foods to improve their nutritive and taste values. Farmers grow fruits and vegetables for particular needs and uses: an easily portable watermelon, for example, small enough to fit in the refrigerator; potatoes with shallow eyes (for easier peeling) developed especially for baking, frying, or mashing. How many other ways can you find that science helps at the kitchen stove?

Operation Lunchbox

This is a good family service project for you. Do any members of your family take lunch to work or school? You could be in charge of making and packing the lunches.

Wrap sandwiches securely, stack them neatly. Close jar and thermos tops firmly. Be artistic and imaginative. Vary sandwich fillings and kinds of bread and rolls. Add honey to hot tea, mint or lime to iced tea. For father, pack his special favorites. For a small brother or sister, try cutting a cupcake in half, putting the frosting in the middle, for non-sticky packing and eating. Make lunch something to anticipate.

Good Hints for Good Cooks

1. Use a meat thermometer to determine when meat is rare, medium, or well done.
2. Before baking, line pan with aluminum foil, for easier cleaning after.
3. To cut sticky foods (marshmallows, candied fruit), use scissors dipped in water.
4. Use a rubber or plastic spatula for folding egg whites into custard or while beating cake batter in a mixer.
5. Learn measurements: Example: One quarter-pound stick of butter or margarine equals eight tablespoons or half a cup. Divide for smaller measures.

Lemon Meat Balls

1½ lbs. ground beef
1 egg, slightly beaten
1 teaspoon grated lemon rind
3 tablespoons lemon juice
2 teaspoons salt
⅛ teaspoon pepper

¼ teaspoon thyme
¼ teaspoon marjoram
3 tablespoons finely chopped onion
⅓ cup uncooked rice
1 (10½ oz.) can tomato soup
2 cups boiling water

Mix all but last two ingredients. Shape mixture into balls about 1½ inches in diameter. The mixture will be soft, but makes tender meat balls. Brown a few at a time in a little hot fat and remove from skillet. When all are browned, pour excess fat from skillet and return meat balls to pan. Cover with tomato soup-boiling water mixture. Cover pan. Simmer 50 to 60 minutes. Remove meat balls. Spoon excess fat from sauce. Pour sauce over meat balls and serve. (4-6 servings)

6. If recipe calls for double boiler and you have none, substitute a small saucepan in a deeper one.
7. Scrape spoon and sides of bowl often for thorough mixing of any ingredients.
8. Obey time and temperature instructions. Don't "hurry" a recipe.
9. Clean up as you go along.

A Family Special

Is there something your mother makes better than anyone else? A dish that's always popular? A party cake or dessert? Or a recipe for traditional holiday fare that has been handed down to your mother or invented by her?

You can master a "special" of your own, perhaps the Lemon Meat Balls recipe. Learn to make one dish so well, that it becomes your specialty, a never-fail favorite.

Preserve "family specials" by writing down the recipes, so you can continue the tradition in your family. There's a space to begin right on this page. Ask your mother for her best recipe, and leave room for one of your own.

Tighten buttons; run elastic thread through ribbing. Outline the sweater on paper, then turn it inside out. Dissolve 1 tsp. detergent in lukewarm water—if very soiled, add 3 more tsps. Wash quickly. Rub soiled spots gently; do not scrub.

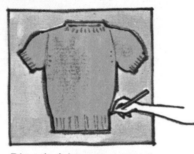

Rinse in lukewarm water at least twice, squeezing gently. Do not wring. Turn right side out. Roll in towel to absorb moisture. Pat into outline shape; dry flat, away from radiator or sun.

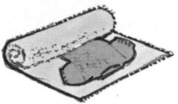

If pills (little wool balls) have formed, brush them away with quick, short strokes as sweater dries. When dry, remove elastic, and touch up with steam iron (or dry iron on damp cloth).

When It's Washday

Sort laundry, separating white and colored articles first. Colors that might run should be washed separately. Before washing, empty pockets, turn down cuffs, and shake out dust and sand. Rinse out egg, milk, blood stains in cool water; hot water will set them. Dampen badly soiled spots, scrub with detergent.

Follow the manufacturer's instructions about the temperature of water and the amount of softener and soap or detergent. Rinse thoroughly. Again follow directions for drying and ironing.

If you can use the family washing machine and dryer, have your mother explain how to operate these appliances. Be sure you clean them thoroughly when you finish.

Sweaters need special care. The specific method depends on the fiber content; for example, wool responds differently from acrilan. In general, follow the steps shown on this page. To keep colors (stripes, checks, patterns) from running together, soak the sweater in cool salt water before washing. This sometimes helps set the colors.

Money Management

Managing money is a sound practice for you now and for the future, when you have your own home. Whether you get an allowance, earn money, or both, use it purposefully. Make a budget. List your needs, your wants, and your sources of income. Be specific. Under "need," you might write "stockings" or "pen." Under ";want," a camera or sweater. Under "future," list your larger goals —a trip, perhaps, or a college education. Make sure the list reflects your wishes and needs. Then plan a saving-and-spending program around it.

A practical plan depends on what you have and what you want. Make provision for fixed expenses first—carfare, troop dues, lunch. Set aside a regular amount to cover recurrent expenses—the stockings or gifts, for instance. Most important, establish a "Future Fund," a plan of saving that will help you, eventually, to pay for your cherished projects. Keep track of your money. Try not to spend it impulsively. Instead, make it buy the things you really want.

Consumer Buying

You can get more for your money, and better quality, too, if you follow a few simple principles. Know what you need. Know what to look for when you shop—size, material, weight. Buy in the proper amount. Learn how to judge quality. For example, when you buy fruits and vegetables, there are ways to tell how good and how ripe they are. Find out which crops are most abundant each season and, therefore, most reasonably priced. Do not be carried away by a bargain, if the "bargain" is something you will never use.

Cadette Scouts should apply these principles to managing troop money, too. For example, if the troop wants a tent for camping, budget funds for the purchase, find out what kind of tent is best for your needs, and shop around to get the best for the least.

The Child in Your Care

All children, no matter their age, have three needs in common. They need understanding, good physical care, and protection. Be prepared to give them all three when you undertake to care for one child or more, by yourself or in a troop child-care project.

Your voice, facial expression, words, and actions are all instruments that convey your attitude. Let a child know you love him and think he's important. In a group, make sure no child is overlooked or slighted. He will be happier, more willing to listen to you if he senses that he has your attention.

Young children of school age are active and demanding. Many of them are spirited and independent and want to be given their own way. You need patience, energy, and a real love of children to direct them without being bossy. You need a sense of humor, too. And it's essential to know a few techniques that will make child care safe, interesting, and enjoyable for the children and for yourself.

Physical care means any number of things, depending on the age you are dealing with and the circumstances in each case. It might mean tucking a child warmly into her crib, with the window opened just so. Or it might mean seeing that a group of children are properly dressed to play in the snow, then giving them cups of hot soup and their afternoon naps.

When you babysit, do your part by arriving promptly and learning what your responsibilities are. You should know the child's name and how to reach the parents or a neighbor in emergency. The child's mother will tell you exactly what to do. If you can, visit the child ahead of time to make friends. If you have had a cold or been exposed to a contagious disease, do not take on a child-care job.

Here are some ways to keep children busily and happily occupied:

o Play guessing games or charades.

o Have a tossing contest, throwing playing cards or cardboard milk bottle caps into a box or basket.

o Pretend you have a sum of money to spend. Look through a mail order catalog, planning what to "buy."

o Tell continued stories. One person starts, stops at an exciting place, and the next one continues the story or ends it.

o Sing songs everybody knows or teach a brand-new one. Try "Mister Rabbit," "Shusti-Fidli," or "The Little Bells." (All from *Sing Together*.)

o Play singing games. Younger children will enjoy "Four in a Boat," "Skip To My Lou," or "The Noble Duke of York." (All from *Skip To My Lou*.)

Teaching games to children will be a success if you choose games to suit the ages and interests of the players. Start with a simple game. Collect the equipment, then arrange the children in game formation, if there is one. Know the game so well that you can explain it briefly and they can play at once. If they make mistakes, wait a while before correcting them. Let them catch the spirit of the game first. Once they know it, let them play by themselves, interrupting only to answer questions or settle disputes. Stop the game before it loses its novelty or the children are tired. If it is a competitive game, lead the cheers and applause for the winners.

Protect children by preventing accidents before they happen. See that window screens are securely locked in. If screens do not have locks, keep children away from them. Don't allow children to run on slippery floors. Put things that might cause injury—matches, sharp and pointed objects, medicines—out of reach. A dresser scarf or tablecloth might tempt a curious child to yank at it, bringing down lamps, hot dishes, things that may hurt him. If something is cooking on the stove, turn the pot handle in, so a child cannot grab it to spill the scalding contents on himself. Know where the child is and what he is doing at all times. Even with the best precautions, accidents sometimes happen. Know your first aid. In addition, have a list of emergency phone numbers handy for quick reference.

"Lullaby and goodnight" are not always welcome words to a youngster. Before his mother leaves, find out what his schedule is and keep to it. This may be difficult when children plead to stay up "just a little bit longer." Be pleasant and friendly, but firm. To get a child to cooperate, let him know in advance what is expected. You may say: "As soon as you finish coloring this page, we need to put away the crayons for the night." A child may be tired and cranky by bedtime. Try to keep the atmosphere quiet and calm. Follow his mother's directions as to prayers, bed coverings, lights, windows, doors, and "special requests" from the child. If you read him a bedtime story, help him choose a favorite, but make sure it is not too exciting to keep him from falling asleep.

MARY MCLEOD BETHUNE won a great many medals and honors during her lifetime. This was neither her ambition nor her aim. Her ambition was to work for the greater good and enlightenment of her people, her aim to build racial dignity, respect, and good will among all mankind.

An educator, Dr. Bethune came from the cotton fields of South Carolina to prove what one woman with faith and courage can do. She founded the Daytona Normal and Industrial School for Negro Girls (now Bethune-Cookman College), became director of the Division of Negro Affairs of the National Youth Administration, and organized and presided over the National Council of Negro Women. Before she died in 1955, she wrote: "If I have a legacy to leave my people, it is my philosophy of living and serving. As I face tomorrow, I am content, for I think I have spent my life well. I pray now that my philosophy may be helpful to those who share my vision of a world of peace."

What Are Your Plans?

Almost everything you learn to do at home has some relation to your future world. New inventions and new products are being developed so fast that no one can possibly foresee what jobs will be available on the day you are ready to begin.

Interest in the kitchen may lead to work as a nutritionist or dietitian. There is opportunity for the science-minded in developing plastic and synthetic materials for fabrics, tableware, and household equipment.

If you live in the country or on a farm, your special interests may center around growing things—either plants or animals. There are opportunities in agronomy, horticulture, bacteriology, entomology, animal husbandry, and veterinary medicine.

There are vocations in designing, interior decorating, teaching home economics, product testing. Or knowledge in these fields can be used in a career in journalism. The home-centered skills and services you learn and practice as a Cadette Girl Scout will help you enjoy the home, husband, children, and job in your future.

People Make the World

If you want to get anything done, with or for others, you should know something about getting along well with people.

Your own attitude can be a great help. Do you view work as a burden? You could say, "I hate housework, it's a bore." Or "I love to make the house fresh and pretty." Which attitude, do you think, produces better results and gives greater satisfaction?

Many of your projects involve other people—your patrol and troop members, your leader, teachers, family and friends. Later in life, you may have a family, work at a job, give service to a school, religious group, or club. Begin now to cultivate ideas and habits to help you work happily with others.

Give help at home in the practical ways shown in this chapter. Do your share well and cheerfully. Be thoughtful in other ways, too. If you go off on an errand, let your family know where you are. Don't complain or criticize your family to outsiders. It is kinder, more dignified, to solve home problems at home.

Be especially courteous to all grownups. It is gracious to rise when an older person enters the room, considerate to place a chair, pick up something she may have dropped. Remember to thank grownups for their kindnesses, to include them in conversations with friends. Address them by name. "Yes, mother," "I'm sorry, Miss Blake," are so much more attractive than a grunt or blunt "yes," "no," or "mmm-hmmm."

It is bad manners to contradict an older person, even when you disagree. State your viewpoint respectfully: "I'm not sure, Aunt Kit, but I think it was May, not June." It may seem unfair to have to restrain yourself just because a person is older. It is not a matter of fairness, but of behaving attractively, instead of rudely. You can get your point across and still be polite.

One important thing to remember about people of all ages is that they like to be praised. When you feel someone deserves praise, be ready to give it. You will earn the same treatment for yourself, while smoothing the road of human relations. You will find that friendly people make the world and the work go better.

How well you get along with others really reflects how well you translate into action your belief in the Girl Scout Promise and Laws.

Service does not stop at your front door. Practice the Promise and Laws by offering your skills to friends and neighbors who need your help. With your troop leader to advise you, you and your patrol can plan, organize, and do wider service projects than before you were Cadette Scouts. Investigate children's agencies, community groups, and your own religious organizations. Find out whether other groups of young people—Boy Scouts, 4-H Clubs, Granges—will work with you.

When you start a project, see it through. Unlike a young child who becomes restless and impatient quickly, you have the ability and vision to stick with a job, though it may get dull at times. This ability is a sure sign of growing up. After every service project set some time aside to ask yourselves, "How can we do better next time?"

Try to find ways for the people to whom you give service to give service, too. If your troop is planning to entertain at a home for the elderly, perhaps some of the ladies could teach you to knit or some of the men could join with you to make toys for the orphanage. Everyone deserves the privilege and pleasure of doing something for others.

Plan an event—a cookout, special troop meeting, or whatever—for the eleven-year-old Junior Scouts who will be joining Cadette Scout troops next year. Confer with your leader to decide from which troops these girls should be invited. Your troop may plan this alone, or cooperatively with one or more other Cadette Scout troops. Organize the activities to help your guests discover for themselves what Challenge and First Class Scout mean. Don't lecture. Let your skills in the arts, the home, and the out-of-doors tell what happens as you earn badges as Cadettes. Display some mementos of your camping and service experiences. Involve your guests in skits, demonstrations, or a wide game. These younger girls are part of your Girl Scout family, and look forward to the day they, too, will be members of a Cadette Scout troop. Welcome them warmly.

our national heritage

A sk yourself: "Who made the United States of America?" You will find a thousand answers in a thousand places; wherever Indians lived and worked; in the southwest, where Spanish settlers brought brilliant designs and deep religious beliefs; on the east coast, where English, Scottish, Irish, and Welsh colonists made homes, sang songs, danced their country dances; from New England to the midwest, explored by French settlers who farmed, set traps, cooked their food inspired by ideas from the old country and the new.

Singing their powerful spirituals, Negroes learned the many skills essential to plantation life, while halfway across the land, German settlers farmed, made cheeses, and sang the *lieder* of their homeland.

More people came. Polish, Japanese, Swedish, Italian, Greek, to mine and sew, to build highways and write books, to weave the threads of their culture into the firm and flexible fabric that is symbolic of the United States of America.

You will find as you explore the story of our country it will give you great satisfaction and pride. Go deeper than dates and events. Learn about your ancestors, how they lived, what they wore, what inspired them to come to this country and to give so much of themselves to it. Some of the spirit of these people has been caught in poetry. Read "American Names," by Stephen Vincent Benet; "The Gift Outright," by Robert Frost; "The Concord Hymn," by Ralph

Waldo Emerson. And a record of the past has been preserved by artists. Look for pictures by Frederic Remington, painter of the Western scene, and by Grandma Moses, the primitive painter, and for prints by Currier and Ives.

The highways and rivers on which you travel have a romance all their own. Before the Revolution the Boston Post Road heard the hoof beats of the riders that kept the Committees of Correspondence in touch. The great National Road, started in 1808, is part of Route 40, which stretches from the Atlantic to the Pacific. The only cross-country highway free of ice and snow year round is built over the old Spanish trails developed in the sixteenth century. Today they all echo the wheels of huge trucks that are so vital to the industrial growth and prosperity of our country. Many are paralleled by the railroads.

Gone are the canoes and the paddle wheel steamers that traveled our rivers, but waterways still play an important part in shipping. Modern engineering has made it possible to link these natural routes and each year the tonnage carried on our inland waterways increases.

The commercial airlines also fol-low routes charted by pioneers—the aviators who flew single-engine planes without the navigational aids we take for granted.

But in each case it was people who made these things possible. People who gave their time, their energy, their money to help build the country in which you live today.

When you visit your state capital or a national monument, think of what it represents in terms of human lives and ideas. When you go to a national park, a wildlife refuge, or a fish hatchery, remember that these are symbols of your government and representative of your country's riches —your riches, to be preserved and protected.

It might be well to think of Baden-Powell's words: "Your forefathers worked hard, fought hard, and died hard, to make your country for you. Don't let them look down from heaven and see you loafing about with your hands in your pockets, doing nothing to keep it up."

Tradition is not a false pride in past glory. It is a heritage from the past that we honor today, not merely in the classrooms or textbooks, but in our hearts and by our actions. That is how we continue a noble heritage into the future of our country.

If your troop were hostess to a Girl Guide from another country or a Girl Scout from another part of our country, how could you acquaint her with the customs and qualities that are characteristic of your region and that give it its unique flavor? The first step, of course, is to find out all you can yourselves.

Learn the songs and legends, the dances and handcrafts, the food and folkways. Talk to people who can help you—the librarian, the curator of the museum, officers of the historical society. Read books, magazines, newspapers. Visit the places of interest. For example, is there a famous historical tree, such as the Cambridge Elm or the Charter Oak, in your locality? What are some of the principal industries? Can you tour the plants? Is yours an agricultural area? Why do some crops grow better there than others? Has any experimental work been done to improve the yield? Have any new varieties been developed?

Take pictures of the places you visit. Be sure some of the troop members write a story about each trip. Collect any printed material available. Using all this information, make a scrapbook and a blueprint for an exhibit which can be assembled quickly when the occasion arises. Plan a party to honor an out-of-town guest. Include local songs and dances, or dramatize a legend. Serve local food specialties. Make small souvenirs from native materials to give to your guest.

Work out a plan for a visit of one day, three days, and a week. If the time is short, use the exhibit and scrapbook. If the visit is longer, include trips to the places of interest. Try out your hostess plan by entertaining a new girl in your school. She needs a welcome tour, too.

Plan imaginary trips to other parts of our country, looking for the similarities in their local heritage. Then you will be ready to give an overseas guest a picture of the whole of your country.

Now you are prepared, and, with a little bit of luck, you might be asked to hostess a visitor to your council. Have you ever noticed that often what looks like a "lucky break" for someone really happens because that someone did a good deal of work to be ready if the chance ever came her way. P.S. You have probably met many badge requirements along the way, and, with this wide view of the fifty states that make up the Union, the song on the next page should have more meaning for you.

America—

Words and Music by Helen Steele

A ALL VOICES *mf*

High tower-ing moun-tains, Fields gold with grain,

B

Rich, fer-tile farm-lands, Flocks on the plain,

C *mp*

Homes blest with peace, with love, with-out fears,

D *mf*

This is the her-it-age we've kept through the years.

E *f*

Stout hearts and true, Hold fast what is ours;

F *mf*

God give us cour-age through dark-est hours;

G *mf*

God give us strength And guide with Thy Hand A

H *ff*

mer-i-ca, Our her-it-age, Our home-land.

I Freely
Sop. *mp*

Wide roll-ing prai-ries, lakes, deep and broad, Can-yons ma-

Alto *mp*

Our Heritage

Arranged by Hawley Ades

Patchwork

Patchwork quilts are examples of an early American art that tells the story of the women who made them. They express the hunger for color and beauty in drab surroundings, the thrift that turned bits and remnants into artistic, useful creations, the patience and skill of needlewomen who took pride in their work. A patchwork quilt was a family affair. It was made from little circles of calico from mother's apron, floral print saved from parts of sister's best dress, a faded strip left from father's shirt after it was worn out.

Many of the original designs were adapted from the beauties of nature; others, equally beautiful, were geometric patterns, arrangements of harmonizing shapes and colors. Perhaps a goose waddling across the yard may have inspired the design on the opposite page. It is called "Goose Tracks."

You can make lovely things from individual squares filled with batting, backed with cotton, and quilted. One square makes a handsome hot plate mat, or, with a loop on one corner, it becames an oversized potholder. Filled with a single layer of batting, a square may be used as a top for a throw pillow, a skirt pocket, or a miniature quilt for a doll's crib.

If your troop decides to make a bed quilt, why not organize an old-fashioned American Quilting Bee? Long ago the ladies combined work with sociability, talking and laughing as they sewed. You can do the same. As you work, you will be part of a chain stretching back into the history of your country to a time when imaginative, spirited women contrived with their needles to turn need into lasting beauty. You will understand the pride and satisfaction of these bygone women as they contemplated their handiwork, radiant with color, warm and cozy against the frosty night. You will know just how they felt, because you will feel the same way. Your pride in your handiwork will be a small reflection of your larger pride as a citizen of the United States of America.

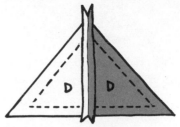

Pin corners of 1 white and 1 colored Unit D. Seam together. Repeat with colored unit on left.

To make one square of the Goose Track quilt you will need:

Unit A (4-inch square) 4 white, 1 colored.

Unit B (4¼-inch square cut in half) 4 colored.

Unit C (2¼-inch square) 4 white.

Unit D (2¼-inch square cut in half) 8 white, 8 colored.

Measurements include the ¼-inch seam allowance on each side of each piece. Join pieces with backstitch.

Make an accurate pattern for each unit on cardboard or sandpaper. Cut the required number of pieces for each unit from sturdy, washable, preshrunk cotton fabric. Assemble the pieces as shown. Press seams flat, not open. The completed piece should be eleven inches square, including ¼-inch seam allowances.

If you make a quilt, put a colored strip (2 or 3 inches wide) between squares and a white block at the intersections. See picture of quilt on page 52. Fill with cotton batting or a worn blanket and then quilt (see Bibliography). A quilt for a single bed requires 5 yards of white and 5 yards of colored fabric.

Sew these two pieces to Unit C to form a triangle.

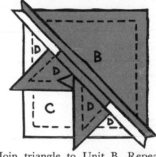

Join triangle to Unit B. Repeat these three steps for remaining corner designs.

Sew corner designs to the 5 Unit A's.

Our
Flag
and
Our
Freedoms

"This flag, which we honor and under which we serve, is the emblem of our unity, our power, our thought and purpose as a nation. . . . And yet, though silent, it speaks to us—speaks to us of the past, of the men and women who went before us, and of the records they wrote upon it." These words of Woodrow Wilson sum up why respect and reverence are due our National flag. And here are some rules that tell you how to honor it.

No flag should be placed above the flag of the United States of America (therefore, always pick it up first, post it last).

When carried in a procession with another flag, the Stars and Stripes should be on the right; or, in a line of other flags, it should be first or in front of the center of that line.

In peacetime, the flags of all nations should be displayed on separate staffs of equal height, with the flag of the United States on the right. The flags of the other nations are usually displayed in alphabetical order. The World Association flag or Girl Scout flags come last and are placed at the left.

When a flag of the United States of America is worn out, dispose of it with due respect. First cut the Union from the flag and then burn the two pieces, which no longer form a flag.

When the flag is raised or lowered

or at the moment it passes you in a parade or in a review, you should face the flag, stand at attention, and salute. Girl Scouts use the citizen's salute—placing the right hand over the heart. Citizens should also salute when the pledge of allegiance is said or when the National Anthem is played and the flag is displayed. The right to salute our flag is one of the privileges reserved to citizens of the United States of America.

Citizenship, with all its privileges and responsibilities, comes automatically to people born in this country, but must be earned by those who come here from another country.

Before an alien can petition the Immigration and Naturalization Service for citizenship, he must meet certain requirements. For example, he must be able to read, write, and speak English and have a knowledge of the history of the United States and its government. Some communities have citizenship classes for these people. Find out if there is a way you can help by preparing materials for classroom use, giving a demonstration, presenting a flag ceremony.

ESTHER HOBART MORRIS was one of the thousands of women who, with their families, came to the boom towns and gold mines of Wyoming after the Civil War. She dressed in calico, worked hard, and lived in a rude cabin, brightened by the flowers she planted. She lived plainly and spoke plainly, but her spirit was rich with the new ideas of feminist reform. In those days, women had few rights. Esther Morris' outspoken requests for women's suffrage was quite a novelty in the Wyoming territory. In fact, many legislators treated it as a joke. But Mrs. Morris, an active, earnest campaigner, won through. Her efforts were directly responsible for the passage of the first equal suffrage bill in history. The bill went further, granting women the right to hold and bequeath property, to conduct a trade or business, and to earn the same teaching salaries as men, if qualified. Esther Morris' fight was won for all the women of the United States, then and now.

The Bill of Rights

AMENDMENTS I TO X OF THE CONSTITUTION OF THE UNITED STATES

I   Congress shall make no law respecting an establishment of religion, or prohibiting the free exercise thereof; or abridging the freedom of speech, or of the press; or the right of the people peacefully to assemble, and to petition the government for a redress of grievances.

II   A well-regulated militia, being necessary to the security of a free State, the right of the people to keep and bear arms, shall not be infringed.

III   No soldier shall, in time of peace, be quartered in any house without the consent of the owner, nor in time of war, but in a manner to be prescribed by law.

IV   The right of the people to be secure in their persons, houses, papers, and effects, against unreasonable searches and seizures, shall not be violated, and no warrants shall issue but upon probable cause, supported by oath or affirmation, and particularly describing the place to be searched, and the persons or things to be seized.

V   No person shall be held to answer for a capital, or otherwise infamous crime, unless on a presentment or indictment of a grand jury except in cases arising in the land or naval forces, or in the militia, when in actual service in time of war or public danger; nor shall any person be subject for the same offence to be twice put in jeopardy of life or limb; nor shall be compelled in any criminal case to be a witness against himself, nor be deprived of life, liberty, or property, without due process of law; nor shall private property be taken for public use without just compensation.

VI   In all criminal prosecutions the accused shall enjoy the right to a speedy and public trial, by an impartial jury of the State and district wherein the crime shall have been committed, which district shall have been previously ascertained by law, and to be informed of the nature and cause of the accusation; to be confronted with the witnesses against him; to have compulsory process for obtaining witnesses in his favor, and to have the assistance of counsel for his defence.

VII   In suits at common law, where the value in controversy shall exceed twenty dollars, the right of trial by jury shall be preserved, and no fact tried by a jury shall be otherwise re-examined in any court of the United States, than according to the rules of the common law.

VIII   Excessive bail shall not be required, nor excessive fines imposed, nor cruel and unusual punishments inflicted.

IX   The enumeration in the Constitution, of certain rights, shall not be construed to deny or disparage others retained by the people.

X   The powers not delegated to the United States by the Constitution, nor prohibited by it to the States, are reserved to the States respectively, or to the people.

The Declaration of Independence states: "That all men are created equal; that they are endowed by their Creator with certain inalienable rights; that among these are life, liberty, and the pursuit of happiness." However, when the Constitution was adopted, many people felt these rights were not clearly spelled out and suggested a bill of rights as a remedy. In 1791, the First Congress adopted the first ten amendments, known as the Bill of Rights.

The Bill of Rights proclaims that you, the individual, have certain rights. You have the right to worship as you choose; to say, write, or print what you please, unless it is libelous. You have the right to read newspapers of your choice, express your opinions about your government. You have a right to own property.

Do you take all this for granted? Do you assume that these freedoms, won for you years ago, are forever yours? History and the daily papers tell you this is not so. These freedoms can be taken away unless you are alert and careful to cherish them.

To keep your rights, you must protect the rights of others. Practice your religion, but respect the right of others to do the same. You are entitled to your thoughts and opinions. So are other people, as long as they do not try to destroy our freedoms. If you force your opinion upon others, you are taking away their freedom. Whenever freedom is taken away from one individual, it is weakened for all.

Take the same care of the property of others as you would of your own. And remember public property—parks, schools—is your property.

You were born with a certain ancestral heritage. You believe in your religion; you love your country. This is true of other people, too. Never accept or join in a bias against people of another race, creed, or national origin. The Bill of Rights is for all.

Right now there is much you can do to show you know what citizenship means. You might try putting some of it into words as you work on the Creative Writer badge. Look at My Country and My Government badges. The Conservation badge will make clear the importance of protecting our natural resources. Stamp collectors will find much of our heritage portrayed in commemorative stamps. It takes work as well as words to understand and serve your country. This is putting into action these words of the Girl Scout Promise: "to do my duty to God and my country." This is part of the Challenge of Active Citizenship.

make the world a better place

Once a year, on her birthday, Juliette Gordon Low wrote a letter to all her beloved Girl Scouts. These birthday letters were, to her, the next best thing to talking directly with every single girl. In them, she showed her pride in Scouting ideals and character, her affection for all Girl Scouts and her belief in them.

In her last letter, she wrote of something very dear to her. "As you gather in your troops to celebrate our Girl Scout Week, think of the girls around the world who are your sister Girl Scouts and Girl Guides. Truly, ours is a circle of friendships, united by our ideals." The letter was signed, "Your friend, Juliette Low."

To Juliette Low, world friendship was a practical goal, something that people could work for and achieve. How did she find her way to this wonderful belief?

Her childhood was filled with sunlight, family love, and laughter. With other children, she attended a schoolhouse in a grove of walnut trees, inventing games and tableaux and, under the pen name of "Daisy," contributing charming poems and illustrations to a magazine. When she was fourteen, she went to a boarding school in Virginia and from there, to a private school in New York City. At eighteen, she became a popular debutante in Savannah.

When she married William Low, she went to live in England and was presented at court wearing a white dress with a silk train six yards long, all brocaded with satin feathers and lined in pink. She met world-famous people. Her life was busy and glamorous.

After the death of her husband, Juliette Low felt that she had accomplished very little in her life. When she met Lord Baden-Powell and heard about Scouting, she recognized something real, something exciting, yet idealistic. And when she came back to Savannah, she telephoned her friend, Nina Pape, and said, "Come right over. I've got something for the girls of Savannah, and all America, and all the world, and we're going to start it tonight."

"And all the world...." Juliette Low knew that good citizenship and peaceful living extend beyond the borders of home to embrace the world. Had she lived to see great jet planes speeding across oceans, linking the peoples of the earth together, she would have felt today, more than ever in the history of mankind, the need for world friendship. Like Lord Baden-Powell, she put her trust in the power of Guiding and Scouting for international understanding. She threw herself, heart and soul, into the work of the International Council of Girl Guides and Girl Scouts, never missing a meeting when she was in Europe and frequently crossing the ocean especially to attend one. It is not strange, therefore, that the Juliette Low World Friendship Fund was set up as a fitting tribute to her memory.

A Fund for Friendship

The Juliette Low World Friendship Fund is just the sort of idea Mrs. Low would have loved. It turns the idea of world friendship into a reality, and it expresses the faith and good will of every single Girl Scout in the United States of America. The Fund is made of the dimes and dollars saved and earned by Girl Scouts of all ages throughout the country. Each year, like the magic purse in the old fairy tale, it is refilled by your voluntary contributions.

This money is spent to weave a network of friendship among girls around the world. Most of the money goes to the Girl Scout international exchange plan. Every year, Senior Girl Scouts and adults are sent abroad, some to international gatherings at Our Chalet in Switzerland or Our Cabaña in Mexico, some to camps and conferences, and some to visit Guides in their own homes. Every year, across our country, Girl Scouts welcome Girl Guides and adults from many member countries of the World Association of Girl Guides and Girl Scouts. Here, the visitors share family living and join in Girl Scout troop and camp activities.

When you contribute to the Juliette Low World Friendship Fund, you help new troops in other parts of the world by providing books and training for leaders. The Fund also buys useful things for Girl Scouts and Girl Guides who have suffered catastrophes.

Some day, you may be a hostess to girls from distant lands. Some day, you may qualify for an international opportunity that will take you to a foreign country. Look up the qualifications on page 278. See where you stand. In the meantime, work for the Juliette Low World Friendship Fund by explaining its purpose to younger troops, your friends, family, and neighbors. Find out whether your troop may help to plan a special ceremony for the collection of contributions to this Fund.

In this way you will help spin the magic thread of which Juliette Low spoke when she said: "Scouting and Guiding can be the magic thread which links the youth of the world together."

The World Is Your Neighborhood

Does the idea of international friendship seem like a contradiction to all that you have learned about devotion to your country? In truth, however, duty to your locality, love of your country, and sincere efforts to practice international friendship are inseparable and indispensable traits of a good citizen.

Naturally, you want to live peacefully and happily, side-by-side with your neighbors, whether they are in the same block, on the same continent, or on the same earth. This is community friendship spread out to include the world. For what happens in other parts of the world will affect you and your life.

Every thinking person, young or old, knows the importance of cultivating good will and understanding wherever people live. The more we understand and respect one another the less inclined we will be to quarrel.

As a Girl Scout, you are in a particularly good position to help strengthen the bonds of world friendship, for you are part of a worldwide movement, the World Association of Girl Guides and Girl Scouts. You have friends and sisters in many lands.

Moreover, international friendship is not something that you do once, and then forget. Never be satisfied with one gesture of cooperation, one international friendship project.

The Founders believed that you and young people like you could do a great deal to promote understanding and appreciation among all people, no matter how different they seem from each other. They hoped you would make the principles of harmony and peace part of your everyday life—saying, thinking, doing as much as you can for world friendship.

Working for the Juliette Low World Friendship Fund is one way to demonstrate your principles. This chapter suggests other ways, too, and of course, you will contribute your own ideas, inspired by the spirited words of the "World Song": "We must unite for what is right In friendship true and strong."

Would you like to have a pen friend in another country? Cadette Scouts are eligible to join the thousands of girls all over the world who are building interesting, worthwhile friendships through the mails, exchanging information and fun, ideas and ideals. See if you meet the requirements. You must:

o Be a registered Girl Scout, at least twelve years old.

o Know how to write a letter that is informative, stimulating and friendly.

o Be willing to make the effort to continue your letter writing long enough and well enough to form a true friendship.

The International Post Box

If you meet the requirements, you may request an international pen pal by writing to: International Post Box Secretary, Girl Scouts of the U.S.A., 830 Third Avenue, New York 22, New York. Do not ask your troop scribe or leader to make a group request. Each individual girl must write her own letter. Write neatly and legibly in ink.

In your letter, include: your full name, age, and address; your troop number; your first, second, and third choice of country.

If you can correspond in the language of the country you have chosen, fine! If not, ask for a pen pal who can write English. Tell something about yourself, such as your special interests and hobbies. Girls in other countries, applying through their own associations, will give the same information about themselves. This helps the International Post Box secretary match pen pals.

Enclose a business-sized envelope, stamped and self-addressed for the reply. It may take some time before you and your friend across the sea are put in touch with each other. Do not be impatient during this waiting period. Instead, use the time to plan letters that will make her look forward to the postman's arrival.

In your first letter introduce yourself, telling about your home and family, what you eat and wear. As the correspondence goes on, write about your troop, school, pets, favorite games, vacations, projects, and plans.

Give her a word picture of your town or city, your country, describing what is interesting, important, colorful. You could tell her about the seasons by sending a snapshot of the same tree as it appears in summer, spring, autumn, and winter. You could show her how you celebrate Thanksgiving and the Fourth of July by sending photographs of your family or pictures from magazines and newspapers.

You might exchange maps, reading material. It costs little to send a subscription to *The American Girl*, for example (see Bibliography). If you send gifts, make them small. Be sure to check with your post office to be certain your pen pal will not have to pay duty.

Always print your name and address on the envelope and the letter. Keep your pen pal's name and address in a safe place. Use airmail postage or the inexpensive airmail stationery sold at the post office. Keep the correspondence going and your friendship alive!

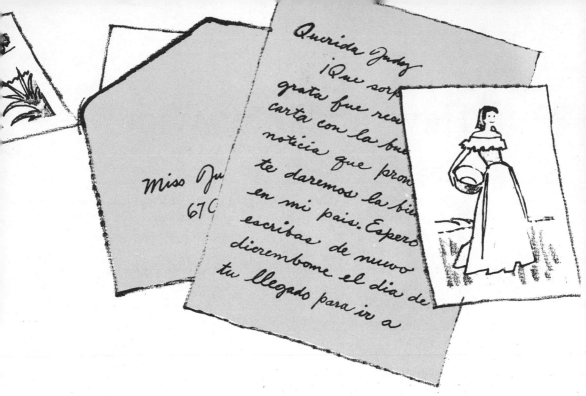

Say It—In Another Language

Amie . . . amiga . . . vriendin . . . freundin . . . amica . . . kaibigan . . . each of these words says "friend." Learn the language of another country and you draw closer to real communication and friendship with its people, for people who speak the same language feel more at home with each other.

If, as a Senior Girl Scout, you visit Our Chalet, you will hear some girls chatting in French or German. At Our Cabaña, the language commonly used is Spanish. Start now, by learning the Promise, the Motto, camping terms, phrases of greeting and courtesy, and songs in another tongue.

If you do not take a language course in school, look for other ways to learn. Start with the Girl Scout record "Say it—In Another Language." Try some of the commercial language teaching records. A foreign student in your town might be willing to teach you, or any person of your acquaintance who speaks a language in addition to English. *Bonne chance!*

Have a "Look-Wide!"

This is a delightful way to see the world right at home. Pick a member country of the World Association of Girl Guides and Girl Scouts and plan an event based on that country, a "Look-Wide." You will find this especially rewarding if you work with another troop in town or several groups at camp.

Here's one way to start. All the patrol leaders of both troops meet to select a country and map out broad plans. Let us say they choose France. Perhaps patrol leaders from different troops pair off to mix and match the plans and assignments.

Now each patrol gets busy, fulfilling its part of the plan. The hostess patrol issues the invitations (in French, of course) and should learn some phrases with which to greet the guests. The refreshment patrol may decide on a supper of eggs stuffed with mushrooms (recipe in *Trefoil Round the World*) with chunks of toasted French bread sprinkled with grated cheese. For dessert, they might offer fresh fruit and French cheeses. They could even write the menu in French!

The music patrols could learn some French Girl Guide songs to sing and teach (see *Chansons de Notre Chalet*).

The costume patrols might make and model the Guide uniforms of the two French Guide Associations. Some girls might learn to give the Promise as *Les Guides de France* do. You may find things at home (a book, a handkerchief, an omelete pan) which reflect life in France.

Teach your audience to applaud in the manner of the Girl Guides in France, who seldom signify their approval by random clapping as is our custom. Instead, each Guide company invents and practices its own special system of rhythmic patterned clapping in unison, interspersed with hand motions and an occasional whistle. Be sure to practice your version until you can demonstrate it with precisioned snap and verve.

Put all these elements together and you have a French "Look-Wide," an event that gives you greater insight into the young people of a fascinating country. You may do the same with any country of your choice. Remember, a "Look-Wide" takes advance planning, research, and cooperation. All this adds to the success of your "Look-Wide" and your enjoyment of it.

And there are other ways to look wide, too. In the community where

you live, there may be opportunities for you to meet people of different countries and races, to get to know something of them and their cultures, and to participate actively in practical projects to promote friendship. Here are some ideas.

If there is an international house or center in your community or close by, find out about the activities there. How can you and your troop be of help? You might offer a sightseeing service to foreign students, based on your hostess plan (see page 215). This project is especially enjoyable if you can speak one of their languages. It's friendlier.

Find out if there are any recently returned members of TOFS (Girl Scout Troops on Foreign Soil) near you. Such girls might have many interesting ideas for troop projects based upon their living experiences in other countries.

There may be nationality organiza-tions or societies in your community. Get in touch with them and see whether you can meet people who have come to this country in recent years. When possible invite the daughters of newcomers to join the Girl Scouts. You may also be able to invite the parents themselves to teach your troop the songs, dances, or food favorites of their homeland.

In a nearby school or college, are there exchange students or teachers? Your troop might "adopt" one for a period of time and interpret to each other present-day living in both countries.

Look at the activities outlined in the World Heritage, World Understanding and World Trefoil badges. Perhaps you will find so many exciting ideas that are possible in your particular community that you will be able to develop an "Our Own Troop's Badge" in international friendship.

"To Help Other People"

In the complex world of today, few of us working alone could make much of an impact on the fundamental problems of mankind. But by pooling our efforts with other organizations in our country that have similar aims, we can take real steps toward international friendship. How can you and your troop take part?

Investigate possible projects and activities which may be open to you. The nature of the projects will vary from place to place, and year to year, because the needs of people change with time and place.

Perhaps the place to start is at your church or synagogue. Religion bids us love our neighbors and share with them. Even your farthest neighbors in other parts of the world can be reached through your religious affiliation. What is your church or synagogue doing about this? Can you as an individual or together with the members of your troop help?

Find out from your Girl Scout council what international friendship projects are currently needed and toward which you could give something of yourself. For example, Girl Scouts your age have worked with the American Friends Service Committee, collecting clothes, school supplies, games, and toys, and knitting scarfs, afghans, and caps. Through the Needlework Guild of America, Inc., Girl Scouts have sent cloth, buttons, zippers, and other sewing notions to young people abroad. In areas where disasters, such as floods or tornadoes occurred, there is often need for clothing and household supplies. Girl Scouts, through their councils, have cooperated with the American National Red Cross to bring emergency help to the people in those areas. Sometimes it is money to buy supplies that is needed, and some Girl Scout troops include a donation to CARE in the troop's budget.

If there is a drive to collect clothes, food, books, writing implements, you may be able to cooperate. Perhaps you will help to organize material, wrap packages and address them to places far away. As you do so, you will begin to think of the people in distant lands as individuals who, like you and everyone you know, must be clothed, warmed, fed, taught to read and write, and encouraged by friendship. It takes more than good will to help people. It takes knowledge, action, and money. Old clothes, for example, must be cleaned. Mailing cartons and postage cost money. When you or your troop plan a service of this kind, remember that even things which are freely given cost money to send. Estimate your costs and allow for them in your budget. See what money-earning projects you can develop. In Chapter 14, Troop Money Earning, you will find some helpful suggestions.

Another way to help is through the specialized agencies of the United Nations which work to improve living conditions and to promote understanding throughout the world. Among those groups that work closely with young people are WHO: World Health Organization; UNICEF: United Nations Children's Fund; FOA: Food and Agricultural Organization; and UNESCO: United Nations Educational, Scientific and Cultural Organization. These agencies provide food for the hungry, medicine for the sick, and teachers for the illiterate. Find out how you can help.

Many years ago, Edward Everett Hale said it this way: "I am only one, but still I am one. I cannot do everything, but still I can do something." These words are just as true today. Look back at the two chapters preceding this one and see how far you have come, from service in your own home into the larger area of your own country, and then into the wider sphere of the world. Be alert to the opportunities for service around you, there is always room, always need for your help. Be well prepared, in attitude and skills, to play a leading part. That is your way of fulfilling the Scouting and Guiding belief in service, your way of meeting the Cadette Challenge of Active Citizenship (see Chapter 16). Accept and meet this Challenge willingly, courageously. It is your chance to do a good turn in a really big way.

troop

Earning your own money is a satisfying experience. When you were a Brownie or a Junior Scout, quite possibly troop dues covered all expenses of troop program. As Cadettes, your troop plans are bigger. You plan a longer troop-camping weekend, for example, or undertake a more expensive service project. The bigger your plans the more money you are likely to need.

Many troops earn the money as a group for their annual national membership dues. Do you know how this money is used? Every year your dollar is added to those of all the other members—girls and adults. It comes back to you in the form of services. Some of these are: development of special national events, the upkeep of Rockwood, publication of the *Leader* magazine, experimentation with pro-

money earning

gram ideas and equipment. Find out about your National Organization—how it works and its relation to your council and your troop.

Troop money earning means making and selling something or doing a service for which you are paid. Soliciting contributions or collecting funds is not money earning. Girls in Girl Scouting are never permitted to solicit money. In considering a money-earning project, take into account the rules and regulations of your council, the abilities of the girls in your troop, and the needs of your particular community. Be sure each girl is willing to take part in the money earning and that all parents approve.

For any troop money-earning project, the troop must have the written permission of the council. When the troop scribe applies she must explain how the money will be earned and what it will be used for. Your leader will know the exact procedure to be followed in your council. Sometimes permission is not granted. This may be because the council knows of another troop nearby doing a similar project and does not want you to fail because of the duplication. Sometimes, a project is considered unsafe or not in accordance with council rules. If your request is not granted, do not be discouraged. Plan a more suitable money-earning project, re-apply, and get to work!

Here are some suggestions to start you thinking and planning.

Sell, Show, Serve

Making things to sell is fine if you enjoy the work and are good at it. Before you decide on the product, find out whether you have the space and facilities to make it in quantity and whether people in your town would want to buy it. Instructions for making a number of things are given in this book (see illustration on page 240). Perhaps some of the following suggestions will suit your purpose.

Any good cooks in your troop? First find out what local ordinances control the sale of home-kitchen foods. If you can meet these regulations, you might enjoy making corn bread, relishes, pickles, or peach leather from recipes in the *Centennial Receipt Book* (see Bibliography).

Any green thumbs in your troop? In city or country, you could grow plants from seeds, bulbs, or cuttings and sell them when they are good size. Pretty containers will make them more saleable. In the country, you might plant a vegetable garden and sell the produce fresh, frozen, or canned.

There are things made by others you may be able to market. If you wish to sell a commercial item, you must get council permission before getting involved with a commercial firm.

How can you go about selling your products? There are two basic methods of marketing which you may use. One is to take advance orders from friends, relatives, people you know, and deliver directly to them. Whenever you take an order or make a delivery, be sure to wear your uniform or pin. Give a receipt for money collected. Always have two troop members work together. Do not enter the homes of strangers or go into strange neighborhoods. These are basic rules of safety.

Another way is to sell your product at a booth. This may be at a Girl Scout neighborhood or district bazaar where you work with other troops, or at a P.T.A. or school function such as a fair. Or a store might allow you to set up a temporary sale booth.

Curtain going up! A theatrical enterprise—a play, puppet show, musical or comedy, a pageant—are all ways of earning money and having a good time, too. Or, consider giving a carnival with sideshows and games. You may give one or more performances, for which you sell tickets. A fashion show is a good money-earning idea, too. Write to Fashion Office, *American Girl*, 830 Third Avenue, New York 22, N. Y. for a copy of *The Girl Scout Troop Stages a Fashion Show*.

You can also arrange a special exhibit of things people are interested in seeing. These may be the products of your own handiwork or a collection loaned to you. Exhibits offer three possibilities of earning money: from entry fees, admissions, and sale of exhibited items.

Other kinds of exhibits are popular, too. For example, you might consider: a community pet show, including everything from turtles to poodles. A flower show, or combine flowers, fruits and vegetables, calling it "Season's Showing." A hobby show, one that demonstrates making the things displayed.

Any entertainment, show, or exhibit needs plans for:

o A place to hold it—a school, community house, church basement, or backyard.

o A "layout." Know in advance where each item is to be placed and how the viewer may identify it. You may need to make signs.

o Publicity, before, during, after the event. You may notify local publications and make posters.

o Invitations. Do you have a mailing list of people you want to invite?

o Ticket-selling. Perhaps a special finance committee is needed?

o Judging. If there are to be ribbons or prizes, who will make the awards?

Money-earning services offer you an interesting choice of projects. Look around your community to see what may be needed. Many people may be glad to pay for services such as washing cars, mowing lawns, and weeding gardens. At spring-cleaning time, you might offer a "helping hand service," assisting housewives in your neighborhood with the furniture and silver polishing. This is a way to turn the skills you practice at home to broader use.

You might develop a group sitting service, in which several Cadettes care for a number of children at one time. This takes real planning and training. You need to arrange a place and facilities and "sitting" hours that do not interfere with your schoolwork and other interests and are convenient for the mothers.

Still another service is based on

your party-giving skills, which may enable you to organize and manage birthday parties for young children. You can arrange decorations, consult with the mothers as to refreshments, and lead the children in games and songs. You might even present a short puppet or shadow play for them.

A catering service is another good idea. Your clients may be either individuals or organizations. For example, you might undertake to prepare and serve a tea for the P.T.A. or a brunch for your troop sponsor or a buffet supper for a local club. Or your troop may initiate the idea of a special meal, a luncheon or tea to friends and neighbors. Here, you set a date and sell tickets as you would to an exhibit or show.

Any money-earning service should be performed by the troop as a whole rather than by individual girls. You must also be clear in your mind as to the difference between a service project and a money-earning service. The activity may be the same but the purpose is different. A service project is offered freely for the benefit of the recipient. A money-earning service is a business enterprise for which you are paid.

When you undertake a money-earning project, do a good job of it.

Be sure that you are giving your customers real value (in both products and services) for the money you are asking in return. This is what makes a fair exchange and a successful enterprise.

Can you think of any other ways for your troop to earn money? A city troop might offer a gift-wrapping service at holiday time, using original gift-wrap paper designed and block printed by the girls. A country troop might find a market for aprons with quiltpatch pockets or the services of a "Stir-and-Sieve Squad" at jelly-making time. Use your imagination. What can you do in your locality?

Since in most communities a troop may undertake only one money-earning project a year, it is important to think your idea through carefully. Can it be part of your regular, ongoing troop program? It should be. Are you capable of seeing the plan through? What is the purpose of the project and how will you spend the money? Are you sure all the girls are participating voluntarily? Do you have the approval and consent of all parents and a go-ahead from the council?

Remember that you will have the advice and help of adults. These will include your troop leaders, the troop committee members, and your parents. One of the fathers, for example, might be called on to give you practical hints on keeping records, handling money, and other good business procedures.

When you have completed your project, you will submit a complete report of it to a representative of your council. This report includes a financial accounting (based on records kept by the troop treasurer during the project) and the girls' evaluation of the success of the project. It is a good idea to keep a record of all aspects of your project as you go along. You will thus remember all the people the troop will want to thank for helping, and be able to look back to see where you went wrong—or right. Even if you have made a mistake or two, next time you will make fewer and you will be gratified by the experience of earning your own money for your own purposes. So allow room on your Time and Events Planning Chart for the troop money-earning project. It's a part of Cadette Girl Scouting.

let's take a trip

One fine troop meeting, someone will say, "Let's *go* somewhere!" and the planning starts. Where can you go? As Cadette Scouts, capable of organizing and doing, you have many choices. You might take a day's outing to view a museum or art gallery, to tour a farm or factory, or to visit your state capital, with time out for lunch at a restaurant. You might plan an overnight trip or one lasting several days. If it's a city trip, consider staying at a hotel, motel, or "Y." If it's a country trip, you might camp in a state or national park. With good planning, you might do some of each.

Troop tripping is a wonderful way to meet other Girl Scouts. You will enjoy making new friends, seeing what they are doing in other communities, sharing interests and ideas.

The exchange trip system is a good way to accomplish this. Your troop arranges to hostess an out-of-town troop, inviting the girls to come and stay a while. Later, the visiting troop returns the compliment. Naturally, an exchange trip must be planned carefully in advance to provide accommodations and an interesting program for all. Turnabout visits may be arranged with the help of your troop leader, friends and relatives in Girl Scouting, and, in some cases, the Girl Scout council. Sometimes, units in established camps plan and carry out a similar exchange-camping venture.

But the program is yours. Remember, your home town is new to your visitors. Entertain them in real "home style." Offer the spirit and flavor of your community. If you have regional dishes, serve them, if you have regional songs, sing them. Use your hostess plan (see Chapter 12).

Troop planning is the basis for a successful trip. As Cadette Scouts you are no longer limited to brief excursions. When you have demonstrated that patrol members can work together as a unit and as part of the troop, and have done a number of projects well, the troop is probably ready to plan a trip. If there is a new member, the girls in her patrol will help her learn her role quickly.

Of course, plans are made through the Court of Honor and in cooperation with the troop leaders and troop committee. Follow your council's requirements for applications and permissions. Be sure to keep your parents posted on the trip plans. For one thing, you will need their permission to go. For another, your parents may contribute greatly to the planning. They may suggest places for you to visit and may know people who can make your trip more eventful.

To start your planning, consult "Steps in Planning" (page 34) and "Inside Outing" (page 155). The first will be useful in the earlier planning stages. The second covers many essential travel details and will help you to plot your course systematically. Then consider the following trip tips.

Planning a budget is basic. Be sure to provide money to cover: transportation, sleeping accommodations, food, insurance, recreation, admission fees, and an emergency fund.

Packing is a skill, and so is the ability to select a minimum of clothing and accessories. Your uniform is a good traveler and should be worn whenever you are in public view.

Simple clothes and comfortable walking shoes are best on trips. Drip-dry materials, fabrics that resist wrinkles, and basic styles pack well and stay neat and good looking. Choose clothes and accessories that mix and match. This will give you more changes with fewer things. Label all your belongings with your name.

If your trip is longer than two days, shop for such conveniences as hangers that inflate, detergents in envelopes, braided elastic clothesline. Before trip day, have a "patrol packing party," to practice folding and packing clothes neatly.

Seeing the sights is more fun when you learn something of your destination in advance—its history, arts, showplaces. Advance knowledge helps you to see the things that interest you most, saves precious trip time.

Always allow time for rest stops, and keep to the curfew hour agreed upon. No matter how exciting the trip, take time out for proper meals.

"*P's and Q's* are always important, but especially on a trip when others are minding your manners. Consider yourself an ambassador from your council and conduct yourself accordingly.

Always look your well groomed best.

Keep with the group, and stick to the plan.

If you are uncertain about etiquette, consult a book on the subject. Tipping customs vary in different parts of the country, so no single rule can be given but a smile and courteous "thank you" is proper accompaniment for a tip everywhere.

Girl Scouts love to sing but choose an appropriate time and place. It is not correct to sing in a public place where other people may be disturbed. Like all good manners, travel manners are based on inconspicuous behavior, quiet bearing, and dignity. You have only to honor the Promise and Laws and you will be acting with good sense and consideration.

Stops for Girl Scouts

Girl Scout National Headquarters: This handsome building, center of Girl Scout administration, is at 830 Third Avenue, between 50th and 51st Street, New York City. During business hours (9:00 A.M. to 5:00 P.M., Monday through Friday,) you may tour the offices. Write in advance for an appointment.

Juliette Low's Birthplace is the charming house where Daisy spent a happy girlhood. Now owned and maintained by the Girl Scouts of the U.S.A., it is filled with mementos, family portraits, Juliette's paintings and handwork, elegant chandeliers, the graceful furniture of the day. Pomegranates and banana shrubs, camellias and pecans grow in the formal garden. In May and June, magnolias blossom lavishly. If you are vacationing with your family, visit the Birthplace. If your troop plans a trip, write first to: Director, The Juliette Gordon Low Birthplace, 142 Bull Street, Savannah, Georgia.

Rockwood National Girl Scout Camp has been called "every Girl Scout's home away from home." It is a year-'round hostel and camping center near Washington, D. C., offering 95 acres of magnificent woodland, primitive camping areas, winter lodges, sleeping accommodations, and facilities for coeducational and Girl Scout family camping, as well as troop camping. Here you can take part in special projects, visit nearby historical landmarks, and meet Girl Scouts from all parts of the country and the world. Members of other youth organizations, such as the 4-H and the Boy Scouts, are welcome, too. For information and reservations, write: Director, Rockwood National Girl Scout Camp, 11001 MacArthur Boulevard, Potomac, Maryland.

Note: Requests for information, appointments, or reservations at all three places should be made by *one* representative of your troop.

Round Trip Ticket

A trip is an adventure, an experience in sight and sound, places and people, flavors and colors. You see things you've never seen before. Learn about them; ask questions. Looking is only part of the fun. Get into the spirit of the trip!

If you are in pecan country, try the pecan pie. In clam chowder country, sample the soup. If something is new to you, don't shy away from it. Explore it. This applies not only to food but to people and customs. Let people know you're interested in their ways. One of the greatest joys of travel is the chance to see and understand things that are different from your own. Respect and enjoy these differences, for they lend variety and enrichment to your life.

Whenever you go, whatever you do, take enthusiasm, curiosity, and friendliness along. Make the most of your trip. Use your eyes *and* your heart as you travel.

Home again! You've kept a diary of the trip, made sketches, taken photographs, collected souvenirs. You're ready to report your impressions and adventures of the trip to the folks at home.

It may be a written report or a prepared talk. But it's more creative and lively to "show" your trip. Set up an exhibit of pictures, with captions describing them. Or present an original play or skit, dramatizing things you saw and did. Invite family and friends, members of the troop committee, possibly someone from your neighborhood service team. You will have the fun of doing; your audience will have the fun of viewing.

After several trips, you may be asked to help a troop with less travel practice. Share your knowledge. You might demonstrate packing techniques or dining car procedures, teach a good game to play on the way, or help with the planning, particularly on the budgeting of time and money.

Experience will convince you that good trips depend on good planning. Budget your time and money. Organize activities. Get set for a glorious time!

WHAT ARE THE CHALLENGES?

Challenges are real-life situations that test your abilities in many ways. There are four Challenges—Social Dependability, Emergency Preparedness, Active Citizenship, and the Girl Scout Promise—each one different and all exciting. They are the steps to becoming a First Class Girl Scout. Challenges are the life and spirit, the high points of your Cadette Girl Scouting career.

the challenges

WHEN CAN YOU START?

It is possible to begin preparing for Challenges as soon as you become a Cadette Scout. Activities which especially interest you, whether in "Program Starters" or badges, plus your troop's plans will point the way toward the Challenge Preps you choose to undertake first. The first three Challenges must be met before you work on the Challenge of the Girl Scout Promise.

HOW DO YOU WORK?

Usually you work with a group of from three to eight girls, planning, sharing, organizing, and accomplishing together. Sometimes an entire patrol becomes a Challenge Group. In some special cases you may seek the cooperation of friends or other troops. Follow the framework for each Challenge as given in this chapter. The Promise and Laws are fundamental to all the Challenges.

HOW LONG WILL IT TAKE?

Each Challenge takes at least six months, including badge work and the Challenge Preps. Challenges are not easy. If you attempt a Challenge but do not successfully meet it, you can try again at another time.

WHEN WILL YOU BE READY TO ACCEPT A CHALLENGE?

When you have successfully completed the Challenge Preps, you will be ready to accept the Challenge itself. Some Challenge Preps you may have learned as part of a badge, or a troop or camp project, or at home or school. Others will be new to you and must be learned from the beginning. It is up to you to keep accurate records of your progress in Challenge Preps as you may be called on at any time to demonstrate your knowledge to your leaders and the other girls in your troop.

WHAT WILL YOUR CHALLENGE BE?

When you have proved that you are ready to accept it, the Challenge itself will be given to you by your leader. This may be a complete sur- prise to you, as in case of the Challenge of Emergency Preparedness when your leader hands you your "sealed orders." Or, it may be that your leader has chosen one Challenge from several ideas submitted by the Challenge Group or suggested by the Court of Honor. Whatever the Challenge, attempting to meet it is certain to include the excitement and suspense of things untried and waiting to be conquered!

HOW WILL YOU KNOW WHEN YOU HAVE SUCCESSFULLY MET A CHALLENGE?

This will be decided by the girls in your Challenge Group, by your troop leaders, and by you. The Challenge of the Girl Scout Promise will also involve the Court of Honor. Using the purpose and evaluation for each Challenge as a guide, you will discuss, evaluate, and decide together. The evaluation covers the Challenge Preps as well as the Challenge itself. As you meet each Challenge, you will receive its insigne—and when you have earned the necessary six badges and completed all four Challenges, you will become a First Class Girl Scout.

the challenge
of social dependability

Can you prove yourself to be a gracious, competent hostess and also a considerate, friendly guest?

PURPOSE:

To show that you have the understanding and skills to get along well with people—older and younger, family and friends, boys and girls, those you already know and new people—and that you can bring them enjoyment and happiness in a social situation.

CHALLENGE PREPS:

Prepare for this Challenge by developing three aspects of your personal life—Health and Good Looks, Know-How as a Hostess, Technique as a Guest.

1. YOUR HEALTH-AND-GOOD-LOOKS PLAN

Develop and follow a personal health and appearance plan that keeps you attractive and fit. Include in your plan the following:

	DATE PLAN STARTED	RESULTS (CHECK ONE) EXCELLENT	GOOD	FAIR
The right kinds and amounts of food to keep you feeling and looking fine.				
Enough fresh air and exercise to keep you feeling vigorous.				
Enough sleep to keep you wide-awake and energetic all day.				
A system of daily care for your hair, skin, nails, and teeth.				
The use of makeup, hair styles, clothes, colors, and accessories most becoming and appropriate to you.				
Practice in the development of a pleasant speaking voice, a pleasant manner.				
Application of good posture habits for good health and good looks.				

2. YOUR KNOW-HOW AS A HOSTESS

Develop the attitudes and skills that make you a gracious, competent hostess. Check to be sure you know how to do the following:

	CIRCUMSTANCE OR PLACE	DATE
Extend invitations appropriate to a variety of social events.		
Plan and arrange an attractive setting in harmony with the spirit or theme of the occasion.		
Plan a menu, shop for food and supplies, help to prepare the food, set the table attractively, and organize the service for at least four of these occasions:		
A family meal.		
A buffet luncheon or supper.		
A party for young children.		
An out-of-door meal.		
A teenage party.		
An event for a larger group, such as a troop supper.		

DATE	CIRCUMSTANCE OR PLACE

Make a plan which is detailed but flexible, with ideas for alternative activities if they are needed, for a party for:

Younger children.

A group your own age.

Parents and adult friends.

Establish guides of etiquette as to chaperons, curfew hour, and so forth, and convey these rules tactfully to your guests.

Help your guests have a good time through your understanding of their tastes, interests, personalities.

Welcome guests hospitably, and say a cordial "Good night and come again."

Organize and direct songs, games, and quiet fun with a group of younger children.

Help produce an informal dramatic presentation.

Organize at least two mixers, two games or contests, one folk dance, one square dance, one social dance.

3. YOUR TECHNIQUE AS A GUEST

Discuss the obligations and responsibilities every good guest has to the hostess and all others at a social event. Check to see that you can be counted on:

	SOMETIMES	OFTEN	ALMOST ALWAYS
o For your good manners. Do you:			
Reply promptly and correctly to invitations?			
Write thank-you notes?			
Respond properly to introductions?			
Reply gracefully to compliments?			
Offer sincere compliments?			
Greet and take leave of your hostess courteously?			
o To start and keep up your part of a pleasant conversation with:			
Girls and boys your age.			
Parents, troop leaders, other adults.			
Younger children.			
VIP's (very important people).			
o To enter enthusiastically into the party plans and contribute your own ideas when asked			
o To be agreeable to:			
Other guests.			
Parents, family, other adults.			
Household help, if any.			
Younger brothers and sisters.			
o To forget yourself, think of others, and help them to have an enjoyable time.			

The Challenge

With others in the Challenge Group, plan and carry out a social event from start to finish!

The Evaluation This checklist will help you, your leader, and the other girls decide how well you have met the Challenge of Social Dependability.

CHECK ONE:			
YES	NO	SO-SO	
			Are your spirits and energies high?
			Do you always look as well as you can?
			At the social event:
			Did you help to make each guest feel liked and welcome?
			Did you give each guest a chance to shine and share in the success of the occasion?
			Was there an activity or series of activities appropriate to the guests and the occasion?
			If food was served:
			Did it look good?
			Taste good?
			Was there enough to go around?
			Was it attractively served?
			Was it comfortably served?
			Did everybody, guests and hostesses, have a good time?

Check the list, then check again. How did you do? Reread the Purpose. Have you met the Challenge of Social Dependability successfully? Or would you like to try it again, giving another social event for another group? It's up to you to decide.

the challenge of emergency preparedness

Can you be depended on to help others in an emergency through quick, sure use of your knowledge and skills?

PURPOSE

To show that you have a good command of the knowledge and skills needed for safe, comfortable living, both indoors and out; that you can get along with a minimum of equipment; that you are enterprising, resourceful; that you can put your skills to good use in an emergency.

CHALLENGE PREPS

Prepare for this Challenge by checking your knowledge and skills in these four areas: First Aid, Communications, Comfort in a Crisis, Enterprise in Entertainment. Use the checklists on the following pages. Just before accepting the Challenge, discuss with the members of your group and your leader the purpose and the kinds of emergencies that might possibly arise in your part of the country. Take into consideration the geography, weather and local conditions.

1. FIRST AID

DATE COMPLETED

Learn or review the objectives of first
aid as outlined in the American
National Red Cross *First Aid Textbook* for each of the following. Keep a
record of when you practiced what to
do in each case. Be prepared to
demonstrate.

Wounds. _____

Shock. _____

Artificial respiration. _____

Poisoning by mouth. _____

Injuries to bones and muscles. _____

Burns. _____

Transporting injured persons. _____

Decide what supplies should go into
the following types of first aid kits,
and, if you do not already have a kit,
help plan and assemble at least one
for your:

Family car. _____

Troop meeting place. _____

Patrol expeditions. _____

Troop camping trips. _____

Consider the hazards young children
may be subjected to in the home. List
at least twenty-five and explain what
should be done to protect against
these hazards. _____

2. COMMUNICATIONS

	LEARNED OR REVIEWED	PRACTICED		
		1	2	3
Demonstrate that you can:				
Use a compass. _____				
Find the North Star. _____				
Draw a sketch map. _____				
Follow a road map and a city street map. _____				
Give directions. _____				
Carry a message accurately in your head. _____				
Using Scout's pace or bicycle, know how to reach the nearest: Police station. _____				
Fire alarm box. _____				
Public telephone. _____				
Develop and use a communication plan to reach all your troop members with speed. _____				

3. COMFORT IN A CRISIS

	LEARNED OR REVIEWED	PRACTICED		
		1	2	3
Demonstrate the safe and resourceful use of:				
Candles.				
Kerosene lamps.				
Lanterns.				
Improvised cooking facilities.				
Fire for warmth.				
Fire for cooking.				
Wash and store dishes, silverware, and cooking utensils in an efficient and sanitary way:				
Indoors.				
Outdoors.				
Using only packaged supplies feed your patrol or family:				
Breakfast.				
Lunch.				
Dinner.				

	LEARNED OR REVIEWED	PRACTICED		
		1	2	3
Know one method to purify water for drinking. ____				
Demonstrate your ability to: Handle simple household upkeep and repairs indoors and outdoors. ____				
Plan, assemble, pack, and transport heavy-duty clothing for yourself for 3 or 4 days. ____				
Choose the items (including food) needed for an emergency utility kit for a 3 or 4 day evacuation of home or camp. ____				

4.●ENTERPRISE IN ENTERTAINMENT

	LEARNED OR REVIEWED	PRACTICED		
		1	2	3
Using games, stories, crafts, and simple dramatics, demonstrate you can keep young children occupied In a confined indoor area. ____				
Outdoors. ____				
Do the same thing for people your own age and older. ____				

The Challenge

Carry out the sealed orders given to you by your leader!

You will be asked to deal with a specific emergency described for the occasion. Here are some examples of the kinds of emergencies you may meet:

8 girls—outdoors: A flood has left many families on your street temporarily homeless. Your patrol is asked to provide a hot meal and drinking water for four families and to take care of ten children (from four to eight years) for the afternoon.

2-4 girls—indoors: An ice storm has caused an electric power failure. Your family consists of your father, who is away at work, your mother, who has a severe cold and should be in bed, and a younger sister and brother. The furnace is not working. The kitchen stove is electric. There is a fireplace in the living room. Take charge for a day. Provide lunch and dinner. Make your mother comfortable. Keep the children warm and happy. Use anything found in the house, basement, garage, outdoors.

6-8 girls, out-of-doors, camp: The buses that take the girls home from day camp cannot get through to them. A forest fire is blocking the bus route. Most of the camp staff have gone to help the fire-fighters. Your patrol is assigned the job of keeping the 32 girls of the Junior Scout unit busy and happy from 2:00 P.M. to 6:30 P.M. They will need a calm atmosphere to counteract the excitement of the day, planned activities, and supper.

Evaluation Could you turn your wish to help into practical, useful action? Were you prepared? Did you meet your emergency?

the challenge of active citizenship

A citizen is a person who by birth or by choice is a member of a state or nation. Do you recognize your rights and responsibilities as a citizen of the United States of America?

PURPOSE

To show that you understand how the rights of citizenship are balanced by the responsibilities, and how you can use this knowledge for the benefit of other people.

CHALLENGE PREPS

With a Challenge Group, review your background information, ponder your past experiences, and bring into focus your training for good citizenship by getting answers to the questions on the following pages.

HOW, WHERE, AND WHEN YOU FOUND AN ANSWER

_____
_____
_____
_____
_____
_____
_____
_____
_____
_____
_____
_____
_____
_____
_____
_____
_____
_____
_____
_____
_____
_____
_____
_____
_____
_____

1. On the basis of your experience in Girl Scout troops and camps, what do you think is needed to make the patrol system operate smoothly?

2. Using a recent student project or concern as an illustration, can you explain how the democratic process works in your school?

3. What is the purpose of local government? What is the governmental structure of your town? Your state?

4. What services are provided by government and voluntary agencies in your community for:

o Handicapped children?
o The aged?
o Teenagers?
o The emotionally disturbed?

5. How is the money raised to support these services?

6. When you want to make a constructive suggestion for the improvement of your town, how do you go about it? What steps would you take if some members of your troop:

o Wished to set up a display or exhibit in a public library?
o Were responsible for arranging for the use of a public school for a Cadette "Look Wide"?

o Wanted to use public land for an intertroop cookout?

_____

_____

7. What are the names and proper forms of address of those who represent you in your state government? In the United States House of Representatives? In the United States Senate?

_____

_____

_____

_____

_____

8. What local and state controversial public issues seem most important to you?

_____

_____

_____

9. What positions in public life at the national, state, or local level now being filled by women seem most interesting to you? What are the qualifications for five of these jobs?

_____

_____

_____

_____

_____

10. In what specific ways can citizens your age demonstrate the qualities of good citizenship in daily living?

_____

_____

_____

11. How can you, either individually or as a troop, through Girl Scout or other organizations:

_____

_____

_____

o Correspond with people from other countries?

_____

o Entertain foreign visitors?

o Give help to people in other countries?

_____

o Receive or exhange information, ideas, or techniques leading to increased international understanding?

_____

_____

_____

The Challenge

Do something for your community in which you give something of yourself. The Challenge Group compiles a list from which your leader will select one. Discover how it might be done and whether anyone else is trying to do it. Then do something about it. Show the relationship of the project you have chosen to the larger community —the state, the nation, or the world.

The Challenge Preps will give you good clues as to where your services may be helpful. Other troop members may participate in the project, but the leadership and follow-through are in the hands of the girls who are working to meet the Challenge. If another organization is concerned with the same need, consider the possibility of combining forces, working together, and doing a bigger and better job. Make a long-term plan for carrying your project through to successful completion. For help in planning, see Chapter 3, page 34.

Evaluation As a Cadette Girl Scout, you understand that service to others is a vital part of Girl Scouting. The Promise you make, the uniform you wear, your badges and insignia, all say, "I am willing and prepared to be of service." Has your citizenship project turned the ideal into a reality for you? How well did your project fulfill the purpose of the Challenge of Active Citizenship?

the challenge of the girl scout promise

This Challenge is the final step toward First Class. Your success in meeting it will be decided by you and all the members of the Court of Honor, rather than only by the troop leader and the Challenge Group, as in the other three Challenges.

PURPOSE

To show you that you have a true understanding of the Girl Scout Promise and its meaning in your daily life; that you are guided by its high standards in relation to yourself and to all other people; that it serves as an ever present guide to you in beliefs and conduct. This Challenge is different, for you began to prepare for it the moment you became a Girl Scout. The first three Challenges test your knowledge, skills, and experience. This Challenge searches your mind and heart, your feelings and attitudes, to discover whether the Girl Scout Promise has become part of you, part of everything you do.

You can see the difference between this Challenge and the others. It is much easier to evaluate your skill in baking a pie or storm-lashing a tent than it is to evaluate your qualities as a person of integrity. It takes time, it takes a sense of values, it takes courage and honesty to learn to live up to the Promise. In some ways, you may find this harder than mastering any specific skill. But the rewards are greater. They are conviction and inner strength, spiritual accomplishments which enrich your life and the lives of everyone around you.

There are no Challenge Preps as such for this Challenge. However, here are two suggestions for you to show the impact that the Girl Scout Promise has made upon you.

One. With others, make up a list of ten or twelve kinds of situations that girls your age meet in which there may be conflicting opinions about the truly ethical way to act. Discuss with the others how your understanding of the Girl Scout Promise helps you decide how to rise to the occasion with honor.

Two. Take an active part in planning and carrying out a Scouts' Own which highlights the ways in which the Girl Scout Promise helps you decide how to act.

After you have completed the other requirements for First Class by earning a minimum of six badges and suc-cessfully meeting the three other Challenges, make application to your troop's Court of Honor. At a meeting which you do not attend, the Court of Honor will decide—on the basis of your everyday actions in and out of Scouting—whether you are ready to accept this Challenge. It will consider the following points:

o Have you demonstrated a real understanding of the Promise and Laws?

o Have you applied this understanding in day-to-day living and thinking?

o Have you shown that you are capable of working, planning, sharing with a group?

o Have you shown through action and attitude, your personal integrity and honor?

Meanwhile, prepare yourself to answer all the questions below. After the Court of Honor has agreed that you are ready to accept the Challenge, you will be asked to answer or demonstrate, alone or with others, one, a few, or all of these questions. You may be confronted with this Challenge at a troop meeting or before the Court of

Honor alone. The Court of Honor will determine how this will be handled.

1. Explain the difference between a movement, an organization, and an institution. Why do you think you join a movement when you become a Girl Scout? Why do you think adult members as well as girls subscribe to the Girl Scout Promise?

2. What is the role of women in the religious group of your choice? What are its marriage customs? What are the purposes and activities of the women's organizations in this group?

3. Explain how the idea for a mean- ingful service project starts, grows, and changes from the Brownie age, through the Junior, Cadette, and Senior age. What service projects in which you have taken part seemed especially satisfying to you? Why?

4. Explain how a ceremony in a troop or camp can convey your feelings about duty to God and your country, and your pledge to be a good citizen. In what way do you think feelings differ as experienced by participants and members of the audience at such a ceremony? Describe an especially satisfactory ceremony in which you have taken part.

The Challenge

Show that you understand and practice the Girl Scout Promise in everything you do and are.

There are no quick and easy short-cuts to successfully meeting the Challenge of the Girl Scout Promise, and no one else can do it for you. For this reason when the time arrives for you and your troop members to recognize that you have achieved that inner strength, that priceless ingredient of your life, you may be justifiably proud. It may be that your Court of Honor will wish to make the meeting especially memorable by planning a special feature for it.

As you successfully meet the Challenge of the Girl Scout Promise, you will become a First Class Girl Scout and a first class person of whom the entire movement will be proud!

To jog your memory in days to come,
Write a few lines of what you've done.

My First Class Record

PROFICIENCY BADGES

Arts

_____

Home

_____

Citizenship

_____

Out-of-doors

_____

Health and Safety

_____

International Friendship

_____

*I,*_____
*completed First Class on*_____
*received First Class insigne on*_____

CHALLENGES

Social Dependability_____

_____
LEADER'S SIGNATURE   DATE

Emergency Preparedness_____

_____
LEADER'S SIGNATURE   DATE

Active Citizenship_____

_____
LEADER'S SIGNATURE   DATE

Girl Scout Promise_____

_____
LEADER'S SIGNATURE   DATE

FLOWERS
ME. MANNING

CADETTE CAREER CLINIC

wider opportunities

One of the great joys of being a Girl Scout is that you always have good company. In your troop, you are at home with your family of sister Scouts. Together, you learn and practice skills, plan and do things. You know the fun and pride of accomplishment, not only as an individual but as part of the troop.

In camp and home, Cadette Scouts join with other troops and groups, to plan and do on a larger scale than ever before. You will enjoy activities beyond your troop or neighborhood which give you a chance to meet

many people and work as a useful member of a big team doing a big job.

Enjoying activities with large groups of other Cadettes is a way of moving into a wider world than you have known, of broadening your knowledge, and strengthening your abilities. It is a way of understanding the deepest values of Girl Scouting.

One way to start things moving is to invite another troop to a special event. For example, if your troop is giving a play, you might ask a nearby troop to join your audience. Or give a gala intertroop performance! If you're planning a ceremony of great interest, you might ask a Junior Scout troop to come. In either case, your troop is hostess to the visitors.

Another good intertroop activity is an event planned by your troop and another. This could be a Look-Wide as described on page 233 or a community service project, such as Operation Deep Freeze on page 85. Or, with another troop, you might arrange for a program consultant, plan an appropriate activity for Girl Scout Week, or create an original troop birthday celebration. Working together, you can develop more ambitious projects, such as a conservation project in your community or a neighborhood play area for children.

And you will find truth in the old saying "The more the merrier."

Your council, too, provides opportunities for activities which make it possible for girls to come together, to meet, work, and share experiences. Such opportunities might include courses in first aid and life saving. Girls with musical interests and abilities should look into chorus or orchestra activities. At day and established camps, or when trip camping, there are days filled with sports and outdoor activities.

Your council may also offer the opportunity to plan and execute events with other groups. Girls who have reached First Class may be asked to serve on planning committees. Pageants, rallies, special celebrations are possibilities for planning on a really large scale.

Sometimes, the council brings girls together to plan a particular program or event. For example, you might be invited to join representatives from several troops to work out an interesting way to collect money for the Juliette Low World Friendship Fund.

Girls working together on such a "thinking cap committee," may hold a single meeting or a series of meetings. When the event is over, the committee is disbanded. When a new event arises, a new committee is formed to plan and see it through. Since "thinking cap committees" are temporary, a great many girls may look forward to the opportunity of serving on one. But there are some permanent committees, too, that you may be asked to join.

Still another activity that may be offered by your council is a meeting that girls and troop leaders attend. A good example of this is a patrol leaders workshop, where patrol leaders and troop leaders exchange ideas, ask questions, and benefit from each other's experiences.

Intercouncil events, too, offer many chances to work and play with other troops—exchange and trip camping, primitive encampments, and special events, such as an arts festival or a dramatics workshop.

There is almost no end to the variety of large specialized events that might be developed just for Cadettes in your neighborhood or council, although only one or two events would be evolved in any given year. Were you one of a group that especially enjoyed meeting the Challenge of Social Dependability? You may find yourself on the planning committee for a winter carnival. Perhaps the stylist who visited your troop

when you were earning the Good Grooming Badge can offer downtown facilities and a large Good Grooming clinic can be launched. If your patrol met the Challenge of Active Citizenship with particular verve, wit and imagination, you might be asked to help at an all day conference for Cadettes preparing to meet Challenges.

When you think of your future, do you dream of certain exciting fields of work? You will have some facts to build those dreams if vocational exploration is the theme for the next large event for Cadette Scouts.

Have you recently held a successful and inspiring ceremony in your troop —a Scouts' Own or a Rededication? Your troop may be asked to share its ideas and the techniques at a Promise and Laws conference for Cadettes.

All these large events should reflect the activities of Cadette troops. The availability of these big events depends upon the willingness and ability of girls to carry them out. Find out the events offered in your council and take advantage of them. Know how you can make requests or offer suggestions to your council. To make wider opportunities really happen is the responsibility of each Cadette Girl Scout.

on to
senior scouting

It's here at last!

This bright day is an occasion for you, one you will always remember. For this is the day you are formally welcomed into a Senior Girl Scout troop. Kinds of welcoming ceremonies are many and varied but one of the most impressive is the capping ceremony. Whatever the ceremony, it is planned by the Seniors themselves, in honor of you and all the other graduating Cadette Scouts and the Girl Scout movement.

There may be many people in the audience, for Senior capping ceremonies are generally held on a neighborhood scale. In addition to friends and family, all Cadette Girl Scouts may be invited.

Your Senior troop may choose the *Panorama* plan, combining a wide variety of indoor and outdoor activities and interests. Or, your troop may choose any one of eight major interests. In addition to Panorama, Senior Scouting's Wheel of Opportunities includes: *Arts* for activities in dramatics, writing, music, or the visual arts; *Community Action* for the satisfaction of being an active force in the life of your community; *Homemaker* for adventuring in food, fashion, interior decorating, home management; *International Friendship* for exploration of people and cultures of other lands; *Mariner* for water skills and sports; *Mounted* for activities on horseback; *TrailBlazer* for camping, hiking, woodcraft, nature; natural science; *Wing* for airborne explorations and the new dimensions of the "space age."

When you are a Senior Scout, your life is filled with action. In addition to troop activities, Seniors have any number of individual opportunities coming their way. You may be troop representative on a Senior Planning Board. You may work with other Seniors at a Senior Conference. You may take part in adult meetings in your council, or at a regional conference, or national convention.

Individual training opportunities are a part of Senior Girl Scouting, too. One, called Leader-in-Training (LIT), teaches you to become a leader in a troop. Another, called Counselor-in-Training (CIT), teaches you to become a counselor in a camp. Service Aide training opens the door to the vocation in your future.

As a small girl, what was it you wanted to be when you grew up?

Have you changed your mind since then and decided upon another career? Would you like to give service to a nurse, teacher, or librarian? Would you rather work in a museum, a department store, or a laboratory? Are you interested in helping handicapped people, working in some phase of public relations, or caring for animals? Senior Service Aide Projects cover these and more. Here are the names: Aquatic Safety Aide, Child Care Aide, Aide to Handicapped Persons, Hospital Aide, International Aide, Laboratory Aide, Office Aide, Merchandising Aide, Museum Aide, Program Aide, Public Relations Aide, Ranger Aide, Library Aide, Teachers Aide, Animal Care Aide.

Start now to prepare for national and international opportunities open to Senior Scouts. Although these events vary from year to year, they are alike in one respect. They are among the most satisfying experiences in Girl Scouting. A Senior Girl Scout representative to any national or international event must be:

o An active, registered member of a Senior Girl Scout troop at the time of the event.

o Able to meet the age requirement and any special requirements for a particular event, such as experience as a camper, facility in another language, proficiency in a specific art or skill.

o In excellent physical condition and willing to have a medical examination and immunizations if needed.

o Endorsed wholeheartedly by her troop members and troop adviser.

o Experienced in the patrol system.

o Able to express ideas, to participate well in discussions.

o Able to adapt quickly to changed plans or unforeseen situations.

o Experienced as an active participant in worthwhile service projects.

o Experienced in sharing program skills with others.

o Able to interpret her own community, region, and country.

o Able to interpret clearly the Girl Scout organization, both local and national.

o Willing to continue her interest in Girl Scouting for at least two more years.

So you see, becoming a Senior Scout means growing up not only in Scouting but in the world beyond.

If you want to know more about choosing from the Wheel of Opportunities, ask Senior Scouts to help you. You might invite some Seniors to a troop meeting to tell you about their experiences. Or have an S.O.S.S. (Survey of Senior Scouting) project with girls in your troop assigned to find out about different phases of Senior Scouting. And if you're invited to see Seniors in action—go!

Congratulations

Now that you are 15, you are ready for Senior Scouting's Wheel of Opportunities and all it has to offer you. You are cordially invited to become a

Senior Girl Scout

INTERNATIONAL

SENIOR PLANNING BOARD

SERVICE AIDES

HOMEMAKER

MOUNTED

MARINER

INTERNATIONAL FRIENDSHIP

WING

PANORAMA

ARTS

COMMUNITY ACTION

TRAILBLAZER

AND

NATIONAL

SENIOR CONFERENCES

OPPORTUNITIES

LIT

CIT

proficiency badges for

A Girl Scout proficiency badge "is a symbol that a girl has done the thing it stands for often enough, thoroughly enough, and well enough to be prepared to give service in it." This description of a badge is as true of Cadette badges today as it was when written by Juliette Low many years ago.

You may begin working on any badge in this *Handbook* as soon as you become a Cadette Girl Scout. How will you decide which badge to select? Reading the purpose stated at the beginning of each badge will help you. Perhaps a badge sounds interesting as you read the requirements. Possibly you want to learn more about an activity you tried in Program Starters. Maybe you want to try something entirely new. Or you may wish to earn a particular badge to complete a Challenge Prep or to meet the requirements for First Class. Whatever the reason for your selection, the list on page 283 shows you the wide variety of badges from which you may choose. Once you have narrowed your choice to two or three, talk it over with your troop leader or camp counselor before making a decision.

You must successfully complete each requirement in order to earn a Cadette badge. Refer to the purpose of the badge as you work; it will help you keep your eye on your goal. As you complete each

cadettes

requirement, whether at troop meeting, camp, or any other place, the person helping you should sign her name and the date in the space next to it. It is up to you to be sure your *Handbook* is available at all times in order to keep your record accurate and up to date.

The three requirements to be filled in by you when you answer the three open-end questions are a special feature of each Cadette badge. An open-end question is one for which there is *no one right answer*. Your answers will depend upon your own experiences as you meet the other requirements of the badge. These are the three questions:

1. *Service.* In what way was I able to use the skills learned to be of service to others?
2. *Health and safety.* What health and safety factors were important?
3. *Promise and Laws.* By my actions and attitudes, how did I demonstrate my understanding of the Girl Scout Promise and Laws?

When you have completed all the requirements, look once again at the purpose of the badge. Do you in truth think you have accomplished the purpose? If so, at this point you and your leader together will evaluate your progress and decide whether you are entitled to wear the badge symbol.

It is impossible to say exactly how much time you will need to complete any specific badge. A great deal depends upon you, the facilities available to you, your consultant, and your past experience. Earning proficiency badges gives you a chance to increase your skills and ability in a particular subject and have fun at the same time. Be sure to allow enough time to complete each requirement with real satisfaction. When you become particularly interested in a subject, seize the opportunity to learn more than is asked by the requirements. If there are people who are outstanding in the field, take time right then to find out who they are and what they have done.

Use the Bibliography and Index in this book to help you find material on your chosen subject. Your leader, badge consultant, and librarian will also help you find resources. Look in the *American Girl* and other magazines.

Where do you work on badges? You may be at troop meeting, at camp, or working with a consultant. Usually you work with other girls as you earn badges. However, you may have an interest or ability not shared by other members of the troop and will work on a badge alone. In that case you should make a special effort to use the skills you acquire to add to the fun of activities all troop members can enjoy.

You will receive the badges you have earned at a Court of Awards. Remember that the little piece of embroidered material you wear on your badge sash is not important in itself. You wear the badge to tell everyone that you are prepared and willing to be of service— that *is* important.

Wear your Cadette Girl Scout badges with pride—the pride of confidence in your ability to be of service with sure skill, the pride of proficiency.

Animal Kingdom
Aviation
Campcraft
Ceramics and Pottery
Chef
Child Care
Clerk
Conservation
Creative Writer
Dressmaker
Explorer
Family Camper
Family Living
First Aid
First Aid to Animals
Folk Dancer
Food Raiser
Games Leader
Good Grooming
Graphic Arts
Handywoman
Hiker
Homemaker
Home Nurse
Horsewoman
Hostess
Interior Decoration
Language
Life Saver
Metal Arts

Minstrel
Music Maker
My Country
My Government
Outdoor Safety
Painting
Photography
Pioneer
Plant Kingdom
Player-Producer
Public Health
Puppeteer
Radio and Television
Reader
Reporter
Rock and Mineral
Science
Small Craft
Social Dancer
Sports
Stamp Collector
Star
Swimmer
Textile Arts
Traveler
Weather
World Heritage
World Trefoil
World Understanding
Our Own Troop's

Animal Kingdom

Purpose: To find out, firsthand, as much as you can about one category of animal life.

1. Choose one of the following categories: Birds. Insects. Mammals. Reptiles and amphibians. Water life. Find out as much as you can about the species in your locality by reading, observing and talking with others.

2. Be able to identify some of the species by their size, shape, color, and other distinguishing marks. Learn about their habits, life cycle, diet, ways of protecting themselves, their calls, how they reproduce and care for their young.

3. Visit a zoo, pet shop, or any place you can see your category being cared for and fed.

4. Make something to attract, protect, or observe your category.

5. Know the state and federal laws that protect animal life, and find out if any species in your category are in danger of extinction. Be able to explain how your category is of value to man.

6. Discover some of the local and national organizations that are concerned with the protection of animal life. Enlist the help of one organization in carrying out a troop project. OR Tell what several people in this field have done to interest others in animals.

7. Make a chart, diorama, or other form of exhibit to show other people some of the information you gathered while working on this badge.

8. Service

9. Health and safety

10. Promise and Laws

MY SIGNATURE   DATE COMPLETED   LEADER'S SIGNATURE

Bird

....
DATE

....
LEADER'S SIGNATURE

Insect

....
DATE

....
LEADER'S SIGNATURE

Mammal

....
DATE

....
LEADER'S SIGNATURE

Water Life

....
DATE

....
LEADER'S SIGNATURE

Reptile and Amphibian

....
DATE

....
LEADER'S SIGNATURE

Aviation

Purpose: To get first-hand experience in the "airman's world" and to explore its dramatic impact on daily living.

1. Outline a brief history on aviation and space exploration. Begin a picture and data file on aircraft and aviation organizations. List resource people and materials in your community. ....

2. Take a guided tour of an airport. Make a model of an airport, a glider, or an airplane. ....

3. Name major parts of an airplane. Define functions of: fuselage, aileron, elevator, rudder, trim tabs, flaps, vertical stabilizer. Identify a glider, helicopter, light single-engine and twin-engine airplane, seaplane, a turboprop and turbojet two or four engine transport. ....

4. Explain some of the uses of airplanes and helicopters. Give three detailed examples. ....

5. Describe some of the ways in which the Federal Government and State Aeronautics Commissions promote civil aviation. Know FAA requirements for a private pilot's license; age when one can solo a glider and airplane. Find out about the work women are doing in aero-space industry. ....

6. Pack a parachute or convert one into a tent. Describe its numerous uses in personal safety. Explain "sky-diving" — observe a meet if possible. OR Make a poster-type chart of safety regulations that must be observed around small aircraft. ....

7. Explain importance of weather knowledge to a pilot. Interpret an aviation weather report; tell how a pilot gets the information. OR Earn the Weather badge. ....

8. Study an aeronautical chart noting aircraft facilities, radio stations, and navigation aids. OR Make a list of navigational and communication aids, ground and air, available to the pilot. ....

9. Service.. ....

10. Health and safety..
....

11. Promise and Laws......................................
....

Campcraft

Purpose: To practice the campcraft skills of an all-round camper.

1. Have the Gypsy badge or the Hiker badge or demonstrate your ability in equivalent skills.
....

2. *Fires and fireplaces:* Gather materials, prepare a site, and build a fire in three minutes, using two matches. Lay and light a ceremonial fire.
....

3. *Outdoor food:* Plan and prepare two dishes using methods of cooking which are new to you. Help plan and carry out a cookout for twelve or more people.
....

4. *Toolcraft:* Learn to handle and care for a tool you never used before. Make something of wood or tin.
....

5. *Ropecraft:* Learn to use four new knots or hitches. Splice a piece of rope. Make a net or a belt or a length of rope.
....

6. *Gear:* With one other girl, pitch, strike, and fold a tent or tarp. Make a piece of group camping gear. Have your own overnight camping gear; pack and carry it at least one-half mile.
....

7. *Compass and map:* Follow directions cross-country for a mile or more. Make a sketch map for someone else to follow. Designate hazards.
....

8. *Safety:* Demonstrate: How to make an emergency stretcher or splint. What to do if lost in your camp or hike locality. How to make water safe for drinking. How to plan and carry out a fire drill.
....

9. *Outdoor citizenship:* Show three ways you have made good use of natural materials. Plan and conduct a quiz on nature or outdoor citizenship for a troop or camp group.
....

10. Service..
....

11. Health and safety...
....

....
....

12. Promise and Laws..
....

....
....

Ceramics and Pottery

Purpose: To explore the history of ceramics and pottery and to try a variety of techniques in making and decorating clay articles.

1. Find out about the development of pottery and ceramics. Collect pictures of Indian and Early American pottery, Chinese porcelain, French and English pottery, and contemporary ware. Tell how clay is used in the folk arts of other countries, such as Peru, Mexico, Japan. ....

2. Visit a potter, brick factory, or commercial china manufacturer to see the processes involved in making pottery and ceramics. ....

3. Visit a museum or art show to see various kinds of ceramics and pottery, including contemporary designs. ....

4. Set up a place to work with clay. Make a wedging board and a plaster bat, and learn how to store clay. Find out about differences in low fire and high firing clay. ....

5. Make: A figure, bowl, or vase, using the coil method. A tile or box by rolling clay flat. A figure by modeling or by carving it or a piece on a potter's wheel. Have the best pieces fired. ....

6. Design and make a small mosaic piece using ceramic tiles, preferably tiles you have made. ....

7. Experiment with several ways of applying one-fire glaze, and with incised or other types of ceramic decoration. ....

8. Learn how to stack a kiln and fire. OR Help set up simple outdoor kiln for bisque firing. If possible, help to dig and process natural clay. ....

9. Find out about various allied uses of ceramics in industry, architecture, and interior design. ....

10. Service.. ....

11. Health and safety...

  ....

12. Promise and Laws...

  ....

....

MY SIGNATURE   DATE COMPLETED   LEADER'S SIGNATURE

Chef

Purpose: To become highly skilled in one kind of cookery.

1. Have the Cook's badge. OR Demonstrate your ability to plan, buy the food for, and prepare a well-balanced family dinner. ....

2. Choose one of the following areas as your specialty: Quantity cooking. International foods. Family cooking. Food preservation. Baking. Look at cookbooks that specialize in your choice and list your favorites. ....

3. List four ingredients or pieces of equipment in your foods area that are new to you. ....

4. Visit an acknowledged authority in your specialty and watch food preparation in her kitchen if possible. Ask her to help you select two recipes suitable for your family or patrol. Prepare the recipes. ....

5. Start a file of recipes you have found successful. Note their sources, yields, and interesting background facts. ....

6. Be able to explain which methods of food preparation retain nutrients. Describe some good nutrition practices in your specialty. Know the basic four food groups. ....

7. Learn how family size recipes must be changed for quantity cooking. OR Discuss foreign food terms used in this country. OR Explore various methods used to freeze and can foods or to make baked goods. Know why these methods are good. ....

8. Keep a record of the products you use and the success you have while doing one of the following: Help plan a well-balanced meal and prepare the main dish for twenty-five people. Plan and prepare an international meal for your patrol or family. Prepare, label, and freeze or can a fruit, a vegetable, meat; preserve jam or jelly. Bake three of the following: cookies, yeast bread or rolls, a cake, pie, quick bread. ....

9. Service.. ....

10. Health and safety... ....

....

11. Promise and Laws.. ....

....

....

Child Care

Purpose: To acquire the know-how of an accomplished babysitter and to test your interest in a career working with children.

1. Choose, with the help of a librarian, at least two books on the development and care of children to use as reference while earning this badge.   *2/9/65 Mrs. B.*

2. Help to collect or make at least five toys for young children. Tell why the toys are safe and describe five others that would be unsafe.   *2/9/65 Mrs. B.*

3. Demonstrate how to bathe, dress, and feed a small child, using a doll as a model.   *2/7/65 Mrs. B.*

4. Explain or discuss with others the signs that indicate health or illness in small children.   *2/7/65 Mrs. B.*

5. Learn two games and two stories that small children would enjoy. Use two of your choices to entertain a group of small children.   *2/9/65 Mrs. B.*

6. Explain ten things that might happen to prove that it is unsafe to leave small children without supervision.   *2/5/65 Mrs. B.*

7. Visit a day nursery or kindergarten to observe the care and attention given the children. OR Help to plan and carry out all the details of a party for preschool children.   *2/5/65 Mrs. B.*

8. Dramatize an interview with a mother who asked you for the first time to care for her child for the afternoon. Include all the things you need to know about the child, the house, the equipment, and what to do in an emergency.   *2/9/65 Mrs. B.*

9. Service   *I was able to care for a child* *2/9/65 Mrs. B*

10. Health and safety   *efficiantly* *I learned the proper care for a child and what and that not a child should play with.* *2/9/65 +1*

11. Promise and Laws   *a girl scouts honor is to be trusted. A Girl Scouts duty is to be useful and to help others.*

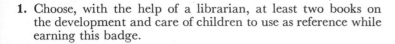

Sherrian Borguink

MY SIGNATURE   DATE COMPLETED   LEADER'S SIGNATURE

Clerk

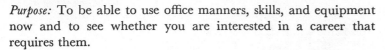

Purpose: To be able to use office manners, skills, and equipment now and to see whether you are interested in a career that requires them.

1. Find out about the various kinds of clerical positions and their importance to business life. Choose one position and learn as much as you can about it. ....

2. Do whichever of the following skills are most closely connected with your choice: Learn how to use and care for a typewriter, a hand stapler, automatic pencil, and postal scale. Know several common filing systems and use one to set up a household file. Learn to cut a stencil, planning an attractive page arrangement, and to use and care for a duplicating machine. ....

3. Dramatize the courteous way to approach sales people, to wait on customers, to receive visitors in an office. ....

4. Demonstrate the correct way to use a home, office, and pay station telephone. Know how to place a long distance, person-to-person call, how to reverse the charges. ....

5. Learn how to write and send a telegram. Find out the difference between fast and deferred service. ....

6. Show that you can write: A bank check and record stub. A bank withdrawal and deposit slip. A receipt. ....

7. Find out what is meant by "time and motion study." Work out a plan to speed up your daily work. ....

8. Practice writing business letters that: Request information. Place an order. Express thanks. Make reservations. ....

9. Write an application letter for a clerical position. Dramatize an interview with a personnel manager. ....

10. Service ....

11. Health and safety ....

....

12. Promise and Laws ....

....

....

MY SIGNATURE   DATE COMPLETED   LEADER'S SIGNATURE

Conservation

Purpose: To find out how our country's natural resources—plants, animals, soil, water—are protected and what you can do to help.

1. With your patrol or troop, plan and carry out one of the following outdoor citizenship projects: Conduct an anti-litter campaign. Make an animal feeding station and maintain it for one year, recording the wildlife that use the station. Set up a soil conservation project at camp, school, meeting place, or home. Help with a reforestation project.

   ....

2. Find out how community, state, and national parks and forests contribute to conservation, including prevention of fire and soil erosion. If possible, visit a conservation agent, forest ranger, or fire warden tower.

   ....

3. Explain how plants and wildlife depend on each other and the relation of soil and water conservation to each. Find out what state and federal laws protect wildlife and combat water pollution.

   ....

4. Know which plants and flowers in your state may never be picked. Be able to identify them.

   ....

5. List the birds and fur-bearing animals that are protected by laws in your state. OR Visit a fish hatchery and find out how state and federal laws protect fish.

   ....

6. Work on a conservation project with a local conservation group. Or With other members of the troop, develop and set up a conservation exhibit.

   ....

7. Learn the Conservation Pledge and be able to explain what it means.

   ....

8. Service.. ....

9. Health and safety..

   ....

10. Promise and Laws..

   ....

....

MY SIGNATURE   DATE COMPLETED   LEADER'S SIGNATURE

Creative Writer

Purpose: To be able to "paint" pictures with words that express your feeling, convey your ideas, and recreate your experiences for others.

1. Read a book on the art of writing. Know how to use the dictionary and other reference books. Add ten words to your vocabulary.

2. Write several poems in one or more of the following forms— limerick, iambic verse, free verse, haiku style.

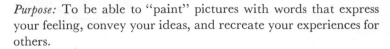

3. Write a story or poem that describes your feelings about something you have seen. OR Give a character picture of someone you know.

4. Write an imaginative story about a character in history or a story that might have been. Write a short play or adapt a favorite story or poem to play form.

5. Write a children's story, letter it, and with a friend illustrate and bind it into a book.

6. Write a story or poem and submit it to a magazine in correct manuscript form.

7. Practice your letter writing skills by corresponding with someone in another community or country. Keep copies of your letters to see how you have improved.

8. Find out how a book is produced—what happens between the time the author completes the manuscript and the book is published.

9. Submit to your council a written description of your most exciting adventure in Girl Scouting.

10. Read several selections written in different styles. Write a short report on which you like best and why.

11. Service

12. Health and safety

13. Promise and Laws

MY SIGNATURE   DATE COMPLETED   LEADER'S SIGNATURE

Dressmaker

Purpose: To increase sewing skills and your ability to choose clothes that fit your figure, budget, and activities.

1. Have the Sewing badge. OR Be able to: Select and care for sewing tools. Do hand stitches. Sew plain seams and finishes. ....

2. Study the elements of dress design to discover which ones are most becoming to you. Plan a basic dress for yourself. Explain your choice as it relates to use, care, cost, wearability, and the accessories you can use. ....

3. Learn terms for garment parts and styles as used on pattern instructions. Practice taking correct size measurements on a friend. Have her take yours to use when you buy a pattern for the dress you planned in No. 2. Know how to alter a pattern for your figure. ....

4. Compare fabrics for summer, winter, dress, or sports clothes; for drapes and linens. Note textures, labels, qualities, care needed. Choose fabric for the outfit you planned in No. 2. ....

5. Demonstrate proper use and care of a sewing machine. ....

6. Know how to: Lay, pin, and cut a garment from a pattern. Make darts, tucks, and curved seams. Mark cloth for sewing (two methods). Put in a hem. Use press-as-you-go construction. Insert a zipper. Demonstrate one of the above. ....

7. Compare the quality of sewing in three ready-made garments. Considering the style, the quality of material used, and the time it would take to make, compare the cost of buying to that of making one of the dresses. ....

8. Prepare fabric for cutting and make the dress you planned in No. 2. Keep a record of the time spent in making it and cost of all materials. Describe: What you feel you did well. Problems you had and how you might improve your work next time. ....

9. Service.. ....

10. Health and safety... ....

....

11. Promise and Laws.. ....

....

....

| MY SIGNATURE | DATE COMPLETED | LEADER'S SIGNATURE |

Explorer

Purpose: To plan and carry out varied types of camping trips.

1. Help to plan and carry out three weekend camping trips, using varied forms of transportation—foot, bicycle, canoe, horse, or car—by working with a group on activities in No. 2 through 9. ....

2. Decide where and how to go. Using road or topographical maps, indicate routes and overnight stops. Arrange for permits, reservations, emergency measures. ....

3. Considering weather expected, activities, and types of trip, decide what group gear and personal gear to take. Plan how to obtain, pack, and carry it. Demonstrate you know how to handle, care for, and make minor repairs on equipment used. ....

4. Plan menus some of which include concentrated and dehydrated foods. Help to obtain, pack, carry, store, prepare and serve food. ....

5. Set up and strike overnight camps, including sanitation, cooking, and sleeping areas. Demonstrate good outdoor living skills, good outdoor citizenship, and emergency preparation. ....

6. Demonstrate two advanced campcraft skills such as use of knots, compass, maps, tools; ability to judge distances, to signal. ....

7. Find out about things to do and points of natural or historic interest to visit. Include some of these in the itinerary. ....

8. Begin or continue an outdoor hobby, such as rock collecting, star study, sketching. ....

9. After each trip, talk over how it went and what could be improved on your next trip. ....

10. Service.. ....

11. Health and safety... ....

....

12. Promise and Laws.. ....

....

....

MY SIGNATURE   DATE COMPLETED   LEADER'S SIGNATURE

Family Camper

Purpose: To use Girl Scout camping skills on camping trips with your family.

1. Help your family plan where to go, what to take and wear, and to make arrangements, including permits, campsite reservations, itinerary for an overnight camp with three meals and two longer camping trips. Go on the trips. ....

2. Help to: Plan food lists and meals, including some you can prepare alone. Obtain, pack, and take care of food at the camp sites. ....

3. Work out a chart to divide jobs of setting up and caring for your campsite. Plan some ways you can give your mother a vacation from housekeeping jobs. ....

4. Know how to pack, care for, and store your family's camping equipment. Be able to take charge of erecting, striking, and rolling one of the tents. ....

5. Use as many of the outdoor skills you have learned as possible. Take care of your own gear. Demonstrate that you know the safe way to use lanterns, stoves, first aid supplies, and other equipment. ....

6. Discuss ways your family can observe good outdoor citizenship. ....

7. Find out about natural and historic points of interest along the way or at the site. If younger children are on the trip, plan activities for them en route or at camp, including some for rainy days. ....

8. Write a letter or a report to your troop, telling about your trip. Sketch or take pictures to illustrate it. ....

9. Service... ....

10. Health and safety... ....

....

11. Promise and Laws..

....

....

MY SIGNATURE   DATE COMPLETED   LEADER'S SIGNATURE

Family Living

Purpose: To make family living more enjoyable by improving your own personality as a family member.

1. List some qualities that you feel make people "good" family members. Check the qualities you usually show and choose one you wish to strengthen. Keep a record for one month to show how you tried to improve. ✓

    3/2/65 Mrs. B.

2. Considering that your family's home is for all to enjoy, practice: Limiting phone calls. Sharing the TV set. Budgeting bathroom time. Caring for your own clothes. Caring for younger brothers or sisters. Note your family's response.

    3/2/65 Mrs. B.
    3/9/65 Mrs. B.

3. Act out a situation showing "actions speak louder than words."

4. Do three of the following: Discuss with your family how decisions about the money you receive are made in relation to the needs of the whole family. Discuss the kinds of insurance carried on home property. Become familiar with a good book on manners and point out examples demonstrating that etiquette is mostly thoughtfulness. Learn about family life in the lands of your ancestors or in another country today. List safety hazards about your home and discuss remedies with your family. Give your parents a night out by preparing dinner, ✓ cleaning up, and watching younger children. Prepare a dish that is a favorite in your family. ✓

    3/9/65 Mrs. B.

5. For three days, write down everything each family member does for your welfare and check those things you took for granted.

    3/9/65 Mrs. B.

6. Act out three of these situations: The telephone rings; the call is for your sister. Someone changes the radio or TV program you are listening to. Your allowance won't cover a new skirt. Your mother needs help and you'd rather swim. You are to watch baby brother on a trip. An elderly relative makes a visit. Make two endings for each situation. Discuss how and why the two endings differ.

    3/9/65 Mrs. B.
    3/9/65 Mrs. B.

7. Service *I helped my family be a better family.*

8. Health and safety *It helped my family to be kind to each other.*

    3/9/65 Mrs B

9. Promise and Laws *all the Laws Except 4 and 1.*

    3/9/65 Mrs. B.

Sharon ____ *3/9/65* ____ *Mrs. Borgunk*

MY SIGNATURE ____ DATE COMPLETED ____ LEADER'S SIGNATURE

First Aid

Purpose: To be able to meet emergencies and to give the right kind of first aid.

Instruction for this badge must be given by a currently authorized American Red Cross First Aid Instructor, a nurse with first aid experience, or a licensed doctor of medicine.

1. Learn and review frequently the objectives of first aid for: Wounds. Shock. Artificial respiration. Poisoning by mouth. Burns. Injuries to bones, joints, muscles. Transporting injured persons. ....

2. Demonstrate: What to do for three types of injuries that require immediate action. How to recognize and care for a patient suffering from shock. Two methods of artificial respiration. ....

3. Apply properly: Roller bandage. Sterile gauze dressing. Triangular bandage. Cravat bandage. ....

4. Demonstrate (with a victim weighing less than you): A chair carry. A two-man carry. How to improvise and use a stretcher. Explain when and why a victim should *not* be moved. ....

5. Tell what to do for a person: Whose clothes are on fire. Who has received an electric shock. Who is drowning. ....

6. Teach someone: Which telephone numbers to post by every home phone in case of emergency. Which items to put in a first aid kit for a hike or trip, and why. ....

7. With others, organize a wide game calling for a demonstration of at least ten of the first aid skills you have learned. ....

8. Service... ....

9. Health and safety.. ....

....

10. Promise and Laws..

....

MY SIGNATURE   DATE COMPLETED   LEADER'S SIGNATURE

First Aid to Animals

Purpose: To be able to care for a sick or injured domestic animal.

1. Find a veterinarian to help you meet the other requirements. Choose one kind of domestic animal with which to work.

2. Know the types of injuries and diseases to which your animal is susceptible and the means of prevention. Learn what is being done in your community for the control of contagious diseases of animals.

3. Demonstrate how to approach the animal if it is injured. Show how to restrain it when giving treatment without risk to you or the animal.

4. Know the parts of your animal. Demonstrate how to take its pulse and temperature. Know how to administer medicine in liquid or tablet form.

5. Be able to give first aid treatment for: Hysteria. Bruises. Suffocation. Burns and scalds. Shock. Wounds. Gases. Drowning. Hemorrhage. Fractures. Electric shock. Internal injuries. Know the care of newborn animals.

6. Make and know how to use: A dog lasso. A restraining stick. An emergency muzzle.

7. Know the local and state laws governing the treatment, use, and ownership of your animal. List the address and telephone number of a veterinarian and of the nearest Society for the Prevention of Cruelty to Animals or other shelter for animals.

8. Know the work and some publications of organizations interested in the humane care of animals. Know location of their nearest units. Visit an animal shelter if there is one nearby.

9. Know the accepted humane method of destroying animals when this becomes necessary.

10. Service

11. Health and safety

12. Promise and Laws

MY SIGNATURE   DATE COMPLETED   LEADER'S SIGNATURE

Folk Dancer

Purpose: To explore the story of folk dances around the world and to be able to dance some well enough to give pleasure to yourself and others.

1. Be able to teach five dances traditional in this country (other than squares) and five folk dances from other countries. ....

2. Know how to call four American square dances. ....

3. Prepare a balanced repertory of singing games, using three different formations, that you could teach to children. ....

4. Discover how collectors of folk music find and record their tunes. Know the names and compilations of several folklorists whose books you can use for source material. ....

5. Take part in a community or intercommunity barn dance. OR Help plan and take part in an international dance festival. ....

6. Play at least four tunes on an instrument to which your troop may dance. OR Help make costumes for a folk dance demonstration. ....

7. With others, plan a basic library of folk dance records for your troop, camp, school, or community. Start to collect records for the library. OR Share your folk dance fun with a group that normally has no folk dancing opportunities. ....

8. Find out about the activities of several famous folk dance groups from this country or from other lands. See at least one performance on TV or elsewhere. OR With the help of a qualified adult, make a study of the dances of one particular nationality and give a performance at which you tell the audience some of the background information. ....

9. Service.. ....

10. Health and safety.. ....

....

11. Promise and Laws..

....

....

MY SIGNATURE   DATE COMPLETED   LEADER'S SIGNATURE

Food Raiser

Purpose: To learn the methods used in raising and preparing one food category for family consumption or market.

1. Choose one product from one of the following food categories: Fruits. Vegetables. Animals. Find out about it by reading, observing, and talking with others. Know the variety of species available.

2. Take full charge of your product for four months. Know how to give it proper nourishment. Make a plan for selecting beginning stock. Set up a checklist to record the care given and the cost.

3. Learn which diseases may attack your product. Explain the local and state laws that govern sanitation and protect against disease.

4. Describe the kinds of tools, equipment, supplies or special housing needed for your product. Find out the correct way to transport it.

5. Find out if your product must be graded before marketing and what the requirements are for each grade. Check on current wholesale and retail price of each grade. Learn how prices are set. Keep a produce and sales record.

6. Know how to prepare your product for cooking, canning, or freezing. Choose two recipes that use your product to serve to your family.

7. Enter some of your produce in a community or state fair. OR Donate some of your produce to an organization or family that needs it.

8. Service...

9. Health and safety..

10. Promise and Laws..

Games Leader

Purpose: To be able to teach a variety of games to children.

1. After clearing with your leader or other adults involved, select a group of children—a neighborhood group, a Brownie troop, handicapped children. Make a plan to work with your group.

2. Teach your group two games from each of the following types: Dramatic and singing games. Circle and line games. Relay team games. Nature games. Guessing games. Games from other countries.

3. Show your group how to make up a game or to make some games equipment.

4. Keep a card file which indicates the games the children liked best, where to find rules for the games, comments which would be helpful to others working with same age group. Share this information with others.

5. Be able to give simple first aid for: Floor burns. A splinter. Twisted ankle. Scraped knee. Know where first aid kit is kept and which adult(s) you need to notify before and after treatment.

6. Plan some festive activity for the last day you work with the group. Evaluate how well you carried out your plan.

7. Service

8. Health and safety

9. Promise and Laws

MY SIGNATURE   DATE COMPLETED   LEADER'S SIGNATURE

Good Grooming

Purpose: To learn the good health and good grooming practices that will make you a more attractive person.

1. Have the Personal Health badge. OR Show how you: Take care of your need for sleep. Observe a proper diet. Get the right kind of exercise.   *4/14/64 Mrs. B.*

2. Ask a beautician to tell your patrol about hair care and styles and nail care. Decide which hair style is best for you.   *1/5/65 Mrs. B.*

3. Discuss how food, rest, cleanliness, exercise, and cosmetics affect your skin. Find out how food and cosmetic product claims are checked by a public health agency.   *1/8/65 Mrs. B.*

4. Find out how care of your teeth and mouth affect total health.   *1/8/65 Mrs. B.*

5. Discuss the kinds of foods a girl your age needs and what happens when they are lacking. Make a dietary plan that meets your needs, follow it for a month, and then evaluate it.   *1/26/65 Mrs. B.*

6. Demonstrate good posture for walking, sitting, lifting, bending, reading, climbing stairs, carrying packages. Discuss: How to care for your feet. Proper footwear for three activities.   *1/19/65 Mrs. B.*

7. Using clothes and accessories you have as the basis, plan a wardrobe that suits your figure, complexion, and activities.   *1/5/65 Mrs. B.*

8. Make a personal grooming kit and a schedule for its use.   *1/13/65 Mrs. B.*

9. Demonstrate how to care for and to pack your Girl Scout uniform. Discuss importance of wearing uniform correctly.   *1/12/65 Mrs. B.*

10. Dramatize how grooming affects your appearance and attitude, and how, in turn, these affect others' impressions of you. OR Give a style show, pointing up importance of good grooming, posture, and appropriateness of clothing.   *11/15/64 Mrs. B.*

11. Service *Give advice to others* / *Help myself be a better person.*   *1/19/65 B. B.*

12. Health and safety *Personal Health, Proper safety in diet and cosmetics.*   *1/19/65 Mrs. B.*

13. Promise and Laws *A Girl Scout is thrifty. A Girl Scout is courteous.*   *1/19/65 Mrs. B.*

Sherian   *1/26/65*   *Mrs. Borgmile*

MY SIGNATURE   DATE COMPLETED   LEADER'S SIGNATURE

Graphic Arts

Purpose: To become acquainted with the many different forms of graphic art; to try your skill with several.

1. Start a collection of prints made by different processes—linoleum block, woodblock, lithography, etching, engraving. Indicate under each the process used and, if known, the artist and his country. ....

2. Find out about the graphic work of early and contemporary artists through books, magazines, art galleries, and museums. Look for etchings, engravings, and lithographs of artists such as Rembrandt, Dürer, Whistler, Toulouse-Lautrec, Roualt, Matisse, Picasso, Bellows. ....

3. Make a drawing using two of the following techniques: Pen and ink. Pencil. Scratchboard. Charcoal. Graphic crayon. ....

4. Design, make, and use a linoleum block for printing on paper or fabric. ....

5. Design and make a silk screen print suitable to use on a poster, program cover, or fabric or as a picture. ....

6. Design, make, and use a stencil to print on fabric, notepaper, wrapping paper, or book cover. Find out how stenciling was used by the early settlers in this country. ....

7. Using one of the three methods of printing above, design and make a print in two colors. ....

8. Create a design for a dry-point type print on celluloid. OR Make a simple lithograph with wax on glass. ....

9. Create a print using objects, impressions, or rubbings; a transfer print; or a monoprint. Find out if there are any print collections in your community, any classes on printing. If possible, attend an exhibit and join a class. ....

10. Service..

11. Health and safety...
   ....

12. Promise and Laws..
   ....

....

MY SIGNATURE   DATE COMPLETED   LEADER'S SIGNATURE

Handywoman

Purpose: To be able to help keep your home in good condition.

1. Have the Housekeeper badge. OR Describe six household activities you do regularly.

2. List the repairs in your home that you could make safely and tell what tools and materials you would need.

3. Visit a utility company to find out how it serves the home. Find out which utility equipment must be installed when a house is built and which can be added later. Compare the cost of two heating methods. Make a list of utility emergency phone numbers. Describe how, when, and under what circumstances utilities should be turned off in your home.

4. Study different kitchen arrangements. On a scaled floor plan, try arrangements that might improve your kitchen. Make a list of small utensils needed in a family kitchen and explain the care each requires.

5. Demonstrate how to: Sharpen knives. Use and care for a dry iron or steam iron. Provide emergency light and heat. Make water safe to drink. Install picture hooks and a utensil rack.

6. Show that you know how to use, care for, and store six garden tools, or household tools, or small appliances such as toaster, mixer, pressure cooker.

7. Demonstrate the safe and correct way to use and care for four major appliances, such as stove, refrigerator, vacuum cleaner, washer, electric rotisserie, dishwasher, dryer.

8. Refinish a small piece of furniture. OR Rewire a lamp. OR Help to paint or paper a room in your home.

9. Service

10. Health and safety

11. Promise and Laws

MY SIGNATURE .... DATE COMPLETED .... LEADER'S SIGNATURE

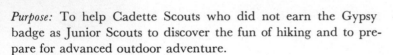

Hiker

Purpose: To help Cadette Scouts who did not earn the Gypsy badge as Junior Scouts to discover the fun of hiking and to prepare for advanced outdoor adventure.

1. Help your patrol, troop, or camp group plan and carry out all the details of two all-day outings on foot, including where to go, what to wear, what to take, permissions required.

....

2. Demonstrate how to: Walk and rest properly. Walk in a group on a sidewalk and a road. Act in a public conveyance. Practice outdoor manners on the way and at the hike site.

....

3. With others: Plan, procure, pack, carry, prepare, and serve food for a cold lunch and for one meal which includes something to cook. Prepare a fire place. Build, use, and put out the fire. Clean up.

....

4. Before each hike, find out what weather to expect. Plan clothing according to activities planned and weather expected.

....

5. Assemble your own hike kit, including a whipped rope, eating utensils, knife, bandana.

....

6. Learn some new campcraft skill such as use of compass, knots, trail signs. Put it to use on the hike.

....

7. Help check contents of first aid kit. Know how to give first aid for: Cut. Burn. Turned ankle. Splinter.

....

8. Plan outdoor fun on the hike—games, songs, nature quest, treasure hunt, campfire program. Do an outdoor good turn on each hike.

....

9. After the hike, discuss what went well and what you would do differently on another hike.

....

10. Service..

....

11. Health and safety..

....

....

12. Promise and Laws...

....

....

....

MY SIGNATURE   DATE COMPLETED   LEADER'S SIGNATURE

Homemaker

Purpose: To learn and practice the skills you will need when you are a homemaker. ✓

1. Have the My Home badge. OR Describe the homemaking activities you do regularly to help your home run smoothly.   ....2/29/64 Mrs. B.

2. List activities your family enjoys doing together at home. Do something to make one of these activities more pleasant.   ....3/2/65 Mrs. B.

3. Discuss time needed and proper method for homemaking activities such as cooking, laundering, ironing, and cleaning. Choose one activity and work out a way to do it better.   ....3/2/65 Mrs. B.

4. Visit a bank to learn about its services and banking terms. Find out how insurance safeguards you and your home. Discuss ways of saving and work out a month's budget for yourself. Develop a personal savings plan.   ....

5. Help your mother shop for and prepare meals for a week to see how she meets the family's nutritional needs.   ....

6. Organize a convenient arrangement for storing things in your room.   ....3/2/65 Mrs. B.

7. Know how to care for floors, walls, furniture, curtains, rugs, kitchen equipment. Demonstrate one.   ....3/2/65 Mrs. B.

8. Discuss the values of comparative shopping. Then do two of the following: Note net weight or fluid measure, servings, ingredients, and price of six container sizes to determine the best buy for your family needs. List qualities to look for in buying or making a school dress. Compare the quality, care needed, and cost of a kitchen utensil or piece of furniture at home with similar ones in two stores. Compare three children's books, noting prices and qualities.   ....

9. Service...........   ....

10. Health and safety...........   ....
....

11. Promise and Laws...........   ....
....

....

MY SIGNATURE   DATE COMPLETED   LEADER'S SIGNATURE

Home Nurse

Purpose: To be able to take care of someone who is ill at home.

1. On a floor plan of a room in your home show how you would adapt its present arrangement to care for a sick person. Show how to set up a bedside table and to arrange trays for medicines, toilet articles, and meals.   *1/19/65 Mrs. B.*

2. Teach someone how to make a comfortable bed for a patient, and how to improvise five of the following: back rest, body supports, waste disposal bag, night light, bed jacket, door silencer, ventilating screen.   *1/19/65 Mrs. B.*

3. Demonstrate how to: Take a pulse. Count respiration. Make hot, moist compresses. Use and care for a mouth thermometer.   *1/19/65 Mrs. B.*

4. Explain six early symptoms of illness and the precautions that must be taken if a doctor diagnoses an illness as contagious.   *1/19/65 Mrs. B.*

5. Make a quiet game, interesting scrapbook, or "do-it-yourself" box and give it to a convalescent.   *1/19/65 Mrs. B.*

6. Show how to help a patient to: Turn over. Sit up. Wash her face and hands. Brush her teeth. Get out of bed.   *1/19/65 Mrs. B.*

7. Explain what is meant by: Liquid diet. Soft diet. Light diet. Prepare and serve a meal from each.   *1/19/65 Mrs. B.*

8. Invite a speaker to your troop meeting to talk about nursing, and make a list of questions to ask her. OR With others, set up a home nursing exhibit or in some way demonstrate what a home nurse does.   *1/19/65 Mrs. B.*

9. Service *I helped a person get well.*   *1/26/65 Mrs. B*

10. Health and safety *Helping others when they are sick or in need of care*   *1/26/65 Mrs. B.*

11. Promise and Laws *a Girl Scout's duty is to be useful and to help others.*   *1/26/65 Mrs. B.*

Sherman	*1/26/65*	*Mrs. Borgwick*
MY SIGNATURE	DATE COMPLETED	LEADER'S SIGNATURE

Horsewoman

Purpose: To be able to ride and care for a horse.

1. Know the daily care of a horse and explain how it varies. Find out approximate cost of the monthly care of a horse. ....

2. Saddle and bridle a horse, explaining care and use of each part. Show how to lead, hitch, and return a horse to stable. ....

3. Name the principal parts of a horse. Find out the symptoms of common ailments and diseases of horses. Explain the proper way to feed a horse, naming types of grain used. Groom a horse and be able to name the implements used. ....

4. Demonstrate how to: Mount and dismount. Ride at a walk, trot, and canter. Lead one horse while riding another. Care for horse after exercise. ....

5. Explain safety regulations for riding and equestrian etiquette. Know how to select and care for your riding equipment and how to dress for Western and park riding. ....

6. Watch a blacksmith shoe a horse. Find out how often a horse should be shod and why. Learn to remove a stone from a hoof. ....

7. Draw or construct to scale a model stall and tack room. ....

8. Make an illustrated booklet on the history and development of the horse. OR Collect or take pictures of four leading breeds and tell about their distinctive features and uses. ....

9. Take part in two: Trail ride. All day cross-country ride. Breakfast or supper ride. Horse show. Riding drill or demonstration. ....

10. Service... ....

11. Health and safety..
    ....

12. Promise and Laws...
    ....

....
MY SIGNATURE   DATE COMPLETED   LEADER'S SIGNATURE

Hostess

Purpose: To know how to be a gracious and thoughtful hostess and guest.

1. Have the Hospitality badge. OR Show that you know how to: Introduce people correctly. Write thank-you notes. Use a book on etiquette.   *3/17/64 Mrs. B.*

2. Describe the qualities you believe are important in friendship. Discuss how they are demonstrated by a hostess and by a guest.   *3/2/65 Mrs. B.*

3. List the things a hostess would need to think of to make a weekend guest comfortable. Discuss the things a weekend guest should do to earn the title "welcome."   *3/2/65 Mrs B.*

4. Write a letter of invitation and one of regret. Explain the difference between social and business stationery.   *3/2/65 Mrs. B.*

5. Make a centerpiece for a table which carries out the theme for a party.   *2/14/65 Mrs. B.*

6. Plan and present skits which show: Mistakes and how to avoid them when a dinner guest in a home or restaurant. How to make friends when the group includes: only one person you know, boys, older people. What to do when unexpected guests arrive.

7. Collect pictures of linens, dishes, glassware, and silverware you like. Tell which ones are suitable for daily use and which for special occasions. Explain the use and care of each article.

8. Make a folder of recipes for food you would like to serve at: A tea. Brunch. Outdoor barbecue. International dinner. Plan imaginative ways to serve this food.

9. Discuss what makes a successful party and why planning is important. Make a detailed plan for a party based on a theme.   *2/25/65 Mrs. B.*

10. Service...

11. Health and safety...

12. Promise and Laws..

MY SIGNATURE   DATE COMPLETED   LEADER'S SIGNATURE

Interior Decoration

Purpose: To be able to make a home more beautiful and comfortable.

1. Make sketches of your dream house exterior and interior. Using these sketches as a base, plan how you would decorate one room—walls, window treatment, floors, lighting, furniture style and arrangement, and accessories. Indicate color scheme with swatches of fabrics, wallpaper, and paint samples. Note what it would cost to carry out your plan. ....

2. Study different decorations for walls and choose two that might fit into your own home. Make a frame for a print, painting, or photograph you have made. ....

3. Make curtains, draperies, or slipcover for some room in your house. OR Embroider, patchwork, or appliqué a quilt. OR Hook or braid a rug. OR Weave, print, or embroider a tablecloth or mat. ....

4. Cover a photograph album or telephone book. OR Make a box portfolio for programs and pamphlets. OR Rebind a book. ....

5. Create two flower and one fruit arrangement appropriate for special occasions. ....

6. List four different types of finishes for wood. Know how to use filler, stain, and paint remover. Finish or refinish a small wooden article or piece of furniture. ....

7. Make a scale model of a room decorated for a girl your age or the room you planned for No. 1. Display at troop meeting. Discuss variations. ....

8. Start a notebook on different periods of furniture. Explain how factors in history, climate, and country affected styles. If possible, find pictures of actual rooms in these periods. ....

9. Service ....

10. Health and safety ....

....

11. Promise and Laws ....

....

....

MY SIGNATURE   DATE COMPLETED   LEADER'S SIGNATURE

Language

Purpose: To "see" the world in terms of the languages people speak and to be able to use one language other than English for some everyday needs.

1. Make a chart which shows in which countries the major languages used today are spoken. Compare the symbols used in writing French, Russian, Arabic, Japanese, or Hebrew with those used in English.   ....

2. Discuss the need for and advantages of learning other languages. List five jobs open to people who know several languages. Find out which five languages are the official languages of the United Nations, which two are the working languages.   ....

3. Know which languages would be most helpful to anyone who wishes to attend a Girl Scout international event.   ....

4. Be able to pronounce correctly the name by which Girl Scouts are known in at least eight countries and to repeat the Girl Scout motto in three languages other than English.   ....

5. Choose one foreign language, list as many countries as you can where it is spoken, and use it to do the following requirements:

   Learn to say six everyday expressions, three words needed for safety, and the Girl Scout Promise.   ....

   Learn two folk songs or games and teach one to your troop.   ....

   Demonstrate you can order a meal from a menu.   ....

   Write a letter about a camping experience. OR Plan and carry out a party, using games, songs, food, and some expressions of a country in which your chosen language is spoken.   ....

6. Service..   ....

7. Health and safety...

   ....

8. Promise and Laws...

   ....

Life Saver

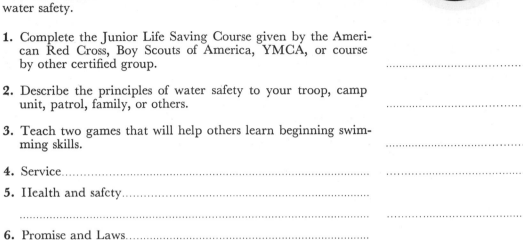

Purpose: To be able to use life saving skills and to teach others water safety.

1. Complete the Junior Life Saving Course given by the American Red Cross, Boy Scouts of America, YMCA, or course by other certified group. ....

2. Describe the principles of water safety to your troop, camp unit, patrol, family, or others. ....

3. Teach two games that will help others learn beginning swimming skills. ....

4. Service.. ....

5. Health and safety...
   ....

6. Promise and Laws...
   ....

Metal Arts

Purpose: To explore the many uses of metal—decorative and practical—and to be able to use some of the techniques of the metal craftsman.

1. Learn how to use and care for the tools generally used in metal work—drill, soldering equipment, jeweler's saw, files, clamps, vise, ballpeen hammer. ....

2. Explain how the properties of gold, silver, tin, copper, pewter, aluminum, and brass affect the choice of the metal you would use to make various articles. Describe one metal in ore form. Tell how it is mined, smelted, and prepared for use. ....

3. List some ways metal is used in your community—in architecture, in sculpture, by industry. Look for examples, in museums or books, of handwrought metal articles. ....

4. Study Early American tinware—its uses and designs. Collect pictures or make sketches of items found in museums or homes. Study the metal work of another country. ....

5. Make: A pewter, copper, silver, or brass bowl. Copper or silver wire jewelry. A silver or copper pin or buckle, using a cutout design. A pewter, copper, or aluminum article on which a design is etched. An article which requires soldering. ....

6. Demonstrate how to clean and polish different kinds of metal. ....

7. Find out about the techniques and materials used in enameling on copper or silver. Make several small disks on which to test color of enamel powder when fired. Make a pin using two colors, then progress to a more advanced technique—painted, stenciled, or cloisonne. ....

8. Service ....

9. Health and safety ....

....

10. Promise and Laws ....

....

....

Minstrel

Purpose: To develop a repertory of songs that you know well enough to sing and teach to others.

1. Sing four typical songs of our country and four from other countries. With others sing a round, canon, part-song or song with a descant. Define these terms. ....

2. Practice simple song-leading directions, then teach a group several songs of different kinds, giving some interesting facts about each. ....

3. Watch a choral or orchestral conductor and see if you can understand his directions. OR Find out about three well-known conductors of symphony orchestras. ....

4. Using Girl Scout songbooks compile and learn to sing a repertory of songs suggestive of a day's activities at camp. OR Weave a number of songs together with dialogue to present a story or dramatic entertainment. ....

5. Start a collection of songs learned at camp or from friends. Discuss qualities of a good song. Explain how the copyright laws protect composers. ....

6. Prepare and take part in an international music program. Give some interesting facts about the songs sung or invite others to do so. ....

7. Prepare a program of representative music of this country to be sung or to be played on records or on instruments. Be able to interpret the music to other people. ....

8. Service ....

9. Health and safety ....

....

10. Promise and Laws ....

....

Music Maker

Purpose: To be able to use your skill as a musician to help your troop have interesting music and dancing activities.

1. Sing and/or play well in a group: Six·folk songs from this country and six from other countries. Four rounds or canons. Four part songs. Tell about their background or explain their musical form. ....

2. Work out the music of six dances with an instrument you play and accompany a group of dancers. OR Work out musical accompaniment to any six songs. OR Work out several folk songs for a mixed chorus. ....

3. Be able to teach fifteen songs that are favorites of Girl Scouts/ Guides. Ask someone who speaks the language well to teach you the correct pronunciation for three songs in another language. ....

4. Find out how American jazz originated. Give your reaction after listening to three kinds. Explain improvisation and try it yourself. ....

5. Listen to several American classical compositions and plan a record concert for your troop. OR Listen to the scores of three musical comedies written by different composers or writing teams. ....

6. Study the score of an oratorio or of a piece of chamber, symphonic, or band music. Sing or play one part of it with a group or with a recording. ....

7. Study the score and libretto and listen to recordings of one opera and one operetta. Put on a marionette or shadowgraph production of one scene from either. OR Take part in an operetta. ....

8. Service.. ....

9. Health and safety..

....

10. Promise and Laws...

....

....

MY SIGNATURE   DATE COMPLETED   LEADER'S SIGNATURE

My Country

Purpose: To explore and understand our country's heritage.

1. Find out the requirements to become a naturalized citizen of our country. See if you and your patrol could meet them.

2. List the freedoms enjoyed by people in our country. Tell in which documents these freedoms are stated, where the documents are kept, and how they affect your daily life.

3. Display pictures of five symbols of our country and be able to explain their origin and meaning.

4. Teach younger girls two songs that express feeling about our country. Explain what the words mean to you.

5. Plan a trip to an historic shrine. Make a display that tells what happened there and how it is being preserved for the future.

6. Choose two Indian tribes and find out about their: History. Folklore. Culture. Present-day whereabouts. Dramatize or write a story to tell some of this to others.

7. Make a display of commemorative United States postage stamps and tell why each subject was selected.

8. Make a scrapbook that would tell someone from another country about our history, arts, agriculture, government, education and industry. Include something about outstanding people in each area.

9. Discuss what "patriotism" means to you.

10. Service

11. Health and safety

12. Promise and Laws

My Government

Purpose: To become an informed citizen—one who understands how our government works and can explain it to other people.

1. Get acquainted with a nonpartisan organization in your community. Ask someone from that organization or a civic group to help you with this badge.

2. Compare your troop elections and government with: Your school elections and government. Your local, state, and national elections and government. Tell how they are alike and how they differ.

3. Discuss: What is meant by a "well informed citizenry." How citizens keep informed. Why it is important that they do so.

4. Find out: Dates for registration, primaries, and election. Who is eligible to vote. Polling places for your neighborhood. How to get an absentee ballot. Why it is important to vote. How Girl Scouts can assist with elections.

5. Make a chart of the kinds of taxes you and your family pay. Tell how three services which are paid for by taxes benefit you as an individual.

6. Make a plan for a trip to your state capital or the national capital that includes what you would do before, during, and after the trip.

7. Explain the meaning of: Legislative, executive, judicial. System of checks and balances. A democracy in a republic.

8. Find out how our country maintains contact with other countries at various levels: State Department, United Nations, commerce and industry, cultural exchanges. Know the functions of an embassy.

9. Visit your town hall, city hall, or county courthouse.

10. Service

11. Health and safety

12. Promise and Laws

MY SIGNATURE   DATE COMPLETED   LEADER'S SIGNATURE

Outdoor Safety

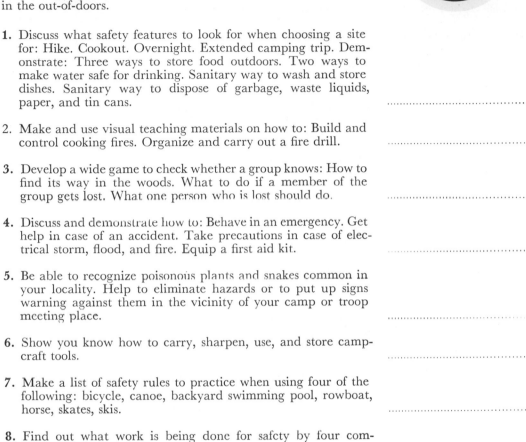

Purpose: To learn and practice how to live safely and comfortably in the out-of-doors.

1. Discuss what safety features to look for when choosing a site for: Hike. Cookout. Overnight. Extended camping trip. Demonstrate: Three ways to store food outdoors. Two ways to make water safe for drinking. Sanitary way to wash and store dishes. Sanitary way to dispose of garbage, waste liquids, paper, and tin cans.

2. Make and use visual teaching materials on how to: Build and control cooking fires. Organize and carry out a fire drill.

3. Develop a wide game to check whether a group knows: How to find its way in the woods. What to do if a member of the group gets lost. What one person who is lost should do.

4. Discuss and demonstrate how to: Behave in an emergency. Get help in case of an accident. Take precautions in case of electrical storm, flood, and fire. Equip a first aid kit.

5. Be able to recognize poisonous plants and snakes common in your locality. Help to eliminate hazards or to put up signs warning against them in the vicinity of your camp or troop meeting place.

6. Show you know how to carry, sharpen, use, and store campcraft tools.

7. Make a list of safety rules to practice when using four of the following: bicycle, canoe, backyard swimming pool, rowboat, horse, skates, skis.

8. Find out what work is being done for safety by four community organizations.

9. Service

10. Health and safety

11. Promise and Laws

MY SIGNATURE   DATE COMPLETED   LEADER'S SIGNATURE

Painting

Purpose: To experiment with different media; to improve techniques; to get experience expressing yourself through painting.

1. Look at examples of the use of oils, watercolors, tempera, gouache, casein, pastel, or oil crayon. Choose two in which you would like to complete some paintings. Find out what equipment and materials are necessary for each. ....

2. With tempera or crayon, do a series of rhythmic lines that suggest parts of body in repose, slow and quick movement. ....

3. Using tempera, or watercolor: Make three sketches of buildings, streets, trees, or camp scenes. OR Make three sketches of scenes that tell a story about your neighborhood. ....

4. Do three paintings that express different moods to you; for example, try painting as you listen to symphony or opera music. ....

5. Do a portrait of someone you know. OR Paint a scene that has people in it. ....

6. Do two paintings of one subject that show the effect of contrast in mood or light. ....

7. Make a notebook as you study and collect pictures. Discuss paintings of various periods to help you understand the development of painting. ....

8. Study the works of contemporary painters and what they are trying to achieve. Visit a painter if possible. ....

9. Mat and mount or frame three of your paintings, each in a different way. ....

10. Help with the arrangement, mounting, labeling, and hostessing at an exhibition of paintings for your troop, council, school or community. ....

11. Service.. ....

12. Health and safety.. ....

....

13. Promise and Laws..

....

....

MY SIGNATURE   DATE COMPLETED   LEADER'S SIGNATURE

Photography

Purpose: To be able to use your camera with artistic and technical skill.

1. Explain emulsion speeds for black and white photography; for color photography. ....

2. Explain: Depth of field. The relationship between F stops and time settings. The relationship between F stops and light source when using an automatic camera. ....

3. Describe what is meant by contrast in a black and white picture. Show some examples. ....

4. Demonstrate how to clean a lens. Explain: When foreground should be in focus. What causes out-of-focus prints. When out-of-focus is desirable. Show some examples. ....

5. Take, develop, and print a picture. Explain how to enlarge a portion of a print. Know the technical term for this process. ....

6. Using prints to illustrate; show the effect of light and shadow on a subject. Explain the following types of lighting: side, flat, flash, strobe. Demonstrate the best way to light a vase of flowers or a person sitting for a portrait. ....

7. Study the works of some well-known photographers, and tell why they are outstanding. Collect pictures of their work. ....

8. Find out about several photographers in your community. If possible, visit one to get his ideas on photography. ....

9. Take a series of pictures that tell a story. OR Take a series of slides or a motion picture, and write a narration for it. ....

10. Take a series of pictures that are purely artistic—that create a feeling or mood through the use of different textures and/or lighting effects. ....

11. Service... ....

12. Health and safety... ....

....

13. Promise and Laws.. ....

....

MY SIGNATURE   DATE COMPLETED   LEADER'S SIGNATURE

Pioneer

Purpose: To put campcraft skills to use in primitive camping.

1. Have the Campcraft badge. OR Demonstrate your ability in each of the campcraft skills. Help to plan and carry out a four-day camping trip on a primitive site by working with a group on activities in No. 2 through 8. ....

2. Select and develop the site. Include the following: Shelters. Food preparation, serving, and clean-up areas. Sanitation facilities. Campfire area. Flag pole. ....

3. Plan the meals, including some that require no cooking and some that require a variety of cooking methods. Procure, pack, transport, store, prepare, and serve food. Take part in all campkeeping. ....

4. Plan, pack, and transport personal gear suitable for the activities, the site, and weather. ....

5. Demonstrate: Skill in the use of tools, knots, lashing, compass, map. Conservation practices. Ability to forecast weather. ....

6. Plan and take part in the daily program, including activities such as, flag ceremonies, Scouts' Own, campcraft tournaments, wide games, outdoor good turns. Allow time to explore and just enjoy the surrounding country and resources. ....

7. Make plans on how to meet emergencies, such as, forest fires, sudden storm, a lost camper, wilderness first aid, evacuation. ....

8. On the last day, strike camp and restore site, as much as possible, to original or better condition. As soon as you return home, return equipment, evaluate the success of the trip, and make a record of your recommendations for your next trip. ....

9. Service... ....

10. Health and safety..

....

11. Promise and Laws..

....

....

MY SIGNATURE   DATE COMPLETED   LEADER'S SIGNATURE

Tree and Shrub

Plant

Plant Kingdom

Purpose: To study trees or wild plants at first hand and to understand their importance to man.

1. Choose one of the following categories: Trees and shrubs. OR Plants. Identify fifteen or more found in your locality.

2. Find out all you can about five by observing, reading and talking with others. Collect pictures or make color sketches of them.

3. Be able to identify your chosen five by shape, size, color and other distinguishing marks. Be able to tell about each: Where it grows. Where in the world it is native. Its life cycle and what happens in each season. How it absorbs food. Method of protection. How used by wild life and by man.

4. Find out which laws in your state were enacted to protect plant life, particularly those which affect your category. Know some of the insects and diseases which are harmful.

5. Visit a tree nursery or plant garden. Plant a tree or find three relatives of wild plants in a local greenhouse.

6. Raise a plant or tree from seed. OR Fill a terrarium with common plants and show how to keep them in healthy condition.

7. Be able to identify poison plants that grow in your locality. Tell how to protect yourself and what to do for such poisoning.

8. Service...

9. Health and safety...

10. Promise and Laws...

Player-Producer

Purpose: To be able to help write and produce a play.

1. With your patrol or others: Attend two or more plays given by a community dramatics group. OR Watch two or more plays on TV. Write reviews of each and look for newspaper reviews for comparison. Discuss the quality of subject matter of the play, the acting, and the stage setting. ....

2. Visit a TV or radio station to see how a play is produced. OR Invite a consultant to a troop meeting to tell about: Terminology of the theatre. Voice and mood projection. Make-up. Mechanics of play production. ....

3. With a group, read aloud plays by three famous playwrights and tell what you liked and disliked about each. Discuss the criteria for a good plot and the techniques of dialogue writing. ....

4. Practice the correct way to walk, sit, stand, rise, run, and relax on stage. Pantomime five characters or actions. Demonstrate voice control by reading short selections from three plays. ....

5. By yourself or with a group: Write a short play. OR Put a story or narrative poem into play form. Prepare the play for production. ....

6. Read about techniques of costuming and staging. Sketch or find pictures that could be used to make costumes for one of the plays in No. 3 or the play in No. 5. ....

7. Help produce the play in No. 5 by helping with two or more of the following jobs: Casting. Acting. Directing. Staging. Costuming. Set construction. Lighting. Publicizing. Make-up. ....

8. Service.. ....

9. Health and safety...
   ....

10. Promise and Laws..
    ....

Public Health

Purpose: To find out what and who contributes to the health of people throughout the world.

1. Learn about ten different professions related to public health and the educational requirements for each. Explore the scope of opportunity for employment in one of these.

   ....

2. Learn about one disease spread by each of four of the following: mosquitoes, wood ticks, flies, fleas, rats, snails, worms. Find out where these diseases are found and what is being done to control them.

   ....

3. Make a chart of the main divisions of your state department of health. Find out what the name of each division means and what each does. OR Investigate the work of the Quarantine Division of the U. S. Public Health Service as it relates to inspection of ships, planes, and people entering the United States of America.

   ....

4. Explore the work of four voluntary health organizations. Tell others of the work of one of these through the written word or through displays.

   ....

5. Visit a camp, restaurant, public market, theatre, or other public building and ask about the health and safety regulations that must be observed.

   ....

6. Learn the background and purpose of the World Health Organization or UNICEF. Tell what it is doing to improve conditions in one country.

   ....

7. For at least six weeks, collect newspaper and magazine articles related to public health. Explain what you discover from these.

   ....

8. Service...   ....

9. Health and safety.......................................

   ....

10. Promise and Laws...

   ....

Puppeteer

Purpose: To learn the story of puppetry and to be able to make puppets and help produce puppet shows.

1. Look up the origin of puppets. This term includes shadow puppets, hand puppets, and marionette (string) puppets. Draw a sketch of three and explain how they operate.

2. Watch a professional puppet show if possible.

3. Talk with a puppeteer or skilled amateur about making and operating puppets. OR Read a book on puppetry.

4. Learn how to make and light stages for shadow, hand, and marionette puppet shows.

5. Make a shadow puppet and use it in a shadowgraph play.

6. Make a simple hand puppet with the features and costume from a story, play, or opera. Do an impromptu skit with your puppet.

7. Make a marionette or hand puppet using a different material for the head than used in No. 6. Know why features need to be exaggerated.

8. Make a marionette puppet and explain the different string arrangements.

9. Practice: Operating a puppet in time with action of the story. Speaking for the puppet as it acts out its part.

10. With your patrol or others, put on a puppet show using puppets, scenery, and stage you helped to make.

11. Service

12. Health and safety

13. Promise and Laws

Radio and Television

Purpose: To discover what makes successful radio and TV programs. To try your hand at some of these jobs.

1. Visit a radio or TV studio. Find out how many people are involved in producing a show, the types of jobs, and the techniques used. Make a list of broadcasting terms and become familiar with language of the trade.   ....

2. Read a variety of scripts (from your local station if possible) of spot announcements, news, commercials, and dramatic shows.   ....

3. Listen to several kinds of programs. Describe what is characteristic about TV, about radio. Go through your local newspaper, classify which news might be appropriate for TV, for radio, for neither.   ....

4. Listen to three programs for children. Outline a program you think children would enjoy. OR Outline a TV show for teenagers and get help from your patrol to put it on for your troop.   ....

5. Prepare a time sheet for radio or TV variety or music show. Explain ways of prompting.   ....

6. Learn about various uses of radio and TV transmission such as ham radios, radio telephone, police radio, closed-circuit TV.   ....

7. Prepare a 15-minute radio program on Girl Scouting featuring news, interview, music, or drama. Include timing, sound effects, editing tape, and, if possible, tape the program.   ....

8. Prepare a TV script for short show on Girl Scouting. Include visuals—film clips, stills, posters—and show how you would handle them.   ....

9. Service...   ....

10. Health and safety..   ....

....

11. Promise and Laws...

....

....

MY SIGNATURE   DATE COMPLETED   LEADER'S SIGNATURE

Reader

Purpose: To stretch your own life and imagination through the writing of other men and to learn something about the history of books, how they are made, and how to take care of yours.

1. Read one book in each of the following categories: Poetry. Essay. Biography. Mystery. Travel. Novel. History. Drama. Autobiography. Write a review of three. ....

2. Start a file of prose and poetry for troop or camp ceremonies. ....

3. Find out what services are offered by the Library of Congress in Washington, D.C., the United States Superintendent of Documents, and your local library. Use the services of one. ....

4. Learn how a book is produced from manuscript to finished book. Discuss how books were made before the printing press. If possible look at rare books in a museum or private collection and visit a printing plant. ....

5. Make a display of books that use different kinds of type. OR Letter a poem or short story. ....

6. Make a display of the works of your favorite illustrators. OR Illustrate a poem or short story. ....

7. Inventory your personal collection of books. Ask a librarian to show you how books are cared for, mended, rebound. Rebind an old book or bind one you have made. ....

8. Select several stories or poems to read aloud with your friends and several to read to children. ....

9. Make an annotated booklist of one subject or one type of literature. ....

10. Read six book reviews in magazines or newspapers. Compare them with those you have written. ....

11. Service.. ....

12. Health and safety..

....

13. Promise and Laws..

....

....

Reporter

Purpose: To explore the story behind the newspapers and to get experience as a journalist.

1. Visit the various departments of a newspaper. Observe how news is gathered, how newspapers are made up and printed. ....

2. Collect and compare a variety of newspapers, different types of reporting, examples of news and feature stories, cartoons, reviews, editorials, headlines, and layouts. ....

3. Help produce a school, troop, or camp newspaper. ....

4. Write a news story about your troop happenings or an adventure you have had in Scouting and submit it to your council, school, or church bulletin. ....

5. Interview someone and write up the interview in newspaper style. OR Write a feature story for one of your community papers. ....

6. Write an editorial on a local or national issue. OR Write a review of a movie or play you have seen or book you have read. ....

7. Be able to recognize two or three printing types and to use proofreader's marks. OR Read about the life of a famous journalist or the history of newspapers. Prepare an exhibit or notebook to share with your troop. ....

8. Write a sample report for your troop leader on your return from an imaginary national or international event. OR Compare makeup of a newspaper from another country with one here. ....

9. Service.. ....
10. Health and safety...
....
11. Promise and Laws...
....

Rock and Mineral

Purpose: To be able to understand the language of the "rock hounds" and perhaps make their fascinating hobby your own.

1. Make a kit of simple equipment, including a good resource book, and begin collecting samples of rocks and minerals. Decide how you will label and store them. ....

2. Be able to identify at least ten rocks with proper name and regional location. Identify ten minerals found in their natural state; tell how they are used. ....

3. Visit one place of geological interest and learn something of its history. OR Collect pictures of other places and tell what rocks and minerals are found there. Visit a museum or a person who has a private collection to learn about rocks and minerals that are not common to your area. ....

4. Know how igneous, metamorphic, and sedimentary rocks are formed; name examples of each. Tell how weather affects rocks and how soil is formed. ....

5. Know three tests for identifying species you have collected. Learn about crystal formation and make some crystals. OR Find a fossil plant or animal and from its appearance be able to tell how and what kind of rock contained it. ....

6. Visit a lapidary for a demonstration of stone cutting. OR Visit a jewelry store to examine and learn about precious and semi-precious stones. ....

7. Make an exhibit based on your discoveries and your collection. ....

8. Service... ....

9. Health and safety...

    ....

10. Promise and Laws..

    ....

....

MY SIGNATURE   DATE COMPLETED   LEADER'S SIGNATURE

Science Badge

Purpose: To use a scientific method to solve problems in the physical and biological sciences.

1. Collect water from a stream or pond and, under a microscope, compare its animal and plant life with the life in water from your tap. Explain why they are different. ....

2. Make a chemical garden; explain what happens and why. ....

3. Add one chemical to the water of each of several plants potted in sand. Tell what has happened to each plant after a week or so, and why. Use chemicals which the plant ordinarily needs. Plant one in an ordinary garden soil for comparison. Describe the connection between the results of the experiment with you and your diet. ....

4. Explain and demonstrate how three classes of levers work. ....

5. Collect newspaper reports of space exploration and peacetime uses of atomic energy and share them with your troop. ....

6. Show in a simple diagram the composition of an atom (not hydrogen), lettering the electron orbits if possible. OR Demonstrate a simple experiment in chemistry for your patrol or troop. ....

7. Explain how we know the length of a year on each of the planets in our solar system. ....

8. Tell how to determine the distance between you and a flash of lightning. During an electrical storm, record the distances of five flashes of lightning. Explain why this method is accurate. ....

9. Design and develop a scientific project. Display it at a Junior Science Fair. OR Help organize and set up a troop science exhibit to be displayed at a Cadette gathering. ....

10. Compare the steps in planning with the scientific method you used. ....

11. Service... ....

12. Health and safety... ....

....

13. Promise and Laws..

....

....

MY SIGNATURE   DATE COMPLETED   LEADER'S SIGNATURE

Small Craft

Purpose: To be able to handle one type of small craft with enough skill to take a one-day trip.

1. Have the Swimmer's badge. OR Show you can jump into water over your head, recover, tread water, and swim with ease. ....

2. Choose one type of craft, such as a rowboat, canoe, or sailboat. With a partner demonstrate: Boarding and casting off. Use of safety equipment. Pivot turns to port and starboard. Maneuvering a triangular course. Landing, debarking, and mooring. ....

3. Draw sketch of craft. Identify all parts and equipment and explain their importance. Describe other classes of your type of craft and explain their advantages and disadvantages. ....

4. Tell about care necessary to keep craft in good condition. Demonstrate making simple repairs. Help recondition a boat. Make an article that will make your craft more comfortable. Tie and demonstrate at least four knots, hitches, or splices used aboard. Show how to whip ends of a line. ....

5. Take part in a deliberate upset and, with the aid of another, right and propel craft to shore. OR Demonstrate rescue of two people clinging to capsized boat. OR Rescue a tired swimmer with a boat. Be able to give artificial respiration. ....

6. Describe important weather and distress signals. OR Forecast weather 24 hours ahead for a one-week period. Discuss rules of the road and boating laws. Find out which boating organizations in your community give help in seamanship. ....

7. Make a list of favorite sea chanteys or stories. Teach two chanteys to your patrol or to younger Girl Scouts. ....

8. Help plan and carry out a day's trip using your craft as transportation. Demonstrate how to pack equipment, dress for the trip, and chart a course. ....

9. Service... ....

10. Health and safety... ....

    ....

11. Promise and Laws... ....

    ....

....

MY SIGNATURE   DATE COMPLETED   LEADER'S SIGNATURE

Social Dancer

Purpose: To increase your dancing ability, poise, and self-confidence.

1. Learn how to dance the waltz, foxtrot, and three other popular dances. ....

2. With your leader or dance consultant, arrange for some social dance lessons for the girls in your troop and boy partners. OR Ask your dance consultant to tell the troop about vocational possibilities in the field of the dance. ....

3. Develop some ideas for getting a dance party off to a quick start. Be able to teach an ice breaker. Know several ways to help guests to mingle. Plan a well balanced dance party. ....

4. Dramatize several situations that demonstrate good manners at a dance. ....

5. Learn some of the history of: One form of stage dancing. OR One famous choreographer. Make an exhibit or plan a skit to share this information with others. ....

6. Find out about several famous dance teams. With others, see at least one performance on TV or elsewhere. Discuss the techniques and interpretations involved in the performances. ....

7. Help create and/or take part in the choreography for an entertainment to be given by your troop or camp. OR Help promote such an event in your community by acting as an usher, selling tickets, or distributing publicity folders. OR Arrange a record concert of dance music past and present. ....

8. Service................................ ....

9. Health and safety................................ ....

....

10. Promise and Laws................................ ....

....

Sports

Purpose: To learn the fine points of one particular sport.

1. Choose one of the following sports: tennis, paddle tennis, badminton, ping-pong, golf, archery, bowling, shuffleboard, skiing, skating. Learn the rules and be able to explain them to others. Practice your sport until you can play it well. ....

2. Tell about the history and development of the sport and the countries in which it is most popular. Know the types of competition or tournaments connected with it. ....

3. Know the points to be considered in selecting, caring for, using, and storing equipment needed for your sport. ....

4. Know the health and safety rules and the proper attire for your sport. Show how to give first aid for the type of injuries which might result from participation. ....

5. Take part in some form of competition. After the event, analyze and discuss with your teammates or other participants how you can improve your play. ....

6. Help plan and run off a competition in any one of the sports listed in the first requirement. ....

7. Officiate as a referee, umpire, timekeeper, or scorekeeper for a competitive event in your particular sport. ....

8. Service... ....

9. Health and safety.. ....

....

10. Promise and Laws...

....

....

MY SIGNATURE   DATE COMPLETED   LEADER'S SIGNATURE

Stamp Collector

Purpose: To start a fascinating hobby and through it increase your knowledge of countries around the world.

1. Mount 350 stamps in an album. Include in the collection: stamps from 20 countries; 75 stamps from one country or 50 stamps depicting one topic, such as heads of states, wildlife, ships. ....

2. Demonstrate how to use: Stamp catalogs. Tongs. Hinges. Magnifying glass. Watermark detector. Perforation gauge. ....

3. Make up two games which use stamps. OR Design a stamp to honor an historical event or famous person. ....

4. Tour a United States Post Office. OR Invite a postal employee to tell your troop how the United States Post Office operates. ....

5. Identify: Five stamps, each from a different country, from the official symbol and the name in Arabic, Cyrillic, or Greek script. Two stamps from their foreign money value. ....

6. Set up an exhibit of two stamps from each of the following classifications: Commemorative. Envelope. Slogan cancellation. Postage due. Air mail. Special delivery. Revenue. Explain the use of each classification. ....

7. Start or belong to a stamp club. OR Visit an experienced collector. OR Order a first day cover and be able to explain its value. ....

8. Make a display of stamps from countries that belong to the World Association. OR Use United States postage stamps and a map of the country to tell a story about our industry, history, or famous people. ....

9. Interest someone else in stamp collecting and help her to remove stamps from envelopes and to mount stamps in an album. ....

10. Service.................................... ....

11. Health and safety.................................... ....
....

12. Promise and Laws.................................... ....
....

....

Star

Purpose: To explore the wonders of the night sky, to learn to recognize some constellations, to begin an interest in astronomy.

1. Locate the Big Dipper and find the North Star. Make a drawing of the Big Dipper and North Star twice in one evening three hours apart. ....

2. Find another constellation. Notice location with respect to same landmark twice in one evening, three hours apart. Read a legend about this constellation, tell the legend to your troop or direct your patrol in a play which dramatizes it. ....

3. Be able to identify ten constellations looking at the sky. ....

4. Once a week, at the same time and place for two months, notice position of constellation you chose in No. 2. Be able to explain what motion of the earth caused the changes you observed. ....

5. Look for the moon each clear evening for a month. With simple materials, demonstrate how and what occurred. ....

6. Note which planets are visible in the sky on one evening and in what constellations they are. Draw a map which shows the position of one planet. Find it in the sky once each month for three months, and draw it in its new position on your map. Explain what the apparent movement of the planet among the stars tells us about its real movement. ....

7. Assist in planning a party using games based on stars and planets. OR Make a device to help younger Girl Scouts learn about stars. ....

8. Service.. ....

9. Health and safety..

....

10. Promise and Laws..

....

....

MY SIGNATURE   DATE COMPLETED   LEADER'S SIGNATURE

Swimmer

Purpose: To learn the basic swimming skills and to qualify for advanced waterfront activities.

1. Explain safety precautions such as buddy board, ring buoy, pole, first aid kit and show you know how to use them. ....

2. Be able to swim 100 yards at one time using three of the following: elementary back stroke, breast stroke, side stroke, crawl stroke. ....

3. Learn one stroke not listed above. OR Play water games with younger children that will help them learn one or two first steps in swimming. ....

4. Rest in a back floating position for two minutes. OR Tread water for two minutes. ....

5. Surface dive to a depth of 6 to 8 feet. OR Swim 10 yards under water. OR Do a standing and running front dive in good form. ....

6. Recover yourself after falling in the water with your clothes on from a boat, canoe, dock, or side of pool. Stay near craft, dock, or edge of pool and remain afloat for five minutes. ....

7. Demonstrate one method of artificial respiration. ....

8. Demonstrate the safe way to get in and out of a rowboat or canoe. ....

9. Take part in a water pageant or play day. OR Practice formation swimming to music. ....

10. Service.. ....

11. Health and safety.. ....

....

12. Promise and Laws.. ....

....

Textile Arts

Purpose: To be able to design and make articles using a variety of textile techniques.

1. Learn five embroidery stitches and work a picture using your own original design.

2. Look at contemporary printed textiles in stores. Collect swatches of several types. Create a design for dress, drapery, or upholstery fabric.

3. Study a variety of kinds of weaving; collect samples. Weave a small original piece on a cardboard or box loom.

4. Learn about needlepoint, quilting, and hooking rugs. Make a needlepoint design on graph paper and work a finished piece. OR Make a quilt square in patchwork or appliqué. OR Make a sample of hooking using your own design.

5. Choose one of the categories below and in addition to the specific requirement do the following: Visit an artist, designer, factory, studio, or museum to find out techniques of production. Collect swatches, samples, pictures, and finished articles. Prepare a scrapbook or an exhibit. Find out about traditional and contemporary works in this country and three other countries.

   Weaving: Complete a piece of original flat weaving on a two-harness or four-harness loom or a box loom and one piece of narrow weaving on an inkle, finger, or card loom.

   Creative Stitchery: Know how to do ten different stitches. Design and make a picture or wall hanging and a household or clothing item.

   Textile Decoration: Design and use two of the following: stencil in more than one color, block print, silk screen, batik, abstract using dowels, sea shells, twigs, and the like.

6. Service

7. Health and safety

8. Promise and Laws

MY SIGNATURE   DATE COMPLETED   LEADER'S SIGNATURE

Traveler

Purpose: To help plan and carry out a three-to-five-day trip on which you travel by bus, car, train, or plane and stay in hotels or motels.

1. Decide where to go and find out all the interesting things to see and do along the way. Using timetable or road maps, plan an itinerary that includes sightseeing and overnight stops. ....

2. Considering the type of trip, season, method of transportation, and activities planned, discuss with other travelers: Clothing and equipment to take and how it should be handled. Meals to be planned. Tipping customs. ....

3. Estimate all expenses (individual and group) and discuss how they will be met. Adjust plans if necessary. Be able to: Send a telegram. Buy and cash a money order or traveler's check. Place a long distance call. ....

4. Practice: Packing and caring for personal equipment. Ordering meals in a restaurant and cafeteria. ....

5. Talk over: Courtesy to other travelers and use of public facilities. How to keep group together and what to do if separated. How to ask for help in a city. What to do in an emergency in a public conveyance or in an automobile. ....

6. Obtain necessary permissions and make all reservations, including those for adults accompanying the group. Go on the trip. ....

7. Help compile a log of the trip by taking photos or sketching pictures, writing an account of one day's activities, collecting printed materials about places of interest. Write an account for the newspaper or a letter to a friend, or tell the story to your class in school. ....

8. After the trip, discuss how it went, write thank-you notes, make a financial report. ....

9. Service ....

10. Health and safety ....

....

11. Promise and Laws ....

....

....

MY SIGNATURE　　　　　　　　DATE COMPLETED　　　　　　　　LEADER'S SIGNATURE

Weather

Purpose: To be able to forecast weather and to avoid or meet any emergencies it causes.

1. Collect pictures or make sketches of sky and clouds for a weather book or weather chart. Identify and explain four different kinds of clouds. Tell which ones come with a warm front and which with a cold front. ....

2. Explain how to read a weather map. Define: "Highs" and "lows." Cold and warm fronts. Weather movements. Tell how movements change the weather around you. ....

3. Make three or more of the following instruments: a hair hygrometer, a wet and dry bulb, a psychrometer, a weather vane, an anemometer, a nephoscope, a barometer. Use them to forecast weather. ....

4. Keep a detailed weather chart for a two-week period in two different seasons. ....

5. Explain what causes the following: storms in your vicinity, tornadoes, hurricanes, typhoons, cyclones, thunderstorms, lightning, snow, hail, and rain. Explain why clothes dry better on certain days and why light-colored clothes are cooler than dark. ....

6. Know two ways to figure wind velocity. Learn four trustworthy weather proverbs. ....

7. Know the rules of safe conduct indoors and outdoors during a storm. Be able to give first aid for: Sunstroke. Heat exhaustion. Shock. Frostbite. ....

8. With others set up a weather station which could be used in a camp setting to help others learn about forecasting. ....

9. Service... ....

10. Health and safety... ....

....

11. Promise and Laws...

....

....

MY SIGNATURE   DATE COMPLETED   LEADER'S SIGNATURE

World Heritage

Purpose: To discover how people from many places and many times have made the world we live in today.

1. Make a map, chart, or poster that shows the number and place of origin of people who immigrated to this country. ....

2. Produce an original skit, play, or choral reading that shows how some of the ideas, customs, and names from other countries have become part of our country. ....

3. Plan an imaginary trip to the country of one of your ancestors. Find out: If you need a passport, visas, immunizations. How much money you need to cover living and travel expenses. Something about the country—the people, language, history, customs, climate, currency, places of interest. ....

4. Plan and carry out a way to tell others: What your state was like before the first settlers arrived. What it is like today. The people and events that brought about the change. ....

5. Prepare and serve a main dish typical of another country. ....

6. Choose two member countries of the World Association of Girl Guides and Girl Scouts and find out how the girls your age live in each. Compare their daily life with yours. ....

7. Learn the story of the Statue of Liberty. Read the poem that is on the base of the statue and explain in your own words what it means. ....

8. Service... ....

9. Health and safety..

   ....

10. Promise and Laws..

    ....

World Trefoil

Purpose: To follow the "magic thread" of Girl Scouting and Girl Guiding around the world.

1. Make a display that shows all the countries that have Girl Scouts/Guides. Include pictures of several uniforms and pins worn by the girls and point out at least two things all Girl Scouts and Guides have in common.

2. Read one publication of the World Association of Girl Guides and Girl Scouts. Discuss and list ways that you think the World Association can contribute to international understanding and peace.

3. Find out where the hostels operated by the World Association of Girl Guides and Girl Scouts are located and who may stay in them. Learn to sing: "Our Chalet Song," "Our Cabana Song," "The World Song."

4. Pretend you are to hostess a Girl Scout/Guide from another country. Explain how you would: Greet her and introduce her to your family and friends. Acquaint her with members of your troop and Girl Scouting in this country. Help her understand life in your community, state, and nation.

5. Plan and carry out a program which will explain the origin, purpose, and use of the Juliette Low World Friendship Fund.

6. Find out: The types of and requirements for national and international events open to Senior Girl Scouts. How girls apply to attend these events.

7. Service

8. Health and safety

9. Promise and Laws

MY SIGNATURE   DATE COMPLETED   LEADER'S SIGNATURE

World Understanding

Purpose: To be a "good neighbor" and to find out about the many organizations that are helping the people of the world understand and appreciate one another.

1. Find out: About two organizations that sponsor international exchanges for young people. The qualifications for exchangees and how to apply.

2. Be familiar with the work of the United States Information Agency and the United States Tourist Service. Show how their activities can further international understanding.

3. Take part in a project that will help Brownie or Junior Girl Scouts learn about children in another country—how they live, play, talk, go to school.

4. Discuss: What a traveler should know about this country and the one in which she travels in order to be a good representative of the United States of America. How the traveler should conduct herself while traveling in another country.

5. Help plan and participate in a project for Pan American Day, Human Rights Day, United Nations Day, or Thinking Day.

6. Find out about three nongovernmental organizations that work for the benefit of people throughout the world. Make a display to show what they do and how individuals can participate.

7. Present a patrol skit to show what it means to be a good neighbor in your community, your country, and in the world.

8. Invite a Senior Girl Scout to tell your troop about International Aides, International Friendship activities of Senior troops, Girl Scout international opportunities.

9. Service...

10. Health and safety...

....

11. Promise and Laws...

....

....

MY SIGNATURE   DATE COMPLETED   LEADER'S SIGNATURE

Our Own Troop's..Badge

When you and other members of your troop have an interest which is not included in any of the badges in this *Handbook*, you can develop a special Our Own Troop's.......................Badge on that subject. An individual girl cannot do this badge by herself. A group must make up the requirements, the name, and the symbol together. No other girls in your troop or any other troop can use your badge. Even if they choose the same subject, they must create their own requirements and symbol.

To earn this badge:

Make sure that your chosen subject is not covered in any of the Cadette badges, and that it does not conflict with the Girl Scout Promise and Laws.

Ask your council for approval of your badge subject. The council approves only the subject of the badge, not its requirements.

With your leader, review the meaning and characteristics of Cadette badges. Then write your own requirements on the next page, agree on a name for the badge and a design for the badge symbol. The name of your subject goes in the blank space in the title Our Own Troop's......................Badge. You put the design for your badge symbol on the blank badge with the gold border.

Do the requirements in a way that satisfies you, your leader, and your consultant (if you have one for this badge). Include the Cadette requirements on service, health and safety, and the Promise and Laws.

When you have completed your badge, send a copy of the requirements and a sample badge symbol to your council and to the National Program Committee at national headquarters for their information and possible display.

Purpose: ....
....
....
....
....
....
....
....
....
....
....
....
....
....
....
....
....

Service ....
Health and safety ....
      ....
Promise and Laws ....
      ....
....

MY SIGNATURE   DATE COMPLETED   LEADER'S SIGNATURE

bibliography

On the following pages are listed a number of publications that you will find useful as you earn proficiency badges, accept Challenges, enjoy troop and patrol activities, go camping, or follow any of the many suggestions in this *Handbook*. Don't think for a moment that all the good books are listed here, for there are literally hundreds of them. Since new titles are published almost daily, you will probably discover other publications not mentioned here that will serve your particular purpose equally well. Most major newspapers have a Sunday book section or page. This is a good source of information about new titles.

Many of these books you will find in your library. There may be some you will want to buy for yourself and some your troop will decide to add to the troop library.

If your troop, patrol, or Challenge group wants information from a publisher or organization or to order a publication, have *one* member write the request. This should be a clear, brief, specific description of exactly what you are seeking. Make sure the return address is complete and legible and, for an order, that a check or money order for the correct amount is enclosed.

For publications available from Girl Scouts of the U.S.A., mail your order to whichever address is nearest to you: Girl Scout National Equipment Service

830 Third Avenue, New York 22, New York

1824 Washington Avenue, St. Louis 3, Missouri

770 Mission Street, San Francisco 3, California

Promise and Laws

STORIES TO LIVE BY edited by Marjorie Vetter (Platt and Munk, New York, N.Y., 1960, $2.95)

A collection of thirty stories, which first appeared in the *American Girl* magazine, offers practical help in meeting the problems of daily living as a Cadette-age girl. Includes a short sketch about the author of each story.

TEENAGERS WHO MADE HISTORY by Russell Freedman (Holiday House, Inc., New York, N.Y., 1961, $3.50)

Interesting stories about people who distinguished themselves in some significant way before they were twenty years old. Each one was deeply stirred by an idea, a cause, or an experience.

THE AMERICAN GIRL (The American Girl, Dept. A, 830 Third Avenue, New York 22, N.Y.)

A magazine published monthly by the Girl Scouts of the U.S.A. for its members and other girls who wish to subscribe. It includes ideas for troop activities, how-to-do-it articles helpful in badges and Challenges, and exciting stories. Special Girl Scout Troop subscription rate is $1.50 for one year, $3 for two years. Regular subscription price is $3 a year, $5 for two years. To cover postage for subscriptions to addresses outside the U.S.A. add 50 cents per year to Canada, $1 per year to all other countries.

Famous American Women

AMERICA AND WOMEN by Marjorie R. Longwell (Dorrance & Company, Philadelphia, Pa., 1962, $3.00)

Fictionized biographies of seven American women to whom all Americans owe much and in whose accomplishments the sweep of American history is reflected.

AMERICAN WOMEN WHO SCORED FIRST by Aylesa Forsee (Macrae Smith Co., Philadelphia, Pa., 1958, $2.95)

The big bright adventure in the lives of ten famous American women.

GREAT AMERICAN HEROINES by Arnold Dolin (Hart Publishing Co., Inc., New York, N.Y., 1960, $1.00 paperback)

Highlights from the life stories of many famous American women from early colonial times to the present.

JULIETTE LOW AND THE GIRL SCOUTS (Girl Scouts of the U.S.A., Cat. No. 19-409, $1.00)

An official biography of the Founder of Girl Scouting. Includes collection of rare photographs of her childhood, married life, and the early days of Scouting.

PIONEERS IN PETTICOATS by David K. Boynick (Thomas Y. Crowell Co., New York, N.Y., 1959, $3.00)

The life stories of eight famous American women who were heroic fighters. (Mary Lyon, Susan B. Anthony, Belva Ann Lockwood, Antoinette Brown, Alice Hamilton, Lillian M. Gilbreth, Amelia Earhart, Dorothy Shaver).

Service

"Do a good turn daily" is the goal of every Girl Scout. As a Cadette, your special goal is to recognize and be prepared to meet the needs of others every day. Your *Handbook* and every title in this Bibliography will help you gain the skills you need to do this.

Troop Management

Chapter 2, "Your Troop," and Chapter 3, "Count Down for Troop Program," in this *Handbook* contain the information you need.

Citizenship

AMERICAN POETRY by Karl Shapiro (Thomas Y. Crowell Co., New York, N.Y., 1960, $5.95)

Appreciation of our national heritage through an excellent collection of American poetry for all occasions—ceremonies, choral readings, reading aloud or reading alone.

GOOD CITIZEN (The American Heritage Foundation, New York, N.Y., 1956, 50 cents)

Booklet that describes the working tools of good citizenship and tells how to use them. Includes definitions, quotations, flag etiquette, and the "nine keys to good citizenship."

A BOOK OF AMERICANS by Stephen Vincent Benet and Rosemary Benet (Holt, Rinehart and Winston, Inc., New York, N.Y., 1953, $3.25)

Fifty-six poems about famous American men and women.

FACTS ABOUT THE UNITED STATES (Superintendent of Documents, U.S. Government Printing Office, Washington 25, D. C., Catalog No. D2.14:5-8A, 1961, 30 cents)

Contains important, interesting, up-to-date facts on the land, people, government, natural resources, living standards, of the United States of America.

OUR AMERICAN GOVERNMENT (Superintendent of Documents, U.S. Government Printing Office, Washington 25, D.C., 1960, 15 cents)

Questions and answers on the history and functions of our government.

POSTAGE STAMPS OF THE UNITED STATES (Superintendent of Documents, U.S. Government Printing Office, Washington 25, D. C. 1962, $1.25)

Booklet illustrates and describes postage issues from 1847. Provides names of designers, engravers, quantities of stamps sold, lists of plate numbers, and other details of interest to stamp collectors.

THE PRESIDENCY by Gerald W. Johnson (William Morrow & Company, Inc., New York, N.Y., 1962, $2.95)

What everyone should know about the highest office of our country.

THE U.S.A. ANSWERS edited by Kenneth E. Beer (U.S. & World Publications, Inc., New York, N.Y., 1961, $2.50 paperback; $5.00 cloth bound)

A guide to understanding the United States of America. 1800 questions and answers divided into categories such as American people and land, education, culture, and how Americans live.

WHAT EVERYONE SHOULD KNOW ABOUT THE CONSTITUTION OF THE UNITED STATES OF AMERICA (Channing L. Bete Co., Inc., Greenfield, Mass., 1960, 50 cents)

A lively, interesting interpretation of the Constitution. Colorful cartoon type illustrations.

THE WHITE HOUSE: AN HISTORIC GUIDE (The White House Historical Association, Room 1013, Interior Department Building, Washington 25, D. C., 1962, $1.00)

More than a guide for those who are fortunate enough to visit the White House, this richly illustrated book includes exciting insight into the lives of the families who have lived there and the things they have left behind in it. Pictures in color of the famous paintings, furniture, and rooms stimulate pride in our national heritage, and new understanding of the role played by many First Ladies.

YOU AND YOUR FLAG (Channing L. Bete Co., Inc., Greenfield, Mass., 1958, 25 cents)

What everyone should know about the National Emblem of the United States of America. Includes official proportions of the flag and flag etiquette.

YOUR RUGGED CONSTITUTION by Bruce Allyn Findlay and Esther Blair Findlay (Stanford University Press, Stanford, Calif., 1952, $3.00)

An illustrated explanation of our country's Constitution, and the ideals behind it.

International Friendship

HI NEIGHBOR Series (Hastings House Publishers, Inc., New York, and U.S. Committee for UNICEF, United Nations, N.Y., $1.50 each)

A series of paperback books with stories, games, songs, illustrations and other information about five different countries. Basic reference for Brownies and Juniors, especially good for Cadettes when they are working with children.

SAY IT—IN ANOTHER LANGUAGE (Girl Scouts of the U.S.A., Cat. No. 19-200, 20 for $1.00)

A pocket card with 33 everyday phrases in English, French, German, Japanese, and Spanish. Each foreign phrase given with simple pronunciation guide. Fits conveniently into uniform pocket.

SAY IT Record (Girl Scout Audio-Visual Materials Service, 830 Third Avenue, New York, N.Y., Cat. No. 18-01, $2.98)

Everyday phrases, folk songs, and "Taps" in French, German, Japanese and Spanish on 12-inch, 33⅓ rpm, unbreakable record.

TRAVEL WITH YOUR HEART (Youth Activities Committee, People-to-People Program, 45 Worth St., New York 13, N.Y., 15 cents)

A guide to happier traveling; good suggestions for guests or hosts.

TREFOIL AROUND THE WORLD (Girl Scouts of the U.S.A., Cat. No. 23-122, $1.50)

Facts about Girl Guiding and Girl Scouting in the member countries of the World Association. Illustrations of membership pins and uniforms; flags of member countries in color. Section on history of worldwide Scouting movement.

THE WHOLE WORLD IN YOUR HANDS (U.S. Dept. of Agriculture, Federal Extension Service, Washington 25, D. C., Catalog No. 4-H-190(10-61), 1961, Single copy free)

A booklet about other countries divided by geographic areas.

YOUNG PEOPLE OF EAST ASIA—AUSTRALIA by Charles A. Joy (Duell Sloan & Pearce, Inc., New York, N.Y., 1961, $3.50)

Interesting up-to-date information about young people in other parts of the world. Other titles by the same author and publisher include Young People of the: Eastern Mediterranean (1959) $3.50; Western Mediterranean (1960) $3.50; West Africa (1961) $3.75.

YOU 'N U.N. (Channing L. Bete Co., Inc., Greenfield, Mass., 1961, 25 cents)

Basic information about what the United Nations is and how it operates, presented in charts and drawings for quick and easy reference.

YOUR UNITED NATIONS (Order from Sales Section, United Nations, New York, N.Y., 75 cents plus 15 cents postage)

The official illustrated guide book of the United Nations Headquarters.

YOUTH AND THE WORLD (Youth Activities Committee, People-to-People Program, 45 Worth St., New York 13, N.Y., $1.00)

Good resource material; includes ideas of things to do, activities of many organizations and bibliography.

Health and Safety

AMERICAN RED CROSS FIRST AID TEXTBOOK (Order from Girl Scouts of the U.S.A., Fourth Edition—Revised 1957, Cat. No. 23-321, 75 cents)

Standard reference book for troop libraries; for use in connection with the First Aid badge and the Challenge of Emergency Preparedness.

HOME NURSING TEXTBOOK, American National Red Cross (Order from your local chapter of Red Cross, 1951, 75 cents)

Basic guide for Home Nurse and Child Care badges.

Sources for Free or Inexpensive Materials

Your own State or County Extension Service, insurance companies, your local chapter of the American National Red Cross often have excellent booklets.

Activities in the Arts

Dancing

BETTY WHITE'S TEEN-AGE DANCE BOOK by Betty White (David McKay Company, Inc., New York, N.Y., 1952, $4.50)

Clear directions for basic fox trot, waltz, polka, mixers, samba, mambo, and others. Ideas for invitations, admissions, decorations, refreshments.

BETTY WHITE'S TEEN-AGE DANCE ETIQUETTE by Betty White (David McKay Company, Inc., New York, N.Y., 1958, $4.50)

How to feel at ease at any dance.

FOLK DANCE SYLLABUS NO. 1 by Michael Herman (Folk Dance House, P.O. Box 201, Flushing, N.Y., $2.00)

Folk dances, contras, squares, suggested menus, recipes, decorations. Write to same address for price lists of folk dance records.

PROMENADE ALL by Janet E. Tobitt (Girl Scouts of the U.S.A., Cat. No. 23-469, 75 cents)

Forty-nine singing games based on American folk songs and songs from other countries. Instructions for dance steps.

SKIP TO MY LOU (Girl Scouts of the U.S.A., Cat. No. 20-199, 25 cents)

Twenty-four singing games from 14 different countries, each with melody line, lyrics, and dance instructions.

SQUARE DANCING FOR EVERYONE by Gene Gowing (Grossett and Dunlap, Inc., New York, N.Y., $1.00)

Clear directions for square dancing with authentic regional variations.

Dramatics

DRAMATICS AND CEREMONIES FOR GIRL SCOUTS (Girl Scouts of the U.S.A., Cat. No. 19-751, $1.50)

Everything needed to conduct troop dramatics and ceremonies.

Four convenient sections contain bibliography, source of all references, and ways to find additional help.

DRAMATIZED BALLADS by Janet E. Tobitt and Alice White (Girl Scouts of the U.S.A., Cat. No. 23-413, $2.95)

Twenty ballads suitable for dramatizing. Includes words and music of each, plus suggestions for staging, costuming and presenting the action.

THE FAMILY BOOK OF VERSE edited by Lewis Gannett (Harper & Brothers, New York, N.Y., 1961, $4.95)

A collection of poems to be read (preferably aloud!) and enjoyed.

PUPPETS AND PLAYS—A CREATIVE APPROACH by Marjorie Batchelder and Virginia Lee Comer (Harper & Brothers, New York, N.Y., 1956, $4.00)

Good source for Puppeter badge. How to make several kinds of puppets and marionettes and stages, scenery and construction of play.

TELEVISION: TECHNIQUES FOR PLANNING AND PERFORMANCE by S. L. Becker and H. C. Harshbarger (Henry Holt & Co., Inc., New York, N.Y., 1958, $4.00)

Excellent basic book for Radio and Television badge.

THE WAY OF UNDERSTANDING by Sarah Louise Arnold (Girl Scouts of the U.S.A., Cat. No. 19-560, $1.00)

Quotations and philosophy useful for troop ceremonies and Scouts' Own.

WONDERFUL WORLD OF THEATRE by J. B. Priestly (Garden City Books, Garden City, N.Y., 1959, $2.95)

Excellent general resource on history of the art of the theatre and various types of theatrical production. Useful for Player-Producer badge and all dramatics interests.

Music

CHANSONS DE NOTRE CHALET (Girl Scouts of the U.S.A., Cat. No. 23-919, 30 cents)

355 /BIBLIOGRAPHY

Pocket-size songbook with songs known to Girl Guides and Girl Scouts around the world.

THE DITTY BAG by Janet E. Tobitt (Girl Scouts of the U.S.A., Cat. No. 23-460, $1.00)
Folk songs, rounds and canons, hymns and carols, art songs. Some for part singing, some with descant.

FIRESIDE BOOK OF FOLKSONGS selected and edited by Margaret Bradford Boni (Simon and Schuster, Inc., New York, N.Y., 1947, $6.00)
Musical arrangements for voice and piano for 147 songs, with brief commentary on origin, background, and history.

THE FIRST BOOK Series (Franklin Watts, Inc., N.Y., $1.95 each)
Each well-illustrated book is written by an expert, for beginners. Titles in the arts include: The First Book of Jazz, First Book of Stage Costumes and Make-up.

GIRL SCOUT POCKET SONGBOOK (Girl Scouts of the U.S.A., Cat. No. 20-192, 20 cents)
Pocket-size book containing 60 favorite songs of Girl Scouts. Convenient on hikes, in camps, or wherever Girl Scouts gather. Includes songs for Girl Scout occasions, fun and action songs, Americana songs from many different sections and groups, and part songs.

LISTENER'S MUSIC LIBRARY Series (Grosset and Dunlap, Inc., New York, N.Y., $1.50 each)
Each book explores a different topic such as orchestral music, folk songs, operas, jazz.

A NEW DICTIONARY OF MUSIC by Arthur Jacob (Penquin Reference Books, Baltimore, Md., $1.25)
Glossary of musical terms, instruments, composers, work. For basic information.

SING TOGETHER — A GIRL SCOUT SONGBOOK (Girl Scouts of the U.S.A., Cat. No. 20-190, 65 cents)

The official Girl Scout songbook. Classified index in four groups; songs for ceremonies and occasions, folk songs, rounds and canons, art songs.

WORLD SONG (Girl Scouts of the U.S.A., words and melody line only, Cat. No. 23-916, 15 cents; words and full music, Cat. No. 23-917, 50 cents)

The official song of the World Association of Girl Guides and Girl Scouts. Music by Jan Sibelius, words in English and French.

Visual Arts

ADVENTURES IN STITCHES AND MORE ADVENTURES—FEWER STITCHES by Mariska Karasz (Funk & Wagnalls Co., New York, N.Y., 1959, $7.50)

Gives instructions and detailed drawings for many stitches with many ideas for creative stitchery. Valuable for Textile Arts badge.

ART FOR YOUNG AMERICA by F. W. Nicholas and M. B. Trilling, M. Lee and E. A. Stephan (Charles A. Bennett Co., Peoria, Ill., Revised 1960 by W. E. Whitford, $4.72)

Resources for art appreciation and an understanding of quality in art in many phases of modern life.

BLOCK PRINTING ON FABRICS by Florence H. Pettit (Hastings House Publishers, Inc., New York; N.Y., 1952, $5.50)

Excellent reource for fabric design, block printing, and the use of design.

BULLETIN BOARDS AND DISPLAY by Randall Haines (Davis Publications, Worcester, Mass., $3.75)

Good ideas for designing and creating artistic exhibits and bulletin boards. Directions for flannelgraphs.

CLAY, WOOD AND WIRE by Harvey Weiss (Scott Publishers, New York, N.Y., 1956, $3.50)

An excellent resource for all phases of sculpture.

CREATIVE HANDS by Doris Cox and Barbara Warren (John Wiley & Sons, Inc., New York, N.Y., 1951, $6.50)

One of the best resources in many media of the visual arts; good instruction, excellent photographs, good approach to creativity. Use for Metal Arts, Graphic Arts, and Textile Arts badges.

CREATIVE PAPER DESIGN by Ernst Rottger (Reinhold Publishing Corporation, New York, N.Y., 1961, $4.00)
Wonderful new resources on arts of paper cutting and paper sculpture.

EXPLORING THE HAND ARTS (Girl Scouts of the U.S.A., Cat. No. 19-304, 65 cents)
Chapters on design, paper, prints, bookbinding, wood, metal, glass, leather, clay, and needlecraft. Basic tools needed in each medium. Suggested projects and many how-to-do illustrations.

HOW TO MAKE POTTERY AND CERAMIC SCULPTURE by Julia H. Duncan and Victor D'Amico (Doubleday & Company, Inc., New York, N.Y., 1961, $1.95)
Excellent resource for work in clay.

JEWELRY AND ENAMELING by Greta Pack (D. Van Nostrand Co., Inc., New York, N.Y., 1961, $4.95)
One of the best and most complete books on the techniques in jewelry making. Use for Metal Arts badge also. Has good section on enameling.

PAPER, INK AND ROLLER by Harvey Weiss (Scott Publishers, New York, N.Y., 1958, $3.50)
Resource for all types of prints including linoleum.

PAPER MAGIC by Robert Harbin (Charles T. Branford Company, Newton Centre, Mass., 1957, $3.50)
Basic resource for paper folding and origami; shows basic folds and leads the reader on to creative paper folding.

STANDARD BOOK OF QUILT-MAKING AND COLLECTING by Margaret Ickis (Dover Publications, Inc., New York, N.Y., 1959, $2.00)
Resource for favorite designs for quilts, includes instructions for patchwork, appliqué and quilting.

WEAVING HANDCRAFT — 15 SIMPLE WAYS by Marthann Alexander (McKnight and McKnight Publishing Company, Bloomington, Ill., 1954, $1.60)

Simple weaving resource includes Hungarian loom, TD-loom, finger weaving, inkle loom weaving. Explains threading of two-harness loom. Good for Textile Arts badge.

Activities in the Home

TEENAGE GUIDE TO HOMEMAKING by M. S. Barclay & E. Champion (McGraw-Hill Book Company, Inc., New York, N.Y., 1961, $5.85)

Basic information on all phases of homemaking: child care, clothing, family living, personal development, foods, grooming, home furnishings and equipment, and management. Includes recommended stain removal chart.

Baby and Child Care

A MANUAL FOR BABY-SITTERS by Marion Lowndes (Little, Brown & Co., Boston, Mass., 1961, $3.50)

How to keep the child in your care safe and happy. Includes a reference section which suggests stories to read and games for children of various ages.

YOUR CHILD FROM ONE TO SIX (Children's Bureau Publication No. 30-1962, Superintendent of Documents, U.S. Government Printing Office, Washington 25, D.C., 1962, 20 cents)

Description of characteristics and typical actions of children from one to six years of age. Includes safety precautions.

Clothing

DRESS by Bess V. Oerke (Charles A. Bennett Co., Peoria, Ill., 1960, $4.69)

Basic resource for grooming, sewing, design, fabric, and clothing buying problems.

HOW YOU LOOK AND DRESS by Byrta Carson (McGraw-Hill Book Company, Inc., New York, N.Y., 1959, $5.50)

"How-to-do-it" on grooming, buying and wearing clothes, sewing and using sewing equipment, remodeling, labeling, how to select and care for clothing.

Foods

CENTENNIAL RECEIPT BOOK (Girl Scouts of the U.S.A., Cat. No. 19-407, 25 cents)

Juliette Low's 32 favorite old-fashioned Southern recipes spiced with 19th century cooking hints.

FAMILY FARE (Home & Garden Bulletin No. 1, Superintendent of Documents, U.S. Government Printing Office, Washington 25, D. C., 1960, 35 cents)

Handy booklet with facts about cooking, planning, buying, and storing foods. Includes ideas for using leftovers.

FAVORITE RECIPES OF THE UNITED NATIONS (U.S. Committee for UN, Washington, D. C., $1.50)

Recipes for international dishes from all the member countries of the United Nations.

FOOD BECOMES YOU by Ruth M. Leverton (Iowa State University Press, Ames, Iowa, 1960, $3.50)

Accurate, up-to-date, useful nutrition information. Includes facts and fallacies about overweight and underweight.

MEAL PLANNING AND TABLE SERVICE by Beth Baily McLean (Charles A. Bennett Co., Peoria, Ill., 1955, $4.40)

Planning and serving meals, how to have attractive table manners, suggestions for entertaining and ideas for meals for various occasions.

YOUNG AMERICA'S COOKBOOK (revised by Dorothy Callahan and Alma Smith Payne, Charles Scribner's Sons, New York, N.Y., 1959, $3.95)

A cookbook for the beginning cook. Recommends recipes that freeze well, and explains how to package, store, and freeze cakes and other prepared food.

Money Management

MONEY MANAGEMENT LIBRARY Series (Household Finance Corp., Chicago, Ill., 15 cents each)

Individual booklets on budgeting, savings, and guides to buying, caring for, and knowing good qualities in food, clothing, household items, home furnishings, also on health care and time management.

Personal Development and Family Living

COMPLETE BOOK OF ETIQUETTE by Amy Vanderbilt (Doubleday & Company, New York, N.Y., 1958, $5.50)

Basic source on etiquette, appropriate dress, and acceptable behavior.

FAMILY LIVING by Evelyn Duvall, edited by D. S. Lewis (The Macmillan Co., Publishers, New York, N.Y., 1961, $3.96)

Many useful suggestions for personal development and good family relations.

FUTURE PERFECT by Bernice Bryant (Bobbs-Merrill Company, Inc., New York, N.Y., 1957, $2.95)

Courtesy, letter writing, entertaining, traveling and grooming are clearly explained.

Source for Inexpensive Material

JUNIOR GUIDANCE Series Booklets (Science Research Associates, Inc., 259 East Erie St., Chicago 11, Ill.)

Gives help on how to succeed in school, get along with family and friends, solve everyday problems and plan for the future. Write for list of titles and prices.

Activities in the Out-of-Doors

Camping Fun and Skills

BE EXPERT WITH MAP AND COMPASS by Bjorn Kjellstrom (American Orienteering Service, 220 Fifth Ave., New York, N.Y., 1955, $2.00)

Basic directions for orienteering.

BETTER HOMES AND GARDENS FAMILY CAMPING (Meredith Publishing Company, New York, N.Y., 1961, $2.95)

Beautifully illustrated book filled with helpful suggestions for making the most of present-day camping equipment for carefree family camping.

COMPASS AND MAPS (Girl Scouts of the U.S.A., Cat. No. 19-630, 25 cents)

A handy pocket-size, how-to-do-it picture booklet that tells how to use a compass and read maps.

COOKING OUT-OF-DOORS (Girl Scouts of the U.S.A., Cat. No. 19-533, $1.95)

The complete book of outdoor cookery—250 recipes for novice and "pro" campers and for all weather and terrain conditions.

CREATIVE CRAFTS FOR CAMPERS by Catherine T. Hammett and Carol M. Horrocks (Association Press, New York, N.Y., $7.95)

Basic resource for camp or council libraries. Directions for splicing a rope and tying a Carrick bend are included among many others.

THE GOLDEN BOOK OF CAMPING AND CAMP CRAFTS by Gordon Lynn (Golden Press, Inc., New York, N.Y., 1959, $1.95)

All sorts of camping skills are described and explained in clear text and colorful illustrations. Includes sections on canoe trips, and out-of-camp expeditions.

KNIFE AND AXE (Girl Scouts of the U.S.A., Cat. No. 19-631, 25 cents)

A handy pocket-size, picture booklet on the care and use of the knife and axe.

TEACHING JOHNNY TO SWIM, American National Red Cross (Order from your local Red Cross Chapter, 1957, 20 cents)

Teaching tips on the fundamentals of swimming and water safety.

YOUR OWN BOOK OF CAMPCRAFT by Catherine T. Hammett (Pocket Books, Inc., New York, N.Y., 1960, 35 cents)

A pocket book of campcraft skills and program for young people. Everything from preparing a bedroll to tent pitching.

United States National Parks and National Forests

Write to Superintendent of Documents, U.S. Government Printing Office, Washington 25, D.C. for price lists of publications, including National Park System Maps and Handbooks of Historical Sites, and to order those listed below:

AREAS ADMINISTERED BY THE NATIONAL PARK SERVICE (Catalog No. I 29.66:962, 1962, 20 cents)

Gives the address and outstanding characteristics for each of the National Parks, Monuments, Battlefields, Historic sites, Recreation areas.

CAMPING (Catalog No. A1.68:502, 1962, 20 cents)

Booklet provides a sampling of some attractions that can be seen and enjoyed on National Forest and Grasslands. Includes answer to questions about camping in National Forests.

CAMPING FACILITIES IN AREAS ADMINISTERED BY THE NATIONAL PARK SERVICE (Catalog No. I.29.2:C15/3/962,1962, 10 cents)

Booklet lists camping accommodations and general information about camping facilities in each area.

Games

GAMES AND SELF-TESTING ACTIVITIES FOR THE CLASSROOM (Superintendent of Documents, U.S. Government Printing Office, Washington 25, D. C., 1961, 10 cents)

Directions for keeping your children happily occupied in a confined space.

GAMES FOR GIRL SCOUTS (Girl Scouts of the U.S.A., Cat. No. 20-632, 35 cents)

More than 100 games that fit in with Girl Scout program. Games for indoors and outdoors; games that teach woodlore; games to use for troop program in nature, music, dancing, international friendship.

GAMES OF MANY NATIONS by Evelyn Oscar Harbin (Abingdon Press, New York, N.Y., 1954, $1.95)

Clear directions for games from different countries. Includes many clever ideas for forfeits, and a classified and alphabetical index.

HANDBOOK FOR RECREATION (Children's Bureau Publication No. 231, Superintendent of Documents, U.S. Government Printing Office, Washington 25, D. C., 1960, 75 cents)

Directions for leading circle games, line games, quiet games, testing games, informal dramatic activities, action songs, suggestions for party mixers. Useful alphabetical and classified index.

WORLD-O-GAME, produced by the World Association of Girl Guides and Girl Scouts (Girl Scouts of the U.S.A., Cat. No. 22-401, $2.00)

A game for six or more in which players learn about Scouting in two languages.

Nature

ALL ABOUT BOOKS Series (Random House, New York, N.Y., $1.95 each)

Illustrated authentic presentations of scientific subjects by authorities in each field. Large variety of subjects including butterflies, electricity, famous scientific expeditions, fish, moths, and radio and television.

THE ART OF FLOWER PRESERVATION by Geneal Condon (A Sunset Book) Lane Book Co., Menlo Park, Calif., 1962, $1.95)

Specific step-by-step directions and clear illustrations explain how to select, preserve, and arrange cut flowers.

COMMON NATIVE ANIMALS (Finding, Identifying, Keeping, Studying) by Matthew F. Vessel and E. J. Harrington, (Chandler Publishing Company, Inc., San Francisco, Calif., 1961, $2.95 in paper, $4.95 in cloth)

Brief descriptions and life data on wild animals (found in or near populated places and those kept by museums). Included are suggestions for care and feeding and for activities with them.

EVERYDAY WEATHER AND HOW IT WORKS by Herman Schneider (Whittlesey House, McGraw-Hill Book Company, Inc., New York, N.Y., 1951, $3.00)

Fascinating facts about weather in nontechnical language, detailed instructions on weather maps, and how to make a home forecasting station out of simple, everyday items around the house.

A FIELD GUIDE TO THE BIRDS by Roger Tory Peterson (Houghton, Mifflin Co., Boston, Mass., 1947, $4.95)

One of a series of illustrated guide books that contains the basic information for which the nature enthusiast is looking. Other titles in the series ($4.50 to $4.95) include Field Guide to: Western Birds; Shells of Our Atlantic and Gulf Coasts; Shells of the Pacific Coast and Hawaii; Butterflies; Mammals; Rocks and Minerals; Animal Tracks; Ferns; Trees and Shrubs; Reptiles and Amphibians.

THE FIRST BOOK Series (Franklin Watts, Inc., New York, N.Y., $1.95 each)

Each well illustrated book is written by an expert, for beginners. Titles in the nature field include: The First Book of: Bees; Birds; Conservation, the Earth, Gardening, Mammals, Plants, Sea Shells, Snakes, Stones, Trees, Weather.

A FRUIT IS BORN by J. M. Guilcher and R. H. Noailles (Sterling Publishing Company, Inc., New York, N.Y., 1960, $2.50)

Remarkable photographs, many of which are magnified, and clear text explain each stage in the transformation of blossom to fruit. Other titles in the series include *A Butterfly Is Born*, *A Tree Is Born*.

THE GOLDEN LIBRARY OF KNOWLEDGE Series (Golden Press, New York, N.Y., 69 cents each)

Colorfully illustrated, inexpensive editions packed with valuable information for the nature enthusiast. Titles include The Insect World, The Sea, and Planets.

GOLDEN NATURE BOOK Series (Simon & Schuster, New York, N.Y., $1.00 paper, $1.95 cloth)

Guide books, fully illustrated in color, present introductory material about a variety of categories of nature, such as birds, fishes, flowers, insects, mammals, stars, trees, reptiles and amphibians, rocks and minerals. Especially useful for Animal Kingdom and Plant Kingdom badges.

HOW AND WHY WONDER BOOK Series (Grosset & Dunlap, Inc., New York, N.Y., 50 cents each)
Introductory information presented in easy-to-read style with many colored pictures. Sample titles include: Dinosaurs, Weather, Electricity, Rockets and Missiles and Stars.

KNOW YOUR WILD FLOWERS by Florence McKinney (Capper Publications, Inc., Topeka, Kan., 1960, 50 cents)
How to see and become acquainted with our common wild flowers.

NATURE ATLAS OF AMERICA by E. L. Jordan (C. S. Hammond and Company, Maplewood, N.J., 1952, $7.50)
In addition to wild life this atlas presents in maps, tables and texts, information about National Parks, National Monuments, and State Parks which keep alive the giant sequoias and redwoods, bald cypresses and white cedars, and rare species.

NORTH AMERICAN SONG BIRDS CARD GAME and NORTH AMERICAN WILD FLOWER CARD GAME edited by Roger Tory Peterson (National Wildlife Federation, Washington 6, D. C., 1961, $1.00 each set of 50 cards.)
Each card includes a reproduction in color of an authentic painting by a leading nature artist, plus descriptive verse in English and in French. For fun while acquiring nature knowledge.

PLANTS THAT CHANGED THE WORLD by Bertha S. Dodge (Little Brown & Company, Boston, Mass., 1959, $3.50)
Some of the plant products that have helped make history and the men who hunted them.

POCKET PLANETARIUM (Girl Scouts of the U.S.A., Cat. No. 23-542, 35 cents)
Four summer and winter luminous sky charts helpful in recognizing stars.

THE STARS—A NEW WAY TO SEE THEM by H. A. Rey (Houghton Mifflin Co., Boston, Mass., 1962, $6.00)

Modern guide to the wonders of the night sky, including charts of the stars' positions throughout the year.

THE STARS FOR SAM by W. Maxwell Reed (Harcourt, Brace & Company, New York, N.Y., Revised 1960, $4.50)

Our own solar system, and the earth's place in it, including new discoveries. One of a series, other titles include: *The Earth for Sam, The Sea for Sam.*

PROJECTS AND ACTIVITIES FOR SUMMER CAMPS, PLAY-GROUNDS, RECREATION GROUPS (National Audubon Society, New York, N.Y., 50 cents)

Directions for many different things to do out-of-doors, such as how to attract birds to a feeder, play nature games, explore a pond.

Science

NEW WORLDS THROUGH THE MICROSCOPE by Robert Disraeli (Viking Press, Inc., New York, N.Y., Revised 1960, $4.00)

Directions for finding specimens, mounting them on slides, and using the microscope. Many fascinating photographs.

SCIENCE EXHIBITS edited by Helen Miles Davis (Science Service, 1719 N Street N. W., Washington 6, D. C., 1959, $2.00)

Helpful suggestions for planning, organizing, or entering local or national science fairs. Actual reports of National Science Fair winners.

YOUNG PEOPLE'S SCIENCE ENCYCLOPEDIA edited by staff of National College of Education, Evanston, Ill. (Children's Press, Inc., Chicago, Ill., 1962)

Look in your library for this up-to-date resource.

OUR WONDERFUL WORLD: YOUNG PEOPLES' ENCYCLOPEDIC ANTHOLOGY edited by Herbert S. Zim (Spencer Press, Inc., Chicago, Ill., 1960)

Illustrated authoritative, up-to-date articles on a variety of subjects of interest to Cadettes. Look for this in your library.

index

Director, Program Department	**Dr. Catherine M. Broderick**
Director, Materials Production Division	**Warren Goodrich**
Director, Program Development Division	**Margery Lawrence**
Editor-in-Chief	**Frances W. Poster**
Art Director	**Salvatore A. Carbone**
Production Manager	**Emanuel A. Lopez**
Age-Level Adviser	**Judy Van Vliet Cook**
Writer	**Patricia Cherr**
Editor	**Margaret C. Manning**
Designer	**Peggy Nakache**
Illustrator	**Jack Burton**
Technical Illustrator	**Charles R. Hunter**

Material for the *Girl Scout Handbooks* was developed by many people including: Betty Gene Alley □ Marion L. Barrett □ Alethea T. Beckhard □ Shirley M. Carson □ Betty H. Collins □ Marian Davis □ Margarite Hall □ Catherine T. Hammett □ Dagmar Edith McGill □ Goldie McGirt □ Carolyn H. Mitchell □ Corinne M. Murphy Madeline S. Murphy □ Helen M. Quackenbush □ Alice S. Rivoire □ Julian H. Salomon □ Mary M. Weeks □ Carol Weiss □ Marian F. Weller □ Alice White

Girl Scouts of the U.S.A. wishes to thank the hundreds of people across the country who have contributed ideas and critical review for the *Handbooks*. Girls, leaders, members of national committees, national board members and officers, other national staff members, as well as educators and educational departments of commercial organizations have all given graciously of their time, effort, and knowledge. In addition, special consultant help has been given by the following: American Camping Association □ The American Forestry Association □ American Home Economics Association □ The American Humane Association □ American Meteorological Society □ American Museum of Natural History □ American National Red Cross American Society of Mammalogists □ American Veterinary Medical Association American Youth Hostels □ Animal Welfare Institute □ Bicycle Institute of America □ Brookhaven National Laboratory □ Evaporated Milk Association □ Griffith Park Zoo, Los Angeles, California □ The National Audubon Society □ National Aviation Education Council □ National Dairy Council □ National Safety Council □ New York Botanical and Brooklyn Botanic Gardens □ New York Public Library □ New York University □ New York Zoological Society □ The Ninety-Nines □ The Soap and Detergent Association □ state departments of public instruction □ Teachers College, Columbia University □ U.S. National Committee for UNESCO □ U.S. Department of Agriculture □ University of Illinois